A PHILOSOPHER AT THE ADMIRALTY

R. G. COLLINGWOOD AND THE FIRST WORLD WAR

A Philosopher at War Volume One

Peter Johnson

imprint-academic

Copyright © Peter Johnson 2012

The moral rights of the author have been asserted.
No part of this publication may be reproduced in any form
without permission, except for the quotation of brief passages
in criticism and discussion.

Published in the UK by
Imprint Academic, PO Box 200, Exeter EX5 5YX, UK
Published in the USA by
Imprint Academic, Philosophy Documentation Center
PO Box 7147, Charlottesville, VA 22906-7147, USA

ISBN 9781845402501

A CIP catalogue record for this book is available from the
British Library and US Library of Congress

TABLE OF CONTENTS

	General Preface	v
	Introduction	1
1	A Life Divided	8
2	Beyond the Sheltered Calm	15
3	Recovery of Belief	21
4	Shadows of War	34
5	I. D. 32 in the Naval Intelligence Division	45
6	Collingwood in I. D. 32	57
7	Preparations for Peace	78
8	Friendships in Wartime	90
9	The War's Critic	101
10	The Christian Philosopher	111
11	A Vision of Life	125
12	Return to Oxford	134
	Afterword	144
	Appendix	147
	Bibliography	149
	Index	168

GENERAL PREFACE

The two volumes of *A Philosopher at War* examine the political thought of the philosopher and archaeologist, R. G. Collingwood, against the background of the First and Second World Wars. Both wars were world shattering and world creating events.

Collingwood served in Admiralty Intelligence during the First World War and was involved with the British preparations for the Peace Conference that followed the end of hostilities. Hopes for a better world and plans for peace and security in the two decades following 1919 were widespread. As the post-war mood turned sour in the 1930s it seemed as if little could be done to avoid another catastrophe. Collingwood's political thought is never far from the sound of battle and, although he was not physically robust enough to play an active role in the Second World War, he was swift to condemn the policies of appeasement which he thought largely responsible for bringing it about.

The guiding principles of Collingwood's philosophical liberalism — freedom, civility and peace — originated primarily from the philosophical problems which troubled him, but they were forged in response to events, in the case of the two major wars of the twentieth century, events of world historical significance. Political practice, Collingwood argued, came before theory, but a theory properly attuned to events holds out the promise of clarifying practice and enlarging it in the name of the political ideals liberals believe in. So to Collingwood's mind political philosophy must be understood in close conjunction with the philosophy of history. My line of approach in both volumes is dictated by these priorities.

I use a blend of political philosophy, history and discussion of political policy to uncover what Collingwood says about the First World War, the Peace Treaty that followed it and the crises that led to the Second World War in 1939, together with the response he mustered to the war before his death in 1943. My aim is to reveal the kind of liberalism he valued and explain why he valued it. Even though some reference to biographical fact is unavoidable, the work is not intended as a biography. Neither is it intended as an intellectual biography, since I set aside much of the context of Collingwood's thought, the influences on it and its overall coherence.

Collingwood wrote about politics in full consciousness that he lived in momentous times. For liberals, whose main focus is peace and the avoidance of war, they were also times in which hard choices were often thought necessary. Collingwood did not believe with Nietzsche that we sail upon open and boundless seas, but he did believe that our choices are our own. No material, either in nature or circumstance, determines the actions of human beings, and if their choices are shaped by history they are not made by it. By 1940 Collingwood came to see that a liberalism separated from Christianity would be unable to meet the combined evils of fascism and Nazism. How Collingwood arrived at this position, and how viable he finally considered it, is the story told in this book.

> And sometimes this third R. G. C. woke right up; for example, on a day soon after the beginning of August, 1914, when a crowd of Northumberland coal-miners, full of patriotic fervour, saw what they imagined to be a German spy on 'the old Roman camp' up the hill, and took appropriate action.
>
> R. G. Collingwood, *An Autobiography*
>
> If I had a big proposition to handle and could have my pick of helpers I'd plump for the Intelligence Department of the British Admiralty. Yes, sir, I take off my hat to your Government sleuths.
>
> John Buchan, *The Adventures of Richard Hannay*

INTRODUCTION

In Britain during the First World War a significant number of academics worked in government departments or as civilians in military planning and administration. As the conflict intensified and the need for government staff increased the universities were seen to be a vital source of qualified personnel. Many academics took leave and volunteered their support, often unpaid, to the war effort. The philosopher and archaeologist, R. G. Collingwood, was one. Between 1916 and 1919 Collingwood worked for the Naval Intelligence Division of the Admiralty, in its Geographical Section, code named I. D. 32, mainly on British preparations for the Peace Conference in Paris which followed the end of the First World War. From being a philosopher at an Oxford college Collingwood became a Temporary Clerk in the Admiralty. Among those who worked in the same section were three philosophers, Hastings Rashdall, Samuel Alexander and H. J. Paton. Geographers, historians and classicists were also employed there. We now know a great deal about the combination of circumstances that took a young philosopher in his mid-twenties from his study to a room in the Admiralty. We also know a lot more about the kind of organisation he joined and the work he did there. On this basis we should be able to go a step further to reconstruct something of his attitudes at the time and the spirit in which he carried out his work. Since the Paris Peace Conference was a decisive event in twentieth-century political history the role played by R. G. Collingwood, one of the twentieth century's foremost philosophers of history, should repay examination.

Philosophers rarely stop being philosophers even when they are doing something entirely different. This was Collingwood's experience during his time at the Admiralty. He continued his work in philosophy not always by publishing his results, but certainly by pondering philosophical questions, as he did during his daily walk through Kensington on his way to work in Naval Intelligence. On the route that became familiar to him, through Kensington Gardens to the Royal

Geographical Society where I. D. 32 was first housed, Collingwood puzzled over the problem of how the Albert Memorial, an object he thought loathsome, could ever have been considered a work of art at all. Out of these musings emerged Collingwood's logic of question and answer, one of his most revolutionary ideas and one that is central to his understanding of historical method. Had they known of these reflections it is doubtful if many of Collingwood's co-workers in the Admiralty would have judged their colleague eccentric. For the Admiralty Intelligence Division was itself not short of quirky, brilliant individuals. It worked in an atmosphere that mixed discordant idiosyncrasy with professionalism and it included more than its fair share of near lunatic genius, such as Ronnie Knox, the cryptographer, who did his best work in the bath, not, possibly, a habit unusual in itself, but made so by his insisting that his bath took place in his office.

Historians of philosophy most commonly restrict themselves to the history of arguments, pausing only briefly to mention some biographical fact that they believe may be illuminating, such as the date of Hobbes' birth coinciding with the arrival of the Armada. Why, then, spend time looking at what a philosopher did outside philosophy? Surely, the sceptical reader will point out, Collingwood's activities at the Admiralty have as much bearing on his thought as, for example, Gilbert Ryle's involvement in counterespionage in the Second World War did on his book, *The Concept of Mind*? Or, to take another instance, the fact that Wittgenstein had some of his best ideas while peeling potatoes in the army does little by way of opening up the more intractable aspects of the *Tractatus*. To switch fields for a moment, art historians tend not to be much bothered by what Michelangelo had for lunch. Well, we might respond, yes, but, then, can the biography of a philosopher afford to be so stereotyped? Surely, the division of a life into compartments risks foreclosing the investigation before it starts. Much more important and, indeed, pressing in Collingwood's case, is the self-understanding of the philosopher himself. For Collingwood in his autobiography discloses his state of mind with such vividness and in such distinctive language that it is impossible to discount. To ignore what Collingwood said about himself erases one of the most valuable sources of evidence we have for his attitudes and beliefs at the time. Thus, Collingwood's autobiographical picture of his wartime life as a struggle against self-segregation is highly pertinent to the story that we have to tell.

Two topics predominate in Collingwood's thinking as it evolved during his formative years, first, the attempt to forge a link between history and politics, second, to unite theory and practice. Together they are a major part of Collingwood's project for reinstating the connection between thought and action. But a quest such as this is conditional on Collingwood's discontentment with the world as he saw it. So it seems highly relevant that the preparations for peace on which Collingwood worked were bedevilled by precisely the divorce between action and theory that he wished to overcome. And there is another twist that complicates the tale. For Collingwood tells us in his autobiography that at that time he was living as if his quest for reconciliation was false. He lived as if his philosophy was untrue. So, again, the exact contribution that Collingwood's Naval Intelligence work made to the Peace Conference is important because whether it was substantial (or insignificant), and why, helps us to understand the priorities that Collingwood was determined to make his own.

Even so, we should be the first to acknowledge that the Confidential Naval Intelligence Manuals on which Collingwood worked in Naval Intelligence are certainly not philosophy. But, then, neither are they the equivalent of Baedeker-style guide books to continental holiday resorts, say, Boulogne-Sur-Mer, complete with train timetables and a potted history of the region. They are closer in format to Collingwood's own *Guide to the Roman Wall* (first published in 1926, and in a number of editions thereafter), but the Manuals are no more works of history than the Guides. Quite obviously, Collingwood was not employed at the Admiralty because he was a philosopher, but like many other academics—classicists, historians, specialists in languages—his value to Intelligence was not bound up with the subject he taught. Mathematicians and logicians may well have had a special aptitude for cryptography, but this was by no means always the case. Classicists sometimes possessed detailed knowledge of the Aegean coast, but this was not the sole reason for their usefulness. It is worth mentioning here that in writing the Manuals Collingwood was not entirely writing to order. There was a template that the authors of the Manuals were expected to follow but, equally, they were given the discretion to form their own opinions and express their own judgements. One of the reasons for Collingwood's value to Naval Intelligence was his ability to assimilate and analyse large amounts of information on a given topic, but his intelligence masters were well aware that, like his cryptographer colleagues in I. D. 25 (Room 40), they would get little of value from him if they kept the bureaucratic chains around his writing drawn too tight.

It is, of course, true that Collingwood's thinking about the war must be discovered not from what he did at the Admiralty, but from the philosophical and political views he expressed at the time.

Collingwood's response to the war must be examined in intellectual terms. In other words, Collingwood understood the war as a philosopher and it is against the background of other philosophical accounts of war that his views need to be located. Among British philosophers German responsibility for the war was much debated and Collingwood contributed to this debate both in his writings at the time and later. For liberal idealists the role of the state in peace and war was a vital topic. In this context, Collingwood's attacks on what he called "Prussianism" are more readily intelligible.

Of equal importance with this line of thought is the connection between theory and practice, or to put it as Collingwood might have done so himself, the capacity of ideas to shape our world for better or for worse. If the war was first and foremost a conflict of ideas then philosophy cannot be a neutral activity wholly disconnected from life, as the "Minute Philosophers" of Collingwood's youth believed. Rather, philosophy, as Collingwood understood and refined it, can become the herald of a better world. For a liberal political philosopher like Collingwood who was also opposed to the realist separation of fact and value this aspiration provided the basis for a lifetime project. If the world was to be called to order through philosophy then it had to be reformulated in thought. In other words, the plan would not work unless a philosophically convincing account of it could be drawn up first. Theory and practice could in principle be drawn together, but only by philosophy laying the foundations for what followed. We have good grounds for thinking of Collingwood as a liberal political philosopher, but he was also an Anglican and as such he did not believe that liberalism could do the work he expected if it was separated too far from religion. As a liberal Anglican, then, Collingwood had a clear idea of the kind of reconstruction needed after the war, but as a philosopher he did not believe that religion could speak solely in its own voice. Thus, in his early works, Collingwood defended a philosophically informed Christianity together with a philosophically informed liberalism.

It is more than tempting to describe Collingwood's work in Naval Intelligence as having no bearing on his philosophy. It was an office job, an activity that was wholly separate from what really tested him, from what gave him his purpose in life. Sometimes in letters Collingwood speaks like this himself. The biographer may find some interest in it, but from the intellectual biographer's point of view it can be quite happily set aside. And, yet, there are a number of reasons why we should consider this conclusion a little too easy. First, to approach a life with this kind of assumption in mind might well lead to a falsification of that life. Imagine someone contemplating a life of Wittgenstein already believing that his choice to become a teacher after the war is perfectly intelligible quite independently of his attitude to philosophy. Teaching in a primary school and doing philosophy simply have no bearing on each other. But writing Wittgenstein's life with that thought in mind would falsify it because a vital element in Wittgenstein's choice would be closed, namely, his belief that he had thought his way through to the end of philosophy. It needs stressing that from this one example it does not follow that connections can always be found between different experiences in life. It is rather that the assumption that they will never be found can, on occasion, lead the biographer astray. The second reason is that too much in life is lost if strict division between activities is assumed at the start. In other words, we lose the perspective that one form of experience can give on another. Collingwood tells us that part of his time at the Admiralty was spent on preparations for the Peace Conference. As I aim to show, it would be a mistake to picture this as something wholly shut off from Collingwood's philosophy, something from which, as a philosopher, he was unable to learn. In fact, in his autobiography Collingwood gives quite the opposite impression. There he says that his wartime experience shaped the direction his thinking was taking. It helped him to identify his life's work. The third reason is that Collingwood's growing philosophical concern in the early period of his life was to show the unity of experience. So to think of Collingwood's life as rigidly compartmentalised is either to deny what became, increasingly during his formative years, his main purpose in philosophy or to say that this had no effect on his life. He lived his life independently of his philosophy. Since any denial of Collingwood's concern with the unity of thought and action is highly unconvincing we are left with the claim that his philosophy had no effect on his life. Indeed, as we shall discover, this was a claim that he later made himself, but the key point is that we could not begin to address this question unless we had some knowledge of his life. Since his Admiralty work is an intrinsic part of his life it is impossible to ignore, even on terms as minimal as these.

The philosophy of war, like the poetry of war, has a long history. War left few of Collingwood's generation untouched. And, yet, the question of how war was to be spoken about by those who had direct experience of it needed an answer. In the voice of Wilfred Owen, one that became highly influential, poetry was the only possible philosophy of war. Collingwood may well have agreed since he thought of poetry as our mother tongue and so uniquely capable of expressing our deepest pain and insecurity. But Collingwood also thought that there were levels of understanding that poetry could not reach. One of these is philosophy and while poetry communicates and, possibly, consoles the feelings, there are conceptual issues that it is unable to address. Collingwood did not believe that war could ever be eliminated. It could, however, be contained, its incidence controlled through understanding it better. Collingwood wrote no single work on war, but he did believe, like Kant and Hegel before him, that war, as a feature of the human world, has to figure in any philosophical account of that world. It is not that war can be spoken about only through philosophy. It is rather that Collingwood did not believe that his Liberal Anglicanism could say what it wanted to say about war without philosophy intervening.

Intellectual biographies are not always about intellectuals, but where they are then some account of the formative influences on their thinking, both negative and positive, is invariably considered essential. Collingwood's slow extrication of his ideas from realism plays an important part in what follows and I indicate the positive direction that was given to his philosophy by Italian idealism. However, this work is not a full-scale intellectual biography of Collingwood, even of his thought in the early period of its development. Collingwood's plans to translate Guido de Ruggiero's work of 1912, *La Filosofia Contemporanea*, were affected by the conflict and publication was postponed until after the war. Similarly, Collingwood's correspondence with Croce begun in 1912 was disrupted during the war years. Neither is it my concern to provide a biography of the young Collingwood. To do that I would have to say a great deal more about his predecessors, his family upbringing, education and experience prior to his starting at Oxford in 1908. Rather, what I have aimed to achieve is something like a snapshot of Collingwood's life and thought during the war, from the time he left Oxford to work at the Admiralty in the late winter of 1915 to his return in 1919. I have had to say a little more about the period from 1912 to 1916 so as to set the scene for what follows, but there my concern ends.

Concentration on a limited period in anyone's life risks appearing arbitrary, even where the starting and finishing points are well-defined as they usually are in the case of war. One powerful reason for this is that the experience of war for the individual concerned is often so completely overwhelming that its effects are felt long after the event. And, yet, exactly how these effects are felt and how they manifest themselves over the course of a life are matters on which generalisation is usually unwise. Even so, in Collingwood's case, what is obviously true is that the war had a quite massive effect on his thought. With this in mind I have, therefore, included a discussion of Collingwood as a critic of the war. This does mean anticipating and, to a degree, trespassing on ideas that only came to him later. While the war did not dictate the actual nature of his thinking, no mere event could do that, it did force him to reflect on the point of his work and why he thought his work, especially on the philosophy of history, had value.

There is another more technical reason for my not wholly respecting the limits I have set myself. It is often the case that evidence of Collingwood's response to the war comes only after the event, in some instances, a considerable time after. *An Autobiography*, written mostly during 1938 and published in 1939, is an obvious and troubling text in this respect, but sometimes single remarks are just as taxing. I have tried to confine my evidence of what Collingwood is saying and thinking about the war to published and unpublished material from the period I am examining. However, unlike his philosophical contemporaries, Bertrand Russell and Ludwig Wittgenstein (both of whom have small parts in the unfolding narrative), Collingwood did not leave a substantial archive of letters and private diaries which record either his thinking about himself or his reaction to public events. The material deposited in the Bodleian Library, Oxford is, of course, extensive, but it is largely philosophical and historical in character and while this is clearly an essential part of the story it does not tell us everything we need to know. Similarly, Collingwood's correspondence, while being highly informative on some points, is small by comparison with Russell's and, to a lesser extent, Wittgenstein's in the same period. Sometimes, therefore, where I think it is necessary or desirable, I have fast forwarded through Collingwood's life to pick up a reflection he makes on a past thought where this seems to throw light on what he was saying and thinking at the time.

CHAPTER 1
A LIFE DIVIDED

R. G. Collingwood is often praised for being one of the most literary of philosophers. Many passages in his writing are highly regarded for lucidity and style. But while there are numerous occasions in Collingwood's writing where his use of metaphor encourages the argument to flow (and Collingwood was the author of a notable analysis of philosophical writing),[1] there are others which are marked by over-ambitiousness and strain. Santayana called Collingwood's autobiography "strangely conceited, but instructive"; we should find this judgement illuminating for although *An Autobiography* aims to tell the story of its author's thought it is inevitably Collingwood himself who draws the reader in.[2]

It is one of the sources of the fascination exerted by *An Autobiography* that it makes us want to discover more, for Collingwood does not lecture his readers, but involves them in his narrative by giving them work to do. To understand what Collingwood is telling us about how his thought developed we have to think, too. Where there are gaps we try to fill them by imagining what Collingwood would want us to say. In this respect, the famous "three R. G. C.s" section reveals Collingwood at his most spellbinding.[3] Here is a passage that tells us more than it says, even though just reading what Collingwood says already sheds light on a great deal. He says that at one time in his life he took up three attitudes towards the division between contemplation and action. In his first attitude he knew from his philosophy that the division was false. In the second attitude he behaved as if it was true. In his third attitude his actions matched his thoughts. The division was false and he no longer behaved as if it was true.

Now we can be sure that this passage is not simply a piece of hyperbole. Collingwood is not inventing an unnecessarily complicated story about himself in order to justify a stance that he wanted to adopt in 1939. For we know from what Collingwood wrote at the time that these divisions perplexed him. The address Collingwood gave at

Coniston on the occasion of Ruskin's centenary in August 1919 provides a good indication of this. Collingwood puts the questions that Ruskin's doctrine of the unity of the spirit was intended to answer: "Why shouldn't a man be a good artist and a bad man? Why shouldn't a virtuous man be artistically incompetent?"[4] Or, to ask the question that Collingwood was surely asking of himself, why shouldn't a philosopher keep his philosophy separate from his life?

If Collingwood's autobiographical reflections are to be believed then in the years running up to his Coniston address he had three attitudes towards the divisions these questions raise. In the first attitude he was with Ruskin in believing them to be false, but in the second he lived as if they were true and in the third attitude, while only occasionally fully on view, actions and thoughts were matched. Here Collingwood reveals more than he says. It is, perhaps, the reason for Santayana thinking *An Autobiography* enlightening. For what Collingwood must surely have wanted his readers to understand is not that he had these three attitudes, but that he had to have them together. To have had one, but not any of the others would have attached quite a different meaning to his life. Or, to put this point differently, in order for Collingwood to tell the story he wanted to tell it was necessary for him to have not just one attitude, but the whole set.

The thoughts he had about himself clearly mattered to Collingwood. *An Autobiography* aims to tell the truth about a life. The story that it tells is certainly one written from a particular historical standpoint, but more important are the terms in which the story is told because it is through these that Collingwood makes sense of his life and expresses that sense to his readers. In other words, the "3 R. G. C.s" picture is a serious one for Collingwood, and for his readers, too. If Collingwood makes his life intelligible in these terms then readers should also be able to see this. But there is one question that Collingwood does not ask — what kind of life was Collingwood living, if it was a life in which all "3 R. G. C.s" had to be present together?

To make sense of Collingwood's life the terms that he uses himself must be transparently clear. Collingwood says that he lived a life in which what he knew to be true in one guise he thought false in another. A life like this does not have to be schizophrenic. Dr Jekyll is not a different version of Mr Hyde, and vice versa. Rather they represent mental states that are wholly disconnected from each other. We should remember, too, that in Collingwood's account there is a fourth R. G. C., namely, the R. G. C. who came to see that he held these attitudes. So the R. G. C. who was the detached scholar was not unknown to R. G. C., the frustrated man of action. Should we see Collingwood, then, as having lived a double life, one in which he lived both as a detached scholar and as a man at odds with himself? But this is no more convincing, for the point of a double life is that the whole individual is engaged in both. Perhaps, we should see Collingwood as having lived a split life, one R. G. C. holding three different attitudes towards the division between theory and life. In this picture Collingwood's life consisted of compartments firmly closed to each other. "My philosophy and my habits were thus in conflict", Collingwood wrote in 1939, but this leaves the fourth R. G. C. intact, namely the R. G. C. who reaches this judgement about himself.[5] There is nevertheless one thing that we can be sure about. At least one of Collingwood's attitudes had to change for him to bring the struggle between them to an end. And this gradual transformation is precisely what *An Autobiography* records. Collingwood thought that philosophical writing was mainly addressed by the philosopher to himself. The purpose was not to report the thought—in its most polished state—back to the philosopher, but rather to deliberately pick out the most awkward and troublesome obstacles to progress. Thus, the third R. G. C., the R. G. C. whose life matched his philosophy, could not come into existence unless the first and second R. G. C.s were reconciled in some way, but when the First World War ended the advances in thought needed to achieve this had still not been reached. A closer rapprochement was required between philosophy and history, a firmer grasp needed of the doctrine of history as self-knowledge and a clearer representation wanted of the forms of experience and the relations between them.

It is unsurprising that Collingwood in his autobiography was able to draw a sharper portrait of his early predicament than was possible for him at the time. For it belonged to the nature of his thought at the time that it was unable to find its way out of the difficulties it had created. And, yet, we misunderstand the stalemate that Collingwood found himself facing if we think of it as arising from a conflict of desires. He was not like Donna Elvira in Mozart's *Don Giovanni* who both wants and does not want to take the monster's hand. Neither would Collingwood's life have been pacified by changes in his behaviour alone. For Collingwood believed that it was the intellect that altered attitudes. It was not an accident that he called his autobiography the story of his thought.

Collingwood was not alone in his belief that history could contribute to a better world after the war. Arnold Toynbee was another who became caught up in the spirit of post-war earnestness. Toynbee shared Collingwood's view that the intellect was a necessary basis for action, and he saw his work for the Survey of International Affairs as highly practical. A political evil such as war is made less likely if its origins and incidence are better understood. Understanding and action are linked. The historian is not remote from present concerns but, in political matters especially, perfectly placed as it is only through historical knowledge that the present can come to understand how it has come to be what it is.[6] Toynbee, however, was not faced with Collingwood's problem of finding a connection between philosophy and life. Collingwood's problem was singular because it arose directly from his particular way of doing philosophy. Thus, Bertrand Russell who was as much concerned as Collingwood with post-war reconstruction showed no concern at all with the questions to do with theory and practice that puzzled Collingwood. Indeed, so little interest did Russell show at this time in the practical value of philosophy that the idea of there being "3 B. R.s" is hard to grasp. For Russell there would be no "first B. R." to disbelieve since he did not take the view that something was necessarily wrong if philosophy played a different tune from life. So, in a lecture delivered at Oxford in November, 1914, Russell argued that

> The scientific philosophy, therefore, which aims only at understanding the world and not directly at any other improvement of human life, cannot take account of ethical notions without being turned aside from that submission to fact which is the essence of the scientific temper.[7]

Philosophy's essence, Russell insisted, was not synthesis, but analysis. So when Collingwood wished a life that reflected his philosophy his wish was not a submission to fact, rather it was the imposition of a synthesis derived from his philosophy on his life, a synthesis, moreover, in which Russell, for one, did not believe.

While Collingwood's "3 R. G. C.s" is a picture he held of his life it is not one that he needed an argument to believe. Collingwood held conflicting attitudes towards himself and the aims in life that he wished to pursue. It is not difficult to think of similar examples. An aspiring writer may simultaneously regard himself as a failure and yet doggedly continue to bombard publishers with work, even though the rejection slips pile up and his self-esteem weakens. There are occasions over the course of a life when individuals struggle to overturn the false picture they have of themselves or find a life that better represents a true one. What is distinctive about Collingwood's picture of himself is its comprehensiveness. To think of one's life in terms of the division between theory and practice leaves little out. Moreover, this way of looking at one's life is distinctive of philosophy because the division between theory and practice is itself a philosophical problem, one that different philosophers will both state and solve in different ways.

Additionally, divisions in one's life that at the time were thought unbridgeable can later be seen as a reason for regret. So, for example, Russell in later years came to see his opposition to the war differently. "When the War was over, I saw that all I had done had been totally useless except to myself. I had not saved a single life or shortened the War by a minute. I had not succeeded in doing anything to diminish the bitterness which caused the Treaty of Versailles."[8]

Russell's determination to give up technical philosophy after the war and to exercise his intelligence for the improvement of the world brings him closer to Collingwood, even though the philosophical gulf between them remained wide and their solutions were very different. Armistice Day saw Russell in Tottenham Court Road surrounded by wildly cheering crowds of Londoners celebrating the end of the war.[9] Collingwood was hard at work on the preparations for the Peace Conference then still a good six months away. Ludwig Wittgenstein, by contrast, was a prisoner of the Italians, and would remain so until August 1919, after the map of Europe had been redrawn. If the circumstances of their lives were different, the philosophical distance between the three philosophers was immense. Russell and Collingwood responded to the war as intellectuals by thinking of it as a problem to be solved. Where the politicians had wrecked any chances of a lasting European peace, philosophers and historians could do better. For Wittgenstein, by contrast, talk of the problems of life and their solutions was talk wasted. Still less did Wittgenstein believe that Christianity was a doctrine that could be reformulated through philosophy. Whatever the job of philosophy was that was not it. As Wittgenstein wrote later in his life, "Christianity is not a doctrine, not, I mean, a theory about what has happened & will happen to the human soul, but a description of something that actually takes place in human life."[10] Only by dissolving the way of talking about life as a problem to be solved could philosophy enlighten practice, and, even then, this would not be a solution to a problem. So does this mean that for Collingwood to make sense of his life he would need to dissolve his picture of himself as "3 R. G. C.s"? We can be sure that the first R. G. C. would certainly have to be dropped, for philosophy, as Wittgenstein understands it, makes no truth claims at all. There would then be nothing for the second R. G. C. to disbelieve. He would also be left with nothing to believe either, since ethics, in Wittgenstein's view, does not consist in a theory of the world's goodness or badness. What remains is Collingwood, the third R. G. C., the man of action, the man whose life can now be lived uncluttered by doctrine. For once the first and second

R. G. C.s have been erased then Collingwood's life can speak for itself. Collingwood's Christian ideals are shown in the way he lived his life.

Endnotes

1   R. G. Collingwood, *An Essay on Philosophical Method*, Clarendon Press, Oxford, 1933, Chapter 10, Philosophy as a Branch of Literature.

2   Cited in Bernard Williams, "An Essay on Collingwood", in Bernard Williams, *The Sense of the Past, Essays in the History of Philosophy*, edited with an introduction by Miles Burnyeat, Princeton University Press, 2006, p341.

3   R. G. Collingwood, *An Autobiography*, Oxford University Press, Oxford, 1939, pp150–53.

4   R. G. Collingwood, *Ruskin's Philosophy*, as reprinted in Alan Donagan (ed.), *Essays in the Philosophy of Art by R. G. Collingwood*, Indiana University Press, Bloomington, 1964, pp5–41, p34; Collingwood's review of Bertrand Russell's *Mysticism and Logic* in *The Oxford Magazine*, 14 February 1919, p129, contains similar, albeit brief, remarks on Russell's criticism of ethics within philosophy.

5   R. G. Collingwood, *An Autobiography*, p151.

6   See Arnold Toynbee, *Experiences*, Oxford University Press, London, 1969, p83, where Toynbee writes, "I have always felt that, in persisting with the Survey, I was not merely helping to expose the major evil of our time (and, indeed, of all times since war began); I have also always felt that I was helping to try to suppress this wicked institution before it annihilated us, its makers." Toynbee, like Collingwood, was much impressed by Croce's contribution to the philosophy of history, see Arnold J. Toynbee, *A Study of History*, vol. 10, Oxford University Press, London, 1954, pp232–3, where he writes, "Alfred Zimmern taught me, eight years before the publication of Benedetto Croce's *Teoria e Storia della Storiografia* in A. D. 1917, that 'all true history is contemporary history'. I learnt this from the intellectual ferment raised in my mind in New College hall in the summer term of A. D. 1909 as I listened to A. E. Z. delivering a course of introductory lectures on Hellenic history, for undergraduates starting to read Literae Humaniores, which was the matrix of The Greek Commonwealth. As I sat listening to those catalytic words, the conventional partitions between 'Past' and 'Present' and between 'Ancient' and 'Modern' dissolved out of my mind and have never since returned to hamper it. I had learnt that life, thought, and feeling in the Hellenic world in the fifth century B. C. were living presences working upon me in a fourteenth century Western Christian hall in which a crowd of twentieth century Western undergraduates was sitting at that moment at the feet of a master." For discussion of Collingwood's criticism of Toynbee's view of history, see William. H. Dray, *History as Re-Enactment, R. G. Collingwood's Idea of History*, Clarendon Press, Oxford, 1995, pp178, 185, 216, 221 and 225.

7   Bertrand Russell, *Mysticism and Logic*, Longmans Green & Co., London, 1918, p109.
8   *The Autobiography of Bertrand Russell*, vol. 2, 1914–44, George Allen and Unwin, London, 1968, p40.
9   Ray Monk, *Bertrand Russell, The Spirit of Solitude*, Jonathan Cape, London, 1996, pp542–3.
10   Ludwig Wittgenstein, *Culture and Value*, revised edition, edited by G. H. von Wright, translated by Peter Winch, Blackwell Publishers, Oxford, 1998, 32e.

CHAPTER 2

BEYOND THE SHELTERED CALM

Unlike Bertrand Russell who gave up philosophy for the duration of the war,[1] Collingwood continued with it insofar as his obligations at the Admiralty allowed. Moreover, whereas Russell at the start of the war had already found a distinctive philosophical voice, Collingwood, in his mid-twenties in 1916 when *Religion and Philosophy* was published and so almost a generation apart, was a philosopher still searching for one. As the nature of Collingwood's writings during the war indicates, this search was neither simple nor immediately fulfilling. Looking back on this time of his life from the perspective of 1939 Collingwood said that it was a period when his struggle to find a rapprochement between theory and practice was radically incomplete.[2] He was surely right to take this view, but the more interesting issue is why. One obvious reason is that the war made serious and sustained philosophical effort extremely difficult. One of the most insistent themes of Wittgenstein's correspondence during his war service in the Austrian army is the thought of the war as a distraction from philosophy, not that this prevented Wittgenstein from taking his military duties extremely seriously, or, indeed, from writing and discussing and making progress with philosophy when the opportunities allowed, rather it is that during the course of a war human energies and anxieties are necessarily directed elsewhere.[3] For Russell, giving up philosophy was a duty since he saw the war as such a monstrous evil that nothing should be allowed to interfere with opposition to it. Whereas for Wittgenstein the demands of military service competed with philosophy, in Russell's case pacifism overrode both.

It is certainly true that the war soaked up energies that both Wittgenstein and Collingwood wished to devote to philosophy. But to leave the matter there would be to fall well short of a full picture in Wittgenstein's case and, interestingly, in that of Collingwood, too. For, as has often been pointed out, there is a sense in which Wittgenstein welcomed the war.[4] In other words, even though the war interrupted his work in philosophy by taking up his time and by wearing him out it was not an interruption that produced nothing of value. On the contrary, as Brian Mc Guinness, the biographer of Wittgenstein's early years, points out,

> In the war—even perhaps because of the war: it is as if the war and its way of thinking came at the right time and put him into the right circumstances, as if he went along with the war anxious...to see what would become of his life. He let it affect, if not dictate, his thought.[5]

Thus, what Wittgenstein learned from the war was not simply the opportunity it gave him to test his religious beliefs or to search out his moral weaknesses by deliberately looking for and finding a combatant role that involved extreme risk. What the war satisfied in Wittgenstein was his need to find meaning in his life and in his belief in God. The war bridged the gap between the philosopher and the man, or, to put the same point slightly differently, the war showed him the impossibility of a philosophy that was purely technical, one that has no bearing on life. From this perspective, the significance of the war for Wittgenstein is neither wholly personal nor wholly philosophical. It is a welding together of both. There is no gap between the ethical and the logical. Thus, here is Brian McGuinness again,

> *Tractatus* and *Notebooks* show how the problems interacted: the philosophical solution was the solution to the problem of life; in both areas it was a matter not simply of not asking for the wrong thing but of not asking for anything.[6]

The war was important to Wittgenstein because it illuminated the nature of value, of what it is to find value in a human life and, for Wittgenstein, how to locate and be certain about his own values. The war showed Wittgenstein how ethics has a bearing on the world. Understood in this way, Wittgenstein's wartime experience does not stand in an instrumental relation to his thought. It is not as if what he gleaned from the war could have been obtained equally effectively from another testing activity, say, mountaineering. However, Collingwood's relation to the war is different. In his *Autobiography*, Collingwood remembers how he needed the time to focus his thought on what was central in the issues that troubled him. He writes,

> And I am not sure that I could ever so have focused it, but for the interruption of my academic life by the war. A man whose mind is always being stirred up by philosophical teaching can hardly be expected to achieve the calm, the inner silence, which is one condition of philosophical thinking.[7]

War is important to Collingwood as a means of escape. It is not what the experience of war uniquely is that figures in Collingwood's account, but what it allows him to avoid. The same end could have been achieved by leave of absence given, say, to care for a sick relative. The point is not that Collingwood exploited the war. Like Wittgenstein, it can be said that Collingwood welcomed it, but in a very different sense. Nor does this distinction depend on the different roles that Wittgenstein and Collingwood played in the war. We know that it mattered a great deal to Wittgenstein that he should see active service. The war would not have had the ethical significance it did in the way Wittgenstein came to understand the meaning of his life if this had been denied. But many sought combat, only to be refused it for a variety of reasons, one of which is the thought that their talents could be better used elsewhere. Thus, the attitude that Wittgenstein took toward his combatant role—that it should make a difference to his understanding of his life—could be taken by someone whose role in the war was in military intelligence, for example. Wittgenstein sought a task in the war that was not an intellectual one and yet managed to show clearly why it was precisely this lack of intellectuality that was important both to his life and to his philosophy. As we shall soon discover, Collingwood's occupation at the Admiralty involving as it did the detailed preparation of regional handbooks and the drawing of maps might be thought little different from academic work, but this surely further underlines Collingwood's picture of himself because it re-introduces the gap between scholarship and life.

The connections we are talking about between philosophy and life are not of the kind arrived at solely by argument. It is not so much the reasons that can be adduced for making particular connections that are important but the spirit in which a philosopher embarks on a course of action together with what is learned once the direction has been set.[8] Indeed, what must also be noted is a point that Wittgenstein and Collingwood might find troubling, namely, that some philosophers simply see no need to make such connections or, if they are willing to acknowledge their possibility, to make them explicit. Russell, for example, was wholly in earnest in his opposition to the war without claiming any link between his philosophy and his pacifism. We should add to this the thought that uncovering interactions between philosophy and life is as much a matter of self-reflection as it is of technical analysis. How a philosopher connects thought with life is not given in advance. Thus, what is especially interesting about the formative period of a philosopher's development is not just how connections are arrived at, but why they are not. In this sense, Collingwood's thought during the period of the war is that of a philosopher searching for a voice. What is worth listening to in others comes more readily to him than saying something himself. Equally, what he does want to say himself he is often unable to say because the concepts he needs remain undiscovered or are present only in imperfect formulations. Voices that offer promising lines of thought later disappoint and we frequently find Collingwood being forced to modify their influence or to look elsewhere, and even where the voice that Collingwood hears is finally his own he frequently turns his ear away in order to change tack or expand what he has said.

During his formative years Collingwood gradually became aware that there was at least one voice that he did not want to listen to. Realism was not simply the object of his attack in 1916, "the year of negative criticism" as he later described it,[9] but a philosophy that could say little to him throughout this early period as well as in much of his subsequent thought.[10] Thus, in his essay, "The Devil", Collingwood looks for a way of speaking about the devil (and, indeed, God), which takes into account the autonomy of religious language.[11] Coming to a belief in God (or the devil), Collingwood argues, is not, as realism teaches, like discovering a new fact, but expresses a change in understanding. Further, if realism can be counted a failure in the philosophy of religion it was no less disastrous in its explanation of moral and political beliefs. For Collingwood, the realist assumption that there exists a realm of facts independent of our understanding succeeds only in perpetuating the gap between philosophy and life that he wished to overcome. Thus, the realist could not be more wrong. Far from it being the case that the world stands aloof from our understanding, it is Collingwood's view that our understanding shapes the character of our world.

That Collingwood had reached this point in his early philosophical work is clear, but what is often left unstressed is his autobiographical account of this period of his life. It is highly significant that for Collingwood at that time any closing of the gap between philosophy and life was radically incomplete. Contrary to realism, Collingwood in his early writings affirmed the close dependence of thought and action. The intellectual life cannot be lived isolated from morality; equally, the moral life cannot be lived in isolation from clear thought. But in 1939 when writing his autobiography Collingwood made it clear that

> this was only a theoretical rapprochement of theory and practice, not a practical one. I did not see that my attempted reconstruction of moral philosophy would remain incomplete so long as my habits were based on the vulgar division of men into thinkers and men of action.[12]

It is surely the case that in this remark Collingwood is telling us something of great importance not only about his thinking in its formative period, but also about his life. For Collingwood is making more than just the claim that there was a time when his thinking about his life and the way he lived it remained unaffected by his philosophy. He is saying, in the words of his autobiography, that "I lived as if I disbelieved my own philosophy, and philosophized as if I had not been the professional thinker that in fact I was."[13]

Endnotes

1   See Bertrand Russell, *The Autobiography of Bertrand Russell*, vol. 2, 1914–44, p18; see Russell's letter to Ottoline Morrell, dated 11 November 1914, where he writes, "What I can do further in philosophy does not interest me, & seems trivial compared to what might be done elsewhere. I can't bear the sheltered calm of university life—I want battle and stress, & the feeling of doing something", cited in Monk, *Bertrand Russell*, p382.

2   See R. G. Collingwood, *An Autobiography*, pp149–50.

3   For discussions of Wittgenstein's war service, see Brian McGuinness, *Young Ludwig, Wittgenstein's Life 1889–1921*, with a new preface, Clarendon Press, Oxford, 2005, especially chapters 7 and 8, and Ray Monk, *Ludwig Wittgenstein, The Duty of Genius*, Jonathan Cape, London, 1990, especially chapters 1, 6 and 7.

4   See, for example, the remark by Wittgenstein's sister, Hermine, "When war broke out in 1914, he returned to Austria and insisted on enlisting in the army, in spite of his previously treated double hernia which had exempted him from military service. I knew very well that he was not only concerned with defending his fatherland, but that he also felt an intense desire to take some difficult task upon himself, and to perform something other than purely intellectual labour." (See Hermine Wittgenstein, "My Brother Ludwig", in Rush Rhees (ed.), *Ludwig Wittgenstein, Personal Recollections*, Basil Blackwell, Oxford, 1981, p3).

5   See McGuinness, *Young Ludwig*, p228.

6   Ibid., p227.

7   See R. G. Collingwood, *An Autobiography*, p28.

8   For a valuable discussion of philosophical biography and autobiography together with the issues at stake, see Ray Monk, "Philosophical Biography: The Very Idea", in James C. Klagge (ed.), *Wittgenstein, Biography and Philosophy*, Cambridge University Press, Cambridge, 2001, pp3–15, and in the same volume, James Conant, "Philosophy and Biography", pp16–50.

9   As quoted in Donald S. Taylor, *R. G. Collingwood, A Bibliography*, Garland Publishing, New York and London, 1988, p90.

10   For discussion of the philosophical context of Collingwood's early attack on realism, see P. M. S. Hacker, *Wittgenstein's Place in Twentieth Century Analytic Philosophy*, Blackwell, Oxford, 1996, pp87-8, and Giuseppina D'Oro, *Collingwood and the Metaphysics of Experience*, Routledge, London and New York, 2002, Chapter 3.
11   R. G. Collingwood, "The Devil", in *Concerning Prayer*, edited by B. H. Streeter and Lily Dougall, Macmillan, London, 1916, pp449-75.
12   R. G. Collingwood, *An Autobiography*, p150.
13   Ibid., p151.

CHAPTER 3

RECOVERY OF BELIEF

We might reasonably think that there is something very curious about Collingwood's statement that he lived as if he disbelieved his own philosophy for Collingwood is not talking about an event in his life, for example, his appointment to a Tutorship in Philosophy at Pembroke in June 1912; neither is he talking about a specific activity in his life, say, archaeology. Collingwood's reference is to his life as a whole, or more precisely, to the task of trying to find a perspective on it. We might imagine a driving instructor saying "I drove as if I disbelieved my own driving manual", without drawing the conclusion that there was something wrong with his life. But this, it would seem, is exactly what Collingwood is suggesting. Second, we should notice that the driving instructor is not implying that the driving instructions contained in the manual are false. Quite the contrary, since in saying that he drove as if he disbelieved them, he is, in fact, asserting his belief in them. In this respect, the affinity between this statement and Collingwood's looks strong. What the driving instructor disbelieved was his own driving manual, but what Collingwood says he disbelieved was his philosophy, and disbelieving a philosophy derives its sense from what you think philosophy is. For some philosophers Collingwood's reference would simply have nothing to grip on to because for them philosophy makes no assertions and so there is nothing to believe or disbelieve. The third feature of Collingwood's statement that is puzzling concerns contradiction. Take, as an example, a socialist who says that they lived as if they disbelieved their own philosophy. This sounds like a clear inconsistency since what they believed in theory is contradicted by the way they lived their life, but it is not just an inconsistency. It is also a self-criticism. We might think of it as an inconsistency because it involves an irresolvable conflict of beliefs. But if the statement is also a self-criticism then things are not so simple since the criticism must mean more than the repetition of the original belief. It might reinforce the original belief by offering an explanation for the discrepancy, possibly some justification for it. Or it might undermine the original belief by refusing to provide anything by way of mitigation. But a statement like Collingwood's surely necessarily implies self-criticism. Consider a cricketer who says, "I played as if I disbelieved my own ability." Clearly, this does not mean that the cricketer surprised himself by the quality of his play for that is consistent with his belief that he had no ability. If the original statement did mean that then the whole point of disbelief would be lost because disbelief depends on the player possessing an ability to disbelieve.

Self-criticism, then, must be a part of Collingwood's meaning, but what exactly is he criticising about himself? What would our response have been if Collingwood had written differently? Say Collingwood had written, "At one time I lived as if I disbelieved my own Christianity", what would we make of that? In addition to the logical difficulties we have encountered we now face a biographical problem. For if we are to make a judgement about the truth of Collingwood's statement we must know something about his Christianity and about how he lived. Now, as a matter of fact, we know very little about how Collingwood lived as a Christian. His *Autobiography* says nothing about his religious life, and although we know something about the place of church going in the Collingwood family way of life when R. G. Collingwood was a young man, this is not of much help.[1] In fact, we know more about the religious way of life of Collingwood's grandfather, William Collingwood, than we do about Collingwood himself.[2] There is evidence in the shape of the religious talks that Collingwood gave during the war, but these tell us about his beliefs, not about how he lived.[3] Unlike Wittgenstein and, indeed, Russell, we have little by way of evidence about how Collingwood lived or about the judgements he made of his life as he was living it. Nor should we think of this state of affairs as accidental. For Wittgenstein, expressing his concerns about his life (in the form of diaries or close correspondence with friends), about, for example, the times when he felt that he had failed to live up to the kind of life that mattered to him, was almost as important as the concern itself. This is a key difficulty since we would be hard pressed to take Collingwood's statement seriously if there had been nothing about his life that mattered to him. To put this point differently, one thing at least must have mattered to him, namely, that at one time he lived as though he disbelieved his own philosophy. Nor is this conclusion weakened when we remember Collingwood's saying that it was his "habits" which were at odds with his philosophy. For if by habits we mean the trivial routines of life then it is hard to understand these as evidence of disbelief. By contrast, if we mean by habit something uninformed by belief then the conclusion is strengthened because Collingwood most emphatically saw his life as a philosopher as consisting of the story of his thought. And, in any case, if there is one characteristic that is common to Wittgenstein, Russell and Collingwood, it is their earnestness.

One solution to the problem of finding a rapprochement between theory and practice is to think of philosophy as the source of ideals whose job is to provide guidance to life. It was the willingness of T. H. Green to take on this task that gave Collingwood his main reason for admiring him. Likewise, one of the reasons Collingwood gave for turning against realism is its inability to see this as an important question. It is noteworthy, however, that in his early reflections on this problem Collingwood had distinct reservations about this picture of the relationship between theory and practice. Initially, these arose because Collingwood found it hard to see philosophy as a source of ideals without first clarifying its relation with history. No rapprochement between theory and practice would be convincing if philosophy was understood as manufacturing ideals unrelated to experience. For the philosopher to try to spin a framework of principles from contemplation alone would be to miss what it is about principles that actually makes them work. Additionally, if human experience is historical experience then an adjustment between philosophy and history is unavoidable. But Collingwood's reservations do not stop there. There would be little point in philosophy attempting to construct principles to guide practice without saying anything about their application. Is this to be left to life or must moral philosophy change into applied ethics? Collingwood tries to avoid both alternatives, arguing instead that without history the bearing of philosophy on life yields only abstractions, and so cannot do the job that Collingwood expects of it.

The origins of Collingwood's turning his attention to history and the course of his early writings on it are well known.[4] Here their significance lies in how they help us to picture Collingwood's aspirations for philosophy and also the kind of philosopher he wanted to be. By 1919 Collingwood knew which voices would not be helpful to him in finding his own. One aspect of this was his growing defence of the autonomy of history and another was his interest in the unity exhibited by distinct forms of experience. Also, by 1919, on his own account, Collingwood had come to see history as central to his activities as a philosopher. This was not simply because the nature and methods of history had been neglected. Rather, it was because in the modern world history was the key mode of existence. Thus, as Collingwood recounted his aims in *An Autobiography*—for him at that time—"the chief business of twentieth century philosophy was to reckon with twentieth century history";[5] it is surely a remarkable statement. For Collingwood is not saying merely that the philosophy of history should be able to stand alongside the philosophy of art, say, or the philosophy of religion, as a natural subject for philosophical enquiry. He is saying that philosophers who do not reckon with history risk ignorance of the problems that face them, but there is more because Collingwood wants us to see that it is twentieth-century philosophers who cannot ignore their own history. Would he have said the same about nineteenth-century philosophy, or any other previous age? Or is it that he is picking out the twentieth century as different, perhaps in its faith in the absolute priority of scientific understanding and the effect this has on the way it conducts its wars? So, by 1919, the year of the Peace Conference that provided Europe and much of the rest of the world with its political parameters for the subsequent two decades, Collingwood had identified history as the key to politics. A political dimension is thereby added to his view that no rapprochement between theory and practice is possible without a similar adjustment between philosophy and history.

At the time Collingwood was struggling to formulate these ideas, his life, by his own account, was at odds with his philosophy. It was a time when he lived as if he disbelieved his own philosophy. Now if we have this statement's logic right it includes a necessary element of self-criticism because it points to a hiatus in his life that needed to be overcome. To live as if you disbelieved everything that philosophy told you would be tolerable only if you thought of philosophy as a wholly technical activity, one that had as little bearing on your life as a philosopher as the investigation of grammar has on the life of a grammarian. Collingwood is not suggesting that he was alienated from himself. It is clear, even so, that he saw this condition as one that he could escape; human life he understands "as a becoming", something not governed by forces outside the individual's control.[6] It can be shaped and re-shaped by self-awareness and choice, but at the time, and this is the key point, Collingwood did not think of his own life in these terms. The freedom to restore lost unity to a life that was inconsistent with itself is true in theory, but Collingwood lived as if he didn't believe it. His philosophy told him that his fate was in his own hands, but he lived as if it wasn't.

We should not underestimate the importance of the doctrine of the unity of experience in the young Collingwood's philosophical imagination. As Lionel Rubinoff has rightly pointed out, at the time he was writing *Religion and Philosophy*, Collingwood's commitment was not just to a defence of Christianity that worked in terms of its rationality, but also to the identity of religious belief with morality and history.⁷ Further, the philosophy of religion was not a neutral enquiry, one conducted independently of the life of the philosopher who is engaged in it. In other words, for Collingwood in this period, no account of the unity of experience would be intellectually and emotionally compelling unless it embraced specifically Christian ideals and aspirations. But Collingwood realised, too, that without history this project would necessarily fail. The web of belief that linked philosophy and religion would be too easily swept away if history was absent. Thus, Rubinoff argues rightly that

> Collingwood emphasizes the importance of coming to know, by means of historical thinking, the mind of Jesus from whom the creed of Christianity is derived. For Collingwood, this means believing in the historical reality as distinct from the myth of Jesus. In re-thinking the mind of the actual Jesus the philosopher is re-living a life that serves as an example of how a human life may satisfy the highest possible moral standards. Only then can a person be expected to imitate that life. The historical life of Jesus, which only history can establish, is thus the guarantee that man can be perfect if he will.⁸

Collingwood's thought on these issues did not arrive on his desk in a finished state for, as he acknowledged in *An Autobiography*, "I have always been a slow and painful thinker", but even so the early works reveal detectable progress in his examination of history and its role in human understanding.⁹ Of course, while many of the substantive ideas belonging to Collingwood's mature philosophy of history, most notably his doctrine of the historical imagination, are absent, his early recognition of the importance of history in human self-understanding is clear. History is too much embedded in human life to be left exclusively to the historians. Thus, Collingwood addresses his argument that Christianity and history are linked not merely to historians of religion, but to religious believers themselves. Without history self-knowledge would be endangered since coming to know ourselves is bound up with our capacity to re-think our own thoughts and actions as well as the thoughts and actions of others.¹⁰ In other words, our capacity to know who we are is intimately connected with our being able to re-trace our steps, to re-think how we came to be what we are. But this capacity is inexplicable on the realist view of history. So the realist can give no account of someone, like our socialist, who lives as if they disbelieve their own ideas. For the realist takes their understanding of knowledge from low-grade thinking. The realist's examples are statements like "This is a rose" or "This house has six windows", and the realist assumption is that it is possible to grasp the truth of these statements without any reference to the active, questioning character of thought. But this assumption is as disastrous for understanding our own history as it is for an historian trying to understand why a builder in ancient Rome constructed his property on one side of a river rather than the other. Knowing why you lived in a certain way is not a matter of straightforward apprehension, but of interrogating the past on the basis of evidence. Statements derive their sense as answers to questions. Contra realism, knowledge is not a matter of pure assertion, but of finding which questions are needed in specific situations. Thus, the past will never be brought alive if it is understood solely as fact, or fact in the shape of testimony, or as the deposition of authorities.

Now suppose that, like Collingwood, we discard realism. Our first benefit will be the knowledge that we do not stand to our past as the scissors and paste historian does to facts. We know also that our past will remain inexplicable to us if we are unable to find the right questions to ask of it. If we have kept pace with Collingwood's disposal of realism then we will be aware, too, that recovering our past beliefs will not be achieved by psychotherapy, if by that is meant a procedure that focuses on sensation rather than thought. Endorsement of Collingwood's anti-realism has produced gains, but there is more. For Collingwood takes his early objections to realism further. "The past", Collingwood writes, "is not a dead past, but a past which in some sense is still living in the present".[11] In other words, if there were no trace of our early life in our current life then we can know nothing about it. Additionally, we will not recover what survives from our early life through memory, even though this may play some part in it, but only by subjecting present evidence to rigorous questioning. Now, if we have been watching Collingwood's rejection of realism closely, then our assets should multiply. For if the past lives on in the present then what seems hidden to the casual eye can now be opened to view. History bears the closest possible relation to practice. Thus, in thinking about our past historically we come to see what traces of our earlier attitudes remain and so understand how it is possible for someone, like Collingwood, to live as if they disbelieved their own philosophy.

There is an added dimension to this. For Collingwood's recognition that there was a time when he lived as if he disbelieved his own philosophy is also a feature of his own self-understanding. However, for a life to be lived in those terms they have to be present to the understanding. They have to inform it. This means that the way Collingwood construed a human life in his thought leading up to 1920 is highly relevant to the story we wish to tell. A human life is not like a building awaiting construction, nor is it derived from a plan spun out of the imagination. For Collingwood, at this time, a human life is neither an event nor a system, but a process; the world inhabited by human beings is not one of facts, but of thoughts.[12] And, as we have seen, for Collingwood, thought and action were inextricably connected. So, whether Collingwood saw his life clearly or dimly is dependent on his grasp of the appropriate concepts. There will be occasions, in other words, where clarity about a life arises only in retrospect because what is seen later was not present to the understanding at the time or was visualised only from a distance. This demonstrates the extent of Collingwood's anti-realism, or, to put the same point another way, his commitment to the idea that self-creation is a matter of self-knowledge.[13]

Now if we are right that Collingwood later came to understand his past life in terms that were unavailable to him at the time it is vitally important that we discover what these are. And, of course, the essential text here is *An Autobiography* in which Collingwood in 1939 provided his readers both with the story of his thought and with his life as it was mediated by his thought at different stages of its development. In drawing on Collingwood's autobiography we are not suggesting that Collingwood re-wrote his past by making it appear other than it was. The point of retrospective understanding is to provide a picture that at the time was absent. Thus, the philosophy of history has a direct bearing on the history of the self. Once again we notice just how far Collingwood had extricated his ideas from realism. The philosophy of history is not the technical analysis of concepts employed by historians, but the elucidation of the ways human beings create and re-create their past.

What was it then about Collingwood's later philosophy of history that enabled him to understand his own past better? In *An Autobiography*, Collingwood says that by around 1930 he had formulated three essential propositions in his thinking about history.[14] First, that history is the history of thought; second, that historical knowledge is the re-enactment in the mind of the historian of the thought he is studying, and, third, that re-enactment involves the encapsulation of a past thought in the present context. Here we should allow Collingwood to speak in his own words,

> If what the historian knows is past thoughts, and if he knows them by re-thinking them himself, it follows that the knowledge he achieves by historical enquiry is not knowledge of his situation as opposed to knowledge of himself, it is a knowledge of his situation which is at the same time knowledge of himself.[15]

Thus, in re-thinking past thought what the historian comes to understand is not the past thought only, but the ability to re-think it. And the discovery of this ability tells the historian who he is. Further, by extending the range of historical thought the historian extends his own self-knowledge, and so, Collingwood argues, his knowledge of how the world has come to be what it is. The science of human affairs is, therefore, history, but not because it imitates natural science. History is the science of human affairs because through it self-knowledge and political action are linked.

We are now in a position to reconstruct Collingwood's self-understanding in terms derived from his philosophy of history. Collingwood says that there was a time when he lived as if he disbelieved his own philosophy. He lived as if the division between the contemplative and the practical life was sound, whereas his philosophy told him it was not. We might say that Collingwood lived as a realist at a time when his philosophy told him that realism was false. This brings out the force of Collingwood's statement that he lived as if he disbelieved his own philosophy. But living as a realist means subscribing to realist philosophy, and if that was the case then Collingwood's own philosophy would be false, and that would leave him with nothing in which to disbelieve. We could try to avoid this impasse by thinking of Collingwood at the time as being half a realist, half not, but this still leaves the difficulty intact, albeit on a diminished scale.

Reconsidering Collingwood's life in terms of his account of historical understanding enables us to solve the problem. It is not just that Collingwood's erasure of realism was a gradual and, sometimes, painful one. It is obviously not the case that at one time Collingwood was a fully paid up realist and at a different time a fully paid up something else. Rather, what ceasing to be a realist meant to Collingwood was taking issue with realism when traces of it remained. In other words, to the extent that Collingwood remained a realist he was unable to ask the questions of realism that his anti-realist side wanted him to ask. The growth in Collingwood's understanding of history gave him concepts such as the living past and methods such as question and answer which allowed him to pursue an anti-realist line, but at the time of the war, and, indeed, up to the mid 1920s, his philosophy of history was still substantially incomplete. We might say that Collingwood had not seen the full implications of his doctrine of the unity of experience and that he had not fully grasped the bearing of his emerging philosophy of history for his own self-understanding.

What Collingwood lacked were the concepts which enabled him to see that his life as he was living it and his philosophy were linked.

Thus, Collingwood's statement that at one time he lived as if he disbelieved his own philosophy can be translated to mean that he remained too much of a realist to ask the questions that his philosophy prompted. When Collingwood further extended his separation from realism as his own philosophy of history matured, then he arrived at the concepts that enabled such questions to be asked. So when Collingwood concluded that historical knowledge is not knowledge of the historian's situation as opposed to knowledge of himself, but both, then it made sense for him to interrogate his life in these terms and to look back on his life with this picture in mind. Collingwood's knowledge of his own past comes from re-thinking it and this is nothing more or less than knowledge of his situation and of who he is. But this, surely, is precisely what Collingwood could not achieve at the time when he lived as if he disbelieved his own philosophy. It is not that he wanted to raise questions about the division in his life and, yet, for some psychological reason was unable to do so, but rather that he lacked the concepts necessary to bring his situation in his life as he was living it and his thought together.

It is fascinating to read Collingwood's address, *Ruskin's Philosophy*, in the light of this interpretation. For not only was *Ruskin's Philosophy* one of Collingwood's first public pronouncements after the war (it was delivered in Coniston on the 8 August 1919, but not published until 1922), it also contains some remarks on the relation between theory and practice as it had been conceived and as Collingwood thought it ought to be conceived. In his address Collingwood identified what he termed the "Victorian heresy" as follows,

> During the whole of the central and later Victorian period it was usual for educated and thoughtful Englishmen to believe as a matter of course that the mind has two faculties, the theoretical and the practical, and that the theoretical was fundamentally unreliable, while the practical was always trustworthy.[16]

In Collingwood's view, the result of this division was that "it inculcated moral narrowness combined with intellectual apathy, and made the Victorian Englishman appear in the eyes of the world as a prig and a Philistine".[17] Naturally, Collingwood admired Ruskin for standing out against this distinction, but what interests us is that the period of *Ruskin's Philosophy* would have been exactly the time when, according to Collingwood's *Autobiography*, his grasp of a rapprochement between theory and practice was incomplete. So when Collingwood says that he lived as if he disbelieved his own philosophy was he saying that, like a Victorian Englishman, his confidence in his own set of values was such that he needed no philosophy to support it? Well, not quite, for Collingwood also says that he knew in his philosophy that the division between theory and practice was false. He did not "want a philosophy that should be a scientific toy guaranteed to amuse professional philosophers safe behind their college gates".[18] His problem was that he had not found a way to live that matched his aspirations. So, unlike the Victorian Englishman whose way of life gave him precisely what he wanted, Collingwood lived his life, at least partially, adrift from his ideals.

Endnotes

1   See Taqui Altounyan, *Chimes from a Wooden Bell, A Memoir*, I. B. Tauris, London, 1990, p56, "Apart from not having to go to church there were many things that were wonderfully different about the Collingwood way of life."

2   For William Collingwood, 1819-1903, see James Patrick, *The Magdalen Metaphysicals, Idealism and Orthodoxy at Oxford, 1901-1945*, Mercer University Press, Macon, 1985, pp83-4; further biographical information about William Collingwood is to be found in Henry Pickering, *Chief Men Among the Brethren*, Pickering and Inglis, London, 1918, pp96-8, including a portrait. William Collingwood was the author of *The Value and Influence of Art as a Branch of General Education*, W. Kent and Co., London, 1862, which consisted of two lectures, part of a course on art he gave at Oxford. There is a remarkable line of continuity between this work, that of his son, W. G. Collingwood, *The Art Teaching of John Ruskin*, Percival and Co., London, 1891, and that of his son, R. G. Collingwood, *The Principles of Art*, Clarendon Press, Oxford, 1938.

3   These include "Lectures on the Philosophy of Religious Evolution", delivered at the Foyer D'Etudiants, Kingsway, March/April, 1916, Dep. Collingwood 1/2; "Lectures on the Philosophy of St. Paul", Somerville College, Oxford, 1918, Dep. Collingwood 1/3; "The Church" (group paper, Oxford 1920 (written at Coniston, 13 April 1920), Dep. Collingwood, 1/4; "The Philosophy of the Christian Religion", 29 September 1920, Dep. Collingwood, 1/5; "Religious Intolerance", Dep. Collingwood, 1/10.

4   For discussion of Collingwood's philosophy of history in the early period, see W. J. Van Der Dussen, *History as a Science, The Philosophy of R. G. Collingwood*, Martinus Nijhoff Publishers, The Hague, 1981, pp11-25; Stein Helgeby, *Action as History, The Historical Thought of R. G. Collingwood*, Imprint Academic, Exeter, 2004; especially Chapter 4 "The Logic of Question and Answer"; Douglas H. Johnson, "W. G. Collingwood and the Beginnings of The Idea of History", *Collingwood Studies*, 1, 1994, pp1-26; Rik Peters, "Collingwood's Logic of Question and Answer, its Relation to Absolute

Presuppositions: another brief history", *Collingwood Studies*, 6, 1999, pp1-28; Rex Martin, "Collingwood's Logic of Question and Answer, its relation to Absolute Presuppositions: A Brief History", *Collingwood Studies*, 5, 1998, pp122-35; Lionel Rubinoff, "The Relation between Philosophy and History in the Thought of R. G. Collingwood", *Collingwood Studies*, 3, 1996, pp137-73, and Lionel Rubinoff, "Review Article: R. G. Collingwood, Religion and Philosophy, *Collingwood Studies*, 4, 1997, pp157-82.

5   R. G. Collingwood, *An Autobiography*, p79.
6   R. G. Collingwood, "The Devil", p474.
7   See Lionel Rubinoff, "The Relation between Philosophy and History in the Thought of R. G. Collingwood", especially pp142-5 and 162-5.
8   See Lionel Rubinoff, "Review Article: R. G. Collingwood, Religion and Philosophy", pp169-70. Rubinoff cites *Religion and Philosophy*, (p53) where Collingwood writes, "The Good Samaritan's action is the kind of thing that any good man might do; it is typical of a kind of conduct which we see around us and know to be both admirable and possible. But if the life of Jesus is a myth, it is more preposterous to ask a man to imitate it than to ask him to imitate Herakles. Any valid command must guarantee the possibility of carrying it out; and the historical life of Jesus is the guarantee that man can be perfect if he will."
9   See R. G. Collingwood, *An Autobiography*, p107.
10 Ibid., Chapter 10 in which Collingwood provides an account of the development of his thought on this subject; see, for example, his letter to his fellow archaeologist and friend, F. G. Simpson, in which Collingwood writes, "to understand history is to understand oneself, which is the Delphic oracle's formula for salvation. That doesn't mean, I think, that if everyone was a historian there would be no wars: I think there still would be: but it does mean that wars wouldn't destroy anyone's faith or the inmost spring of their happiness." As cited in Van Der Dussen, p442, see Peter Johnson, *Correspondence*, S1v, letter dated 6 October 1922. For the germ of these ideas in 1916, see R. G. Collingwood, *Religion and Philosophy*, Macmillan, London, 1916, p160 where Collingwood writes, "The spirit of truth is not circumscribed by the limits of space and time. If a real community of life is possible between two men who share each others outward presence and inward thoughts, it is possible no less between two who have never met; between the ancient poet and his modern reader, or the dead scientist and the living man who continues his work. The earlier in point of time lives on in the life of the later; each deriving the benefit from such intercourse."
11 R. G. Collingwood, *An Autobiography*, p97.
12 For a discussion of Collingwood's ideas of process and becoming in the early period that bring out his indebtedness to Hegel's logic, see Gary K. Browning, *Rethinking R. G. Collingwood, Philosophy, Politics and the Unity of Theory and Practice*, Palgrave Macmillan, London, 2004, pp35-8.

13   All these ideas point forward to their more complete and dialectically organised expression in *Speculum Mentis*.
14   R. G. Collingwood, *An Autobiography*, pp110–15.
15   Ibid., p114.
16   See R. G. Collingwood, *Ruskin's Philosophy*, p26. The conference at Coniston where Collingwood delivered his address was one of a number held in 1919 to commemorate the centenary of Ruskin's birth. The first of these was the public meeting organised by the Ruskin Centenary Council and held at the Royal Society of Arts on 8 February 1919, the day of the centenary. The addresses given on that occasion were published in a volume entitled, *Ruskin Centenary Addresses 1919*, edited by J. Howard Whitehouse, Oxford University Press, London, 1919. There is no doubting the Ruskinian atmosphere of the event. For example, one of the contributors, Henry Wilson, then president of the Arts and Crafts Exhibition Society, writes, "The thought of national service reminds me of what has been called reconstruction, though no one seems to agree on what the word really means. To some it appears to mean the re-constitution of all the destructive agencies which have produced the present disaster; it seems to mean intensified machine production, new industrial towns, vast exports, colossal trusts, immense profits, and at the end of it all another cataclysm bringing more opportunities of more unscrupulous profiteering out of the bitter need of suffering humanity. But to Ruskin's followers reconstruction means other things. He has shown us, and we have discovered for ourselves, that national prosperity does not and cannot consist in the multitude of material possessions, but it does consist, and always will, in the quality and extent of its creative capacity" (pp30–31). There is also little doubt that Collingwood counted himself one of Ruskin's followers in respect of this ideal. The conference at Coniston would have been especially significant because of Ruskin's residence at Brantwood, the house near Coniston where he lived for the final years of his life, and the closeness of the Collingwood family to Ruskin in this period, see Tim Hilton, *John Ruskin The Later Years*, Yale University Press, New Haven and London, 2000, especially Chapter 27. There is useful information on John Howard Whitehouse and his role in the Ruskin Centenary Committee in Robert Hewison's Lecture to the Royal Society of Arts, entitled, "Ruskin To-Morrow" (dated 19 April 2000). In the course of his Lecture Hewison refers to Collingwood's address and he links it specifically with Ruskin's love of contradiction, quoting his remark, "Perhaps some of my hearers this evening may occasionally have heard it stated of me that I am rather apt to contradict myself. I hope I am exceedingly apt to do so. I never met with a question yet, of any importance, which did not need for the right solution of it, at least one positive and one negative answer" (*Works*, vol. 16, p187). Is it too fanciful to see Ruskin on contradiction as one of the sources of

Collingwood's own logic of question and answer? Those who are doubtful should consult *Ruskin's Philosophy*, p22.
17   Ibid., p27.
18   R. G. Collingwood, *An Autobiography*, p153.

CHAPTER 4

SHADOWS OF WAR

R. G. Collingwood was not a German spy, as the Northumberland miners mistakenly thought he was, nor, indeed, was he a British one either. Espionage, however, is just one of the devices employed by a state's intelligence services. All governments depend on intelligence in one form or another and in times of war good intelligence is at a premium. During the First World War there were plenty of John Buchan's "big propositions" for British Intelligence Staff to get their teeth into. Not only did the conflict challenge human will and resourcefulness in terms of the sheer intensity of the fighting, it required governments to conduct policy on a global scale. The intelligence war was certainly a battle of wits, but it was also a race in which the participants in the conflict competed with each other to develop and utilise new technologies. Collingwood was neither one of Buchan's "sleuths", if by that is meant someone who engages in covertly discovering the enemy's secrets, nor was he engaged in the complex and increasingly vital task of intercepting foreign government's communications, but he did spend much of the First World War working in the Naval Intelligence Division of the Admiralty and the work he did there contributed, if not to military operations in the war, then certainly the peace that followed it. As the demands of war multiplied successive British governments became more aware that if the war effort was to be effective and if the preparations for peace were to be well directed then good intelligence was essential. It was also realised, if not always with equal force, that for intelligence to be both accurate and usable then recruitment must be as broadly based as possible. To achieve this end the intelligence services cast their nets widely, attracting talent from a variety of occupations including the universities. What combination of circumstances, then, took a young Oxford philosopher and archaeologist from his rooms at an Oxford college to a role in Naval Intelligence?

When Collingwood became a Fellow and Tutor in Philosophy at Pembroke College, Oxford in the summer of 1912 his life's work seemed secure. He was beginning work on *Religion and Philosophy*, one of his earliest investigations into the nature of religious belief.[1] He had already encountered Croce, perhaps the most influential of the figures who shaped his thought in its formative years.[2] And, like any new university teacher he was preparing lectures, in Collingwood's case on Aristotle's *de Anima* and on the theory of knowledge that he would deliver from 1913 to 1915.[3] In Collingwood's life philosophy was studied side by side with history and archaeology.[4] The summer of 1912 is important here, too, because in June that year Collingwood read one of his earliest archaeological reports, on the excavations at the Roman fort at Papcastle, so establishing a distribution of labour between philosophy and archaeology which set a pattern for much of his life.[5]

The year 1913 saw this routine taking shape. Writing lectures on the theory of knowledge, translating and preparing lectures on Aristotle's *de Anima* followed an August part of which was spent on a walking tour in Switzerland.[6] In this year Collingwood was given "his first independent command" in excavation by F. J. Haverfield, his mentor in archaeology, in the exploration of the Roman fort at Ambleside, the reports of which were given in September 1913 and March/April 1914.[7] With the start of the Michaelmas Term in October 1913 philosophy once again becomes the dominant interest. We find Collingwood putting the finishing touches to his translation of Croce's work on Vico, indeed, at the end of October he wrote to Croce expressing his hopes that he will find it worthwhile and that his thought will become more widely known outside Italy as a result.[8] When the translation appeared towards the end of 1913 it repaid a debt to Croce incurred when Collingwood first asked for Croce's permission to translate it in the December of the previous year.[9] More importantly, perhaps, Collingwood, by responding positively to Croce's treatment of Vico, was signposting the themes in the philosophy of history that were to preoccupy him in his future work.

This pattern is repeated in 1914. *Religion and Philosophy* is completed, but it has not yet been published. The Trinity Term finds Collingwood in Oxford delivering his lectures on the theory on knowledge, then during the spring and in the glorious summer of that year Collingwood is heavily involved in the Ambleside excavations.[10] At the start of the war he was at Ambleside being sharply woken up when a crowd of Northumberland coal-miners thought him a German spy.[11] In spite of this incident, in the autumn of 1914 what Collingwood later described as the "shadow of the war" was not so keenly felt. Even so, Collingwood could not have missed the first indications of changes to the order of his life. L. B. Freeston, the archaeologist with whom Collingwood collaborated on the Ambleside explorations, joined the army in September 1914 with the result that his contribution to their report had to be curtailed.[12] Indeed, the 1914 report, a very substantial piece of work containing an extensive text, detailed analysis of evidence, maps and photographs by Collingwood himself, was completed by Collingwood more or less single-handed.[13]

Michaelmas Term 1914 saw Collingwood lecturing once again on *de Anima*. Similarly, after the first Christmas of the war, in Trinity Term 1915, lectures on the theory of knowledge are resumed and during August and September he returned to Ambleside for a third year of excavation although for reasons of economy it was not possible to carry out the work on a large scale.[14] The effects of the war, even in small matters like this, were being noticed. More seriously, in 1915 the Michaelmas Term lectures on the philosophy of religion mark a change in the subjects his teaching had been concerned with so far. Now the themes of the reasonableness of Christianity and the need for spiritual renewal in a time of national crisis become more pressing since they arise from the division between thought and action that Collingwood in these early years was struggling to overcome.[15] And so there is urgency in Collingwood's prose which reflects more than just the seriousness of the topic.

The following year, 1915, was a sombre and frustrating year on the Western Front. As John Keegan puts it, "much blood spilt for little gain and any prospect of success postponed until 1916".[16] In the autumn of 1915 Collingwood was working in an Oxford that had changed utterly from the one he entered in 1908. Undergraduate numbers were severely depleted, university buildings were used as hospitals, and the colleges became training grounds for officer cadets.[17] Both from the influence of military events and from government policy the war was taking on the character of a national purpose. Attrition on the battlefield demanded resources and resources could only be utilised efficiently if they were made subject to government control. Conscription reflects this acknowledgement of necessity, but from a liberal perspective it was important because it made individuals confront the justice of the war and the authority of the state that was forcing them to fight. There were, of course, hard military reasons behind the new policy. Too few were enlisting and an increase in recruitment was needed for the campaigns planned for 1916. Certainly, the Military Service Act of January 1916 contained exemptions, but even so it is hard to disagree with David Stevenson's judgement that taken overall the conscription policy that became law early in 1916 "hastened Britain's commitment to a form of total war".[18]

Total war is not an expression that is likely to gain the approval of liberal intellectuals. Even so, Collingwood, as both a liberal and an intellectual, could not easily set aside the question of service to a democratic state at war. Unlike Russell, whose open opposition to government war policies continued throughout the conflict, Collingwood served the government in ways that were intended to lead to the more efficient prosecution of its policies. Unlike the No Conscription Fellowship of which Russell was an active member and which discouraged its supporters from engaging not only in combatant roles in the war, but also any other alternative form of service, Collingwood supported and contributed to the war effort, and would have wanted to enlist, but for a serious knee injury.[19] In 1942, three years into the Second World War, Collingwood described his work in the First World War as "such service as I was able to do", a phrase that is not, perhaps, as clear as it appears.[20] We might reasonably understand "service" as implying a degree of volunteering, even, perhaps, an obligation on Collingwood's part, but "able to do" requires further exploration. Is Collingwood being reticent here, simply and appropriately modest about his wartime contribution, or is he suggesting that he could have done more? For if Collingwood is hinting that he could have done more then there must surely be a story to tell. Was it, for instance, that his role in intelligence was limited, so curtailing his wish to do more? Was there something about the organisation he worked for, possibly its rivalry with other branches of government, which reduced its effect? By contrast, when Collingwood informs us that he worked on the preparations for the Peace Conference, the words he uses are quite exact. He wants us to see that it was the preparations he worked on, that he did not participate in the Conference itself. But, once again, the clear indication is that there is a story to tell. Perhaps, Collingwood did not attend because the organisation he worked for was not invited. Or was it standard procedure only for specific personnel to be included?

Like many liberal academics Collingwood tended to see the war as a conflict of ideas, but in order to discover the nature of his own involvement in it we need a more finely tuned approach. We know that by 1919 Collingwood had analysed the First War as embodying a crisis of civilisation, the result of a spiritual malaise that would signal the barbaric doctrines that would come to dominate twentieth-century political history.[21] Did Collingwood develop this kind of thinking independently of his war service or were they in some way related? To tackle this question we need to know what Collingwood's war service actually was. When did his service in the war start? Where and with whom did he work? What kind of work was he responsible for?

From the outset Collingwood responded to the war from the perspective of a committed liberal, one who had been impressed by the political intelligence of the Boer War settlement, particularly the sensitivity it showed to the ideals of national self-determination.[22] In Collingwood's hands liberalism does not shy away from the proper authority of the state, but neither does it neglect the role of community and nationality in the establishment of a legitimate political identity. Liberals in wartime are as much concerned as anyone else to counter aggression, but they also wish to know who is responsible for it since it makes a difference to the apportioning of blame and, hence, to the construction of a just peace once the conflict is over. Here the debates that took place at the time about the role of the governing Prussian elite in sparking the war are relevant because they rely on a distinction between state and society that liberals take extremely seriously.[23]

As a liberal and also a philosophical idealist Collingwood was well aware of the Hegelian influences on the political philosophers he admired; in fact, he had once contemplated writing a study of nineteenth-century political thought in which T. H. Green, for one, would have figured prominently. And, yet, it is not Green's roots in German philosophy that interested Collingwood, but his Englishness. Green's political thinking arises from the mid-Victorian polity which forms its background.[24] As the war ground on what interested liberals, however, was not Englishness, but Prussianism. Should liberals think of the war as being fought not against the German people, but the "ring of German war-lords" that plotted it?[25] For many liberals Prussianism was convenient shorthand for answering this question. It enabled them to portray the war as a conflict with the German military caste that had caused it rather than with the German people themselves. As a way of thinking about the war Prussianism was highly influential, pervading British war aims and also the nature of the settlement to be reached with Germany once the conflict was concluded.[26] Not everyone found this doctrine persuasive, however. For it rested on a distinction between the German government and the German people which many found unconvincing.

When we consider Collingwood's response to the war in the light of these attitudes and beliefs we might well expect him to be sympathetic to an understanding of the conflict that depicts it as a crusade against a military elite ruling over a subjugated people. And it is true that in his *Autobiography* Collingwood identifies the territorial ambition of an enclosed Prussian military class as one of the immediate causes of the war.[27] Even so, Prussianism, in Collingwood's usage, is notable as much for the questions it doesn't answer as it is for those it does. It does tell us that it is a false imperialism that is at the heart of German aggressiveness and that it is a false conception of the state that lies behind it, but what it does not take a view on is the collective guilt (or lack of it) of the German people.[28] Collingwood argues that the idea of the state which Prussianism subscribes to is false because it collapses the distinction between state and society, but this tells us little about the actual circumstances in any given case. We should consider this omission significant because it is indicative of Collingwood's thinking in its formative stage. A philosophical idea of the state (what Collingwood calls the spirit of Prussianism) gives us an account of the state as a concept. What it does not do is trace the instantiation of the state as an historical idea. But historical understanding is exactly what a doctrine like Prussianism calls for. How could we know if Prussianism was a consoling liberal myth or a plausible explanation of the German people's predicament without an historical awareness of the contemporary situation then existing in Germany? Similarly, the debate over the immediate causes of the war versus its deeper origins could only be addressed on the basis of historical knowledge. Philosophy, in other words, needed to be brought into a closer relation with history, but in 1919 Collingwood's thinking had not yet reached a point where this could be achieved.

One of the features of Prussianism as a political doctrine is that it contains a credible motive for action. It will do so, however, only if the facts of the situation match the assumptions of the theory. To treat Germany as a united nation when it was not would lead to mistaken policies. By the same token, to treat Germany as if the distinction between the government and the people was true when in this case it was not would equally lead to mistaken policies. In 1919 Collingwood argued that the solution to Prussianism was a strong and active League of Nations.[29] Later, as we shall see, Collingwood retracted this position just as he also moved much closer towards explaining German expansionism in terms of a collective German identity.[30] A conception of history that delivers it from realism promises a closer relation between history and politics. In 1919, however, Collingwood was just at the start of his search for a unified theory—one that he hoped would bring about a satisfactory rapprochement between philosophy and history and between theory and practice.

The bald facts concerning Collingwood's service in the war have often been stated.[31] We know that Collingwood served in the Naval

Intelligence Division of the Admiralty.[32] We know that he was involved in the preparations for the Peace Conference.[33] We know also because Collingwood tells us in his "List of Work Done" what publications this led to. What we do not know, however, is the background to the Naval Intelligence Division and the role Collingwood played in it. Nor do we know where and how Collingwood worked or who worked with him. More importantly, we know nothing about the significance of Collingwood's contribution, "such service as I was able to do", as he tells us, either at that stage of the war effort or in terms of the development of his thought. In what follows I will answer these questions in turn by drawing together new historical research on Admiralty Intelligence and its personnel in this period of the war with our knowledge of Collingwood's life and thought at the time.[34]

Endnotes

1   See R. G. Collingwood, "List of Work Done", Collingwood MS, DEP 22, p15. See also W. J. Van Der Dussen, *History as a Science: The Philosophy of R. G. Collingwood*, p448.

2   See Amedeo Vigorelli, "Lettere Di Robin George Collingwood A Benedetto Croce (1912-39)", *Rivista di storia della filosofia*, n.3, 1991, p549; Collingwood's letter to Croce is dated 14 December 1912.

3   For details of the lectures Collingwood gave in the period I have followed Van Der Dussen, *History as a Science*, Appendix 2, p 433.

4   Van Der Dussen (*History as a Science*, p202) writes, "Collingwood always worked—from his days at College till near the end of his life—on the three tracks of philosophy, archaeology and history." This is clearly right.

5   R. G. Collingwood, "Report of the Excavations at Papcastle, 1912", *Transactions of the Cumberland and Westmorland Antiquarian and Archaeological Society*, 13, 1913, pp131–41.

6   Letter from Collingwood to his sister, Barbara, dated 3 July 1913 (in private possession).

7   See R. G. Collingwood, "Report on the Excavation of the Roman Fort at Ambleside, 1913 (with Professor Haverfield), with a Preliminary Report of the Excavation in March and April 1914 (with L. B. Freeston)", *Transactions of the Cumberland and Westmorland Antiquarian and Archaeological Society*, 14, 1914, pp433–65; see also Collingwood's obituary of Francis Haverfield, *Proceedings of the Society of Antiquaries of Newcastle-upon-Tyne*, (third series), vol. 9, no. 9, 1919, pp117–18. William M. Johnston, *The Formative Years of R. G. Collingwood*, Martinus Nijhoff, The Hague, 1967, reports that "Haverfield had been greatly distressed by World War 1 because it cut him off from many intimate friends on the Continent (see F. Haverfield, *The Roman Occupation of Britain*, Clarendon

Press, Oxford, 1924, p30). It is possible that this experience of Haverfield's contributed to Collingwood's intense repugnance to the War as a disruption of civilised life" (pp37-8n2). It would seem that Johnston has a point because in George Macdonald's *Biographical Notice* which he is citing we find the following, "He was one of the large number of people on this side of the Channel upon whom the violation of Belgium's neutrality reacted most powerfully, leaving the moral issue so stark and clear that doubt or hesitation was impossible" (see F. Haverfield, *The Roman Occupation of Britain*, p30). There is a detailed discussion of Haverfield's response to the war in P. M. W. Freeman, *The Best Training Ground for Archaeologists, Francis Haverfield and the Invention of Romano-British Archaeology*, Oxbow Books, Oxford, 2007, pp349ff. For Collingwood's debt to Haverfield, see R. G. Collingwood and J. N. L. Myres, *Roman Britain and the English Settlements*, Clarendon Press, Oxford, 1936, ppvi-vii.

8   Vigorelli, "Lettere", p550; Collingwood's letter to Croce is dated 27 October 1913; Collingwood's translation was published as Benedetto Croce, *The Philosophy of Giambattista Vico*, Howard Latimer, London, 1913.

9   Vigorelli, "Lettere", p549; letter dated 14 December 1912.

10   See R. G. Collingwood, "The Exploration of the Roman Fort at Ambleside: Report on the second year's Work (1914)", *Transactions of the Cumberland and Westmorland Antiquarian and Archaeological Society*, vol. 15, 1915, pp1-62.

11   R. G. Collingwood, *An Autobiography*, p152; were these the same Northumberland miners that Arthur Ransome mentions in a letter to W. G. Collingwood? Speaking of his younger brother, Geoffrey Ransome, who had just received a commission in the West Yorkshire Regiment, Arthur writes, "he gets on very well with his men, and when the regiment as a whole refused to go on parade, his platoon sent him a note to say that they intended to turn up, and did so, to Geoffrey's lasting honour. They are mostly Northumberland miners, and he likes them very much." Letter dated 27 November 1914, see *Signalling from Mars, The Letters of Arthur Ransome*, selected and introduced by Hugh Brogan, Jonathan Cape, London, 1997, pp16-17. On spy scares in the early days of the war generally, see Christopher Andrew, *Secret Service, The Making of the British Intelligence Community*, William Heinemann Ltd, London, 1985, pp35-85; Richard Deacon, *A History of the British Secret Service*, Frederick Muller Limited, London, 1969, pp160-73, and for spy scares in the Lake District more particularly, see, for example, Linda Lear, *Beatrix Potter, A Life in Nature*, Allen Lane, London, 2007, p269.

12   *Transactions*, 1915, pp3-4; Collingwood's reference to the "shadow of war" comes from *The Book of the Pilgrimage of Hadrian's Wall*, 1-4 July 1930, p3.

13   Professor Haverfield contributed a great deal to the work, but the report was written by Collingwood.

14   See R. G. Collingwood, "The Exploration of the Roman Fort at Ambleside: Report on the third year's work (1915)", *Transactions of the Cumberland and Westmorland Antiquarian and Archaeological Society*, vol. 15, 1915, pp56–90.
15   For discussion of the influences on Collingwood's thought in the period I am examining, see James Patrick, *The Magdalen Metaphysicals, Idealism and Orthodoxy at Oxford, 1901–1945*, pp83–92.
16   See John Keegan, *The First World War*, Hutchinson, London, 1999, p219.
17   For three descriptions of this, see Arthur Lionel Smith Master of Balliol (1916–24), *A Biography and Some Reminiscences by His Wife*, John Murray, London, 1928, p221ff; and Margaret Leigh, *The Fruit in the Seed, Chapters of Autobiography*, Phoenix House Limited, London, 1952. Leigh's impressions of Oxford in Easter 1915 are contained in the following passage, "Meantime the war had tightened its hold on Oxford. The Examination Schools became a base hospital; the younger male dons felt for their swords, and undergraduates dwindled to a handful of crocks, Indians and Irishmen" (p59). George Macdonald's description in his Biographical Note of Collingwood's friend and mentor in archaeology, Francis Haverfield, has greater personal resonance: "To those who had been familiar with the city under its normal aspect, Oxford during the long years of war presented a strange and melancholy spectacle. Of the younger generation there remained only the women students, and a handful of undergraduates too young to serve or physically unfit. The lecture rooms were all but empty; the river and the playing fields were deserted; the Examination Schools were filled with wounded men. And the sounds were as unusual as the sights. The streets echoed to the rumble of army wagons and the tramp of marching feet; the quiet of the most retired of college gardens was broken by the harsh and insistent droning of aeroplanes. The whole atmosphere was depressing in the extreme. In these surroundings the older members of the teaching staff, or such of them that had not been claimed for emergency duty in London, did their best to forget their anxiety as to what was happening overseas, and strove manfully to prevent the total collapse of academic activity" (Francis Haverfield, pp30–31). There is a good discussion of the impact of the war on Oxford by J. M. Winter, "Oxford and the First World War", in Brian Harrison (ed.), *The History of the University of Oxford*, vol. 8, *The Twentieth Century*, Oxford University Press, Oxford, 1994, pp3–27.
18   David Stevenson, 1914–1918 The History of the First World War, Penguin Books, London, 2004, p203; for the move towards conscription, see John Rae, Conscience and Politics, The British Government and the Conscientious Objector to Military Service 1916-1919, Oxford University Press, London, 1970.
19   For Russell's involvement in the anti-war movement, see Ray Monk, *Bertrand Russell, The Spirit of Solitude*, pp456ff.

20   See R. G. Collingwood, *The New Leviathan*, The Clarendon Press, Oxford, 1942, pv.

21   See the discussion in David Boucher, *The Social and Political Thought of R. G. Collingwood*, Cambridge University Press, Cambridge, 1989, pp184-94.

22   R. G. Collingwood, *An Autobiography*, pp155-6. Another who saw the disparity between the two settlements was General Sir Ian Hamilton who had commanded British troops at Gallipoli. In an address given in 1922 he asked a fundamental question, "How is it that the Boer War put an end to the feuds, race hatreds, bankruptcies, disorders and bloodshed which had paralysed South African progress for a generation, whilst the Great War has on the contrary inflicted race hatred, bankruptcy and murder over the best part of the old world from Ireland in the West to the Near East? I'll tell you why it is; it is because our Politicians entirely ignored the ideals…by making a vindictive instead of a generous peace", as cited in John Pollock, *Kitchener*, Robinson, London, 2002, p209.

23   See the very useful discussion in Lorna S. Jaffe, *The Decision to Disarm Germany, British Policy Towards Postwar German Disarmament 1914-1919*, Chapter 1, "Destroying Prussian Militarism", Allen and Unwin, London, 1985, pp3-20.

24   R. G. Collingwood, letter to G. de Ruggiero 29 May 1921, as published in Alessandra Greppi Olivetti, *Due Saggi Su R. G. Collingwood*, Liviana Editrice, Padova, 1977, p93; and R. G. Collingwood, Report to the Clarendon Press on J. W. Gough, *Social Contract Theory*, 15 and 17 February, 1936, see Donald S. Taylor, *R. G. Collingwood A Bibliography*, 1.164 (I am grateful to Stein Helgeby for his transcription of this item).

25   R. G. Collingwood, *An Autobiography*, p90.

26   See Jaffe, *Decision to Disarm*, pp12ff; also valuable is David French, "'Had We Known How Bad Things Were In Germany, We Might Have Got Stiffer Terms': Great Britain and the German Armistice", in Manfred F. Boemeke, Gerald D. Feldman, and Elizabeth Glaser (eds), *The Treaty of Versailles, A Reassessment After 75 Years*, German Historical Institute, Washington, D. C. and Cambridge University Press, Cambridge, 1998, p69.

27   R. G. Collingwood, *An Autobiography*, p90. Another who thought in a similar vein was Thomas Hardy. In a letter to Florence Henniker (23 March 1915) Hardy wrote, "I, too, like you, think the Germans happy and contented as a people: but the group of oligarchs & munition-makers whose interest is war, have stirred them up to their purposes-at least so it seems." As cited in Michael Millgate, *Thomas Hardy A Biography*, Oxford University Press, Oxford, 1985, pp502-03.

28   See the discussion by David Boucher in his editor's introduction in R. G. Collingwood, *The New Leviathan*, revised edition, with an introduction and additional material edited by David Boucher, Clarendon Press, Oxford, 1992, ppxlvii-lvii.

29   See R. G. Collingwood, "The Spiritual Basis of Reconstruction", Address to the Belgian Students' Conference at Fladbury, 10 May, 1919, as reprinted in R. G. Collingwood, *Essays in Political Philosophy*, edited with introduction by David Boucher, Clarendon Press, Oxford, 1989, p204.

30   For Collingwood's retraction of his earlier support for the League of Nations see, for example, R. G. Collingwood, *The New Leviathan*, 29.69, and for his later judgement of the German collective will, see, for example, *The New Leviathan*, 45.88.

31   Even though obituaries of Collingwood almost invariably refer to his war service there are noticeable differences in their dating of it. For example, R. B. McCallum, "Robin George Collingwood 1889-1943", *Proceedings of the British Academy*, vol. 29, 1943, pp463-68, says that Collingwood's service at the Admiralty began in 1914 with the outbreak of the war, (p464); T. M. Knox, "R. G. Collingwood", *Dictionary of National Biography*, 1941-50, pp168-70, simply says "In the war of 1914-1918 Collingwood worked in the intelligence department of the Admiralty" (p169). The authors of the article on Collingwood in the *New Oxford Dictionary of National Biography*, Stefan Collini and Bernard Williams, deploy the phrase "During the First World War" to describe the period of Collingwood's service, see "Collingwood, Robin George (1889-1943), *New Oxford Dictionary of National Biography*, 2004, 12, pp677-81. In his edited collection, *R. G. Collingwood Essays in Political Philosophy*, edited with an introduction by David Boucher, Clarendon Press, Oxford, 1989, Boucher dates Collingwood's service as beginning in 1915. Fred Inglis in his recent biography, too, seems to date Collingwood's war service from 1915, see Fred Inglis, *History Man, The Life of R. G. Collingwood*, Princeton University Press, Princeton and Oxford, 2009, p87.

32   See R. G. Collingwood, *An Autobiography*, p29. R. G. Collingwood is listed under Naval Staff, Intelligence Division in the Navy List, see *The Navy List*, H. M. S. O., London, November 1918; see also Viscount Jellicoe of Scapa, *The Crisis of the Naval War*, Cassell and Company Ltd. London, 1920, p298.

33   R. G. Collingwood, *An Autobiography*, p89.

34   See Michael Heffernan, "Geography, Cartography and Military Intelligence: The Royal Geographical Society and the First World War", *Transactions of the Institute of British Geography*, NS 21, 1996, pp504-33; Erik Goldstein, "Hertford House: The Naval Intelligence Geographical Section and Peace Conference Planning 1917-1919", *Mariner's Mirror*, 72, 1986, pp85-8 and Erik Goldstein, *Winning the Peace, British Diplomatic Strategy and the Paris Peace Conference 1916-1920*, Clarendon Press, Oxford, 1991. I wish to acknowledge the very considerable usefulness of Goldstein's work.

CHAPTER 5

I. D. 32 IN THE NAVAL INTELLIGENCE DIVISION

In his "List of Work Done" Collingwood refers to "a great quantity of work done in I. D. 32, 1915-1919."[1] To understand this statement fully we need a little of the historical background. In the final quarter of the nineteenth century a number of continental European states created powerful intelligence gathering agencies within their military establishments. Successive British governments were in no position to ignore these developments and so they engaged with the task of reorganising their intelligence gathering operations. To this end a separate naval intelligence division was created and ordered "to collect, classify and record with a complete index all information which bears a naval character or which may be of value during naval matters, and to preserve the information in a form available for reference".[2] From this reorganisation emerged the structure of naval intelligence as it stood at the start of the First World War, and, yet, although adequate in times of peace, the intelligence services in the early days of the war quickly realised how unprepared they were for the demands of the conflict to come.[3]

From the appointment of Admiral Sir Reginald "Blinker" Hall as Director of Naval Intelligence at the Admiralty in November 1914, intelligence gathering was soon transformed.[4] Hall, so-called because of his unmistakeable facial twitch, was charismatic, devious, innovative and entirely ruthless in achieving his aims. An empire builder, the new Director of Naval Intelligence, had no qualms about concerning himself with matters well outside the strictly naval. Hall wanted a finger in every pie and it is largely because of his remarkable drive and insistence on a totally free hand that naval intelligence became by far the most powerful of the main British intelligence gathering organisations during the First World War. Political, economic and military affairs were rapidly, and contentiously, made to feel Hall's influence. On his appointment as Director of the Naval Intelligence Division Hall found an organisation that was mainly concerned with cryptography, the analysis of intercepted radio signals and diplomatic messages. Room 40, as it became known, was the domain of the cryptographers, but vitally important though this work was, under Hall's influence the Naval Intelligence Division expanded rapidly to include a number of wider and, perhaps, surprising responsibilities, including, as we shall discover, the early preparations for Britain's involvement in the post-war peace conference.[5]

The role played by Hall in the expansion of the responsibilities of the Naval Intelligence Division was decisive. As Patrick Beesley puts it, "Hall had seen that not only Room 40 but also he himself and his Intelligence Division, faced with a hundred and one problems never foreseen in peacetime, needed a very considerable injection of civilian talent."[6] For a large part of 1915, in other words, Hall was on the look out for skilled individuals who could perform the complex intelligence gathering required by a naval power that was conducting a war on a global scale.[7]

We now need to shift the background a little more. The unit of Naval Intelligence that Collingwood was assigned to was known as I. D. 32, and both the origin and evolution of I. D. 32 are important for understanding the work that Collingwood did. I. D. 32 originated from a suggestion by Professor H. N. Dickson, at the time professor of Geography at University College, Reading. I will let Erik Goldstein, whose research on this topic has proved invaluable, take the discussion forward.

> The idea for a geographical section had initially been proposed to Hall by Professor H. N. Dickson of University College, Reading. Hall agreed with Dickson's proposal and the Geographical Section of the Naval Intelligence Division, codenamed I.D.32, was established.[8]

Dickson had initially approached the War Office, but on finding it both crowded with similar activities and also largely unresponsive, he had contacted the Admiralty. Once formed, I. D. 32 needed a home and, like many quasi-governmental organisations in wartime, as it expanded it found that each home was too small for its needs. From tiny and rather cramped beginnings in rooms at the Royal Geographical Society in Kensington in July 1915 I. D. 32 moved, as its personnel and functions grew, first, in April 1917, to much larger premises in Hertford House,

I. D. 32 IN THE NAVAL INTELLIGENCE DIVISION 47

the home of the Wallace Collection, in Manchester Square and, then, in September 1918, to 41 Berkeley Square.[9]

I. D. 32's function was to act as the geographical arm of Naval Intelligence. To a degree this meant topographical intelligence but, in fact, the organisation's remit was much wider. Map production for operational purposes was largely the responsibility of the Geographical Section of the War Office and neither the War Office nor the Foreign Office had the personnel to provide the breadth of geographical information that was wanted by the War Cabinet as the war spread.[10] H. C. Darby provides us with a succinct account of the Geographical Section's origin and work:

> the War that was raging at the time generated an increased interest in geography not as an academic discipline but as a subject of practical importance. In 1915 a Geographical Section was formed in the Naval Intelligence Division of the Admiralty to write geographical handbooks on various parts of the world. About seventy writers were involved together with over a dozen draughtsmen, and they produced more than 50 handbooks and manuals and also some 130 short geographical reports. Topographical description loomed large in the content of these. The Director of the Section was H. N. Dickson who had taken a science degree at Edinburgh before lecturing in physical geography at Oxford (from 1899) and becoming a professor of geography at Reading in 1906. Most of the staff were not professional geographers, but there were a few from a small band of university geographers: R. N. Rudmose Brown (Sheffield), O. J. R. Howarth (Oxford), John McFarlane (Aberdeen), and O. H. T. Rishbeth (Southampton).[11]

From its beginning the organisation was conceived as an information providing agency. It was to provide the basis for discussion of military, diplomatic and political questions, not to answer those questions itself.[12] However, our most detailed account of the work of I. D. 32 comes from the reports written by Major Douglas Johnson, the representative of the American Inquiry, whose job it was to determine the best method for the collection of information preparatory to the Peace Conference.[13] From Johnson's reports we see that I. D. 32 had five main functions—first, to prepare a series of Geographical Handbooks giving brief descriptions of an individual country's climate, topography, history and economic resources; second, to prepare a series of Manuals which are more substantial and elaborate than the Handbooks, each with an accompanying atlas; third, to provide special maps required at short notice, often where there was a need to collate different sets of information; fourth, to compile short geographical reports for specific military, political and diplomatic purposes, and, fifth, to provide meteorological data for the services.[14]

Recruitment to I. D. 32 was mainly, but not exclusively, based on the universities.[15] As the official history of the section stresses,

> the nature of the work made it clear at an early stage that the staff of the section should consist of scholars accustomed to collect and weigh scientific evidence rather than of travellers or other persons with first hand knowledge of the areas under investigation.[16]

However, if wanderers in foreign parts were discouraged then philosophers were not. The official history comments that "it may be of interest to note that the new principles and methods were absorbed and applied with great readiness and success by students of philosophy—roughly men of the 'Oxford Greats' type".[17] Indeed, Dickson's Geographical Section attracted a significant number of volunteers from the universities. William Calder, Professor of Greek at Manchester, 1912-30 and W. B. Stevenson, Professor of Greek and Semitic Languages at Glasgow, 1907-37, are two, but, as Stuart Wallace has noted, there were many more. Wallace writes, "Collingwood's colleagues included the Kantian scholar Norman Kemp Smith and two Oxford moral philosophers, H. J. Paton and Hastings Rashdall."[18] Jane Garnett comments of Rashdall that in 1914 he "yearned to find a way of getting personally involved in the war effort. He joined the volunteer corps in Oxford in 1915 and in 1917 finally obtained employment in the Admiralty Intelligence department."[19] Paton was more closely involved with Collingwood's work since, as W. H. Walsh writes,

> he was employed in the Intelligence Division of the Admiralty, along with his fellow philosopher, R.G.Collingwood. In 1919 Paton attended the Versailles Peace Conference as a British expert on Polish affairs, later he wrote about the Polish settlement in the official History of the Peace Conference in Paris.[20]

Later, Samuel Alexander, a philosopher whose work Collingwood admired, joined the organisation.

One snapshot of the kind of work that academics undertook for Admiralty Intelligence comes from the autobiography of the Oxford ancient historian, G. B. Grundy who worked for the War Office from October 1914 to 1915 making maps of Greece and Macedonia. Grundy tells how, in 1915, Hall, then, as we have seen, Director of Naval Intelligence, summoned him to draw up a more detailed map of the coasts of Greece than the Admiralty had available, to see if there were bays or inlets where U-boats might hide. We should let Grundy tell the story himself.

I. D. 32 IN THE NAVAL INTELLIGENCE DIVISION

On thinking over the matter, I recognised that at different times I had got to know all the coasts except on the outside of Euboea. I made a lucky shot at the outset of the work. I mentioned to him a small bay just to the north of the Bay of Navarino as an ideal place for U-boats. Unknown to me, Hall passed on that piece of information to the Mediterranean Fleet, and a little more than a week after I had told him, informed me that they had caught and destroyed a U-boat there. I doubt whether the rest of my information was equally useful.[21]

Not all intelligence work had such a dramatic outcome, as Grundy's final remark implies. Margaret Leigh, who was an undergraduate at Somerville College, Oxford, from 1913 to 1915 studying philosophy and ancient history, tells how she was recruited to intelligence and how frustrating work at Hertford House could often be. She writes,

In the early summer of 1917 my late philosophy tutor asked me to go with him to the Admiralty Intelligence Department, at that time mainly staffed by Oxford dons unfit for military service and their more promising girl pupils. We worked among the shrouded remains of the Wallace Collection, watched over by innumerable commissionaires who, when the sirens went, collected our precious papers and shepherded us into the basement, where we played pitch-and-toss or marbles until the All-clear sounded. The department was under the charge of a geographer, and had little to do with the Admiralty: I and my immediate neighbours were kept busy compiling handbooks on various eastern and central European countries. I have never discovered what use, if any, was made of them.[22]

We get a clear picture of what the day-to-day work of the geographical section was like after it moved to Hertford House from the reports to the "Inquiry". Once the Wallace Collection was placed in store the vacant spaces that remained offered an excellent opportunity for the preparation of maps. As this source explains:

One large gallery is filled with large tables, each table devoted to a special region (such as Mexico, Belgium, Serbia, etc.), is filled with books and maps relating to that region, and is presided over by the specialist assigned to prepare the report on that region. Several assistants, most of them men and several of them army officers, serve under each specialist. Another large room is equipped with tables where a corps of translators, mostly women, is at work, translating and abstracting such foreign reports as the specialists and their assistants may desire. Two other rooms were equipped with drawing tables, and perhaps a dozen or more draughtsmen and cartographers were busy preparing maps.[23]

In the First World War intelligence gathering largely meant maps and maps meant the Royal Geographical Society, an organisation whose involvement in intelligence activities in the First War was, as Michael Heffernan has persuasively shown, both detailed and extensive.[24] Only the Royal Geographical Society had the facilities and the resources that geographical intelligence needed. What it lacked, however, were qualified personnel. British universities were seen as the recruiting grounds that would overcome this, and so throughout 1915 a number of academics were drafted in to remedy this deficiency. Of the many university recruits to naval intelligence in this period one figure is especially important to our appreciation of the organisation that Collingwood joined, also to our knowledge of when he joined it and why.

This was D. G. Hogarth who was Keeper of Antiquities at the Ashmolean Museum, Oxford, a close friend of T. E. Lawrence and a major influence on British military strategy in the Middle East. He was a member of the Council of the Royal Geographical Society and since January 1915 had been working on maps relating to Turkey and the surrounding areas. Hogarth was in the Middle East until the last few weeks of December 1915 when he was contacted by Hall and asked to return to Britain to take charge of a recently recruited intelligence team whose purpose was, as Michael Heffernan explains, "to research strategic alternatives with respect to different localities around the world where naval power could be deployed."[25] We should let Heffernan take up the story.

> The new NID team installed itself alongside the GSGS cartographers in Kensington Gore where the RGS map and reference library proved perfectly suited to its needs. By October 1915, there were twenty NID academics working full-time at the RGS squeezed into four large rooms, under the immediate command of Lieutenant-Commander Cozens-Hardy.[26]

As the functions and personnel of I. D. 32 increased so also did its productivity. Transfer to more spacious accommodation facilitated this to such a degree that by the end of the war the output of the Geographical Section counted in terms of Manuals, Handbooks and Geographical Reports, in addition to the production of atlases, maps and specific reports on areas or topics of urgent strategic or political interest, was very considerable. An obituary of H. N. Dickson comments that "it was the pride of I. D. 32 that there was no corner of the known world about which it failed on demand to produce information at the shortest notice", a claim which, assessed by reference to the volume of work completed, is not difficult to understand.[27] Dickson's accomplishment has been described as a kind of "universal geography" in which systematically organised data is made available

I. D. 32 IN THE NAVAL INTELLIGENCE DIVISION 51

on the topography and geography of the main theatres of war.[28] For example, Handbooks were completed on Arabia, (C. B. 910); the Danube River, (I. D. 01020); Libya, (I. D. 1162), and Portuguese Nyasaland, (I. D. 1161), with Short Geographical Reports on a huge range of territories ranging from the Coast Provinces of Asia Minor, (I. D. 92) to Russian Poland, (I. D. 1174). Since the war had a global reach then the information had to be as comprehensive as possible. Further, the information needed to be presented in a standard format so that the physical, historical, ethnographic, economic, and political features of the countries to be described were uniformly accessible. In some of the volumes the organising focus was a theme or topic such as roads, rivers or the main modes of communication, rather than the country itself. But, overall, the aim of the series was to create a body of expertly assembled material that would provide the basis for informed military and political decision-making, but without determining the decision itself. The series, in other words, aimed to be objective, accurate and impartial.

The Geographical Section also found itself responsible for the early British preparations for what became the Paris Peace Conference. When, then, did the British preparations for the peace start? Harold Nicolson who as a young diplomat attended the Paris Conference says it was in the spring of 1917 that "a special organisation was created for the collection of material and the training of a peace staff".[29] Prior to that date any detailed planning for the conclusion of the war would have been difficult, first, because all energies were devoted to winning it, second, because the exact circumstances of the end game were near impossible to predict and, third, because no government would have been willing to make detailed commitments in advance. During 1917, however, information gathering by a variety of government agencies proceeded apace. The Geographical Section of the Admiralty in which Collingwood was employed was one among a number of government departments engaged on similar intelligence tasks. Of the material produced by the War Office, the War Trade Intelligence Department, the Foreign Office and the Historical Section of the Foreign Office, in addition to the Admiralty, Nicolson comments

> Should any historian doubt the quality of our preparation, I should urge him to obtain the whole collection from the London Library and peruse their contents. He will agree that no more authoritative, comprehensive or lucid basis of information could possibly have been compiled.[30]

Once again Goldstein is helpful because he tells us exactly how the involvement of I. D. 32 came about. He writes,

Hall also came to be responsible for the initial stages of Britain's preparations for a post-war peace conference. This rather curious task for Naval Intelligence originated in a proposal to the War Cabinet Secretariat in January 1917 by two young historians, Arnold Toynbee and Alfred Zimmern, for the creation of a Peace Terms Intelligence Section which would gather useful background information for use at any subsequent peace negotiations. They succeeded in convincing Leo Amery, the assistant secretary to the War Cabinet, to support the plan, and it was Amery who cast about for a way to establish and staff such an operation. The Foreign Office, the obvious home for such work, was not viewed with favour by many of those around the Prime Minister, and so Amery turned instead to Admiral Hall as the man best able to implement the plan for a department to gather geographical, historical, economic, and statistical material. Hall accomplished this by expanding the work of the Naval Intelligence Geographical Section, establishing a Historical Section, and assisting the War Trade Intelligence Section to expand its capabilities. It was the Geographical Section though which was the hub of Hall's foray into peace planning.[31]

In his Report of May 1918 on British plans for collecting information for use at the Peace Conference, Douglas Johnson took the view that Dickson "was the first to begin systematic accumulation of data for use at the peace table".[32] For even though Dickson's organisation had started with the aim of amassing information on territories as the war spread, from March/April 1917 its main duties were to do with preparations for peace. From that time, then, I. D. 32 was part of the highly elaborate, not to say labyrinthine, British planning for peace. It was intended that the Geographical Section should be at the centre of the collection and dissemination of the massive amount of data relevant to the decisions that would determine the political shape of the world once the war ended. Staffed by experts, but not responsible for policy, I. D. 32 aimed to link theory with action by encouraging informed decision-making. As we shall discover, however, this was to be an aspiration more easily conceived than realised. This was the organisation that Collingwood joined early in 1916 and it is to his specific role in it that we must now turn.

Endnotes

1   R. G. Collingwood, "List of Work Done", Collingwood MS, DEP 22, p16
2   As quoted in F. H. Hinsley, *British Intelligence in the Second World War*, vol. 1, HMSO, London, 1979, p7.
3   On the Naval Intelligence Division and its origins, see Patrick Beesly, "British Naval Intelligence in Two World Wars—Some Similarities and

Differences" in Christopher Andrew and Jeremy Noakes (eds), *Intelligence and International Relations 1900–1945*, Exeter Studies in History no. 15, Exeter, 1987, pp253–73; Deacon, *British Secret Service*, pp174–89, 203-217; David Stafford, *Churchill and Secret Service*, John Murray (Publishers) Ltd, London, 1997, reprinted Abacus, 2001, pp69ff; Christopher Andrew, *Secret Service*, pp87ff; Alan Judd, *The Quest for Mansfield Cumming and the Founding of the Secret Service*, Harper Collins, London, 1999, p289ff; Patrick Beesley, *Very Special Intelligence, The Story of the Admiralty's Operational Intelligence Centre 1939-1945*, Hamish Hamilton, London, 1977, pp1–9; Donald McLachlan, *Room 39, Naval Intelligence in Action, 1939-1945*, Weidenfeld and Nicolson, London, 1968, although mainly concerned with the Second World War, is also useful because it discusses geographical intelligence and its strategic value.

4   For Hall, see Sir William James, The Eyes of the Navy: A Biographical Study of Admiral Sir Reginald Hall, Methuen and Co. Ltd, London, 1953, and David Ramsay, 'Blinker' Hall, Spymaster, The Man Who Brought America into World War One, Spellmount, The History Press, Stroud, revised edition, 2009.

5   For Room 40, see Patrick Beesly, *Room 40 British Naval Intelligence 1914–1918*, Hamish Hamilton, London, 1982, which also contains a List of Staff serving in Room 40 (Appendix 2) and a valuable bibliography of further reading, (pp321–3); there is a fine impression of life in Room 40 in Penelope Fitzgerald, *The Knox Brothers*, Coward, McCann and Geoghegan, New York, 1977, pp135ff and 142ff. See also Arthur J. Marder, *From the Dreadnought to Scapa Flow, The Royal Navy in the Fisher Era, 1904–1919*, vol. 2 *The War Years: To the Eve of Jutland*, Oxford University Press, London, 1965, pp133-4, and also vol. 3, *Jutland and After*, (May 1916–December 1916), second edition (revised and enlarged), Oxford University Press, London, 1978, pp269–70.

6   Patrick Beesly, *Room 40*, p125.

7   For Hall's recruitment policies in the wider business and academic communities see C. M. Andrew, "The Mobilization of British Intelligence for the Two World Wars", in N. F. Dreisziger (ed.), *Mobilization for Total War, the Canadian, American and British Experience 1914–1918, 1939–1945*, Wilfred Laurier University Press, Waterloo, Ontario, Canada, 1981, pp96-7.

8   See Goldstein, "Hertford House", p85, and *Winning the Peace*, p27.

9   For the changing locations of I. D. 32 see *The Geographical Work of the Naval Intelligence Division, Naval Staff, 1915–1919*, Technical History Section, Admiralty, December 1919, ADM223/90 303339, p1.

10 See T. D., "Handbooks of the Geographical Section, Naval Intelligence Division, Admiralty", *The Geographical Journal*, vol. 57, no. 1 (Jan. 1921), pp51-2.

11 See H. C. Darby, "Academic Geography in Britain 1918-1946", *Transactions of the Institute of British Geographers*, new series, vol. 8, no. 1, 1983, pp14–26.

12 The Geographical Work, p1.

13   *Inquiry Document 984*, Confidential Report on the Arrangements made by the British Government for Collecting Data for the Peace Conference, June 1918, pp3–5, Records of the Inquiry, National Archives, Washington, D. C. For detailed discussion of the Inquiry, see Lawrence E. Gelfand, *The Inquiry, American Preparations for Peace 1917–1919*, Yale University Press, New Haven and London, 1963.

14   *Inquiry Document 984*, see the discussion in Goldstein, "Hertford House", p85.

15   A. R. Wells illuminates the background to Hall's insistence on going outside traditional naval recruitment sources. He writes, "The basic argument against the scholar-intelligence worker at the Admiralty stemmed from the premise that the kind of knowledge that was useful in solving intelligence problems comes almost entirely from practical first hand, 'experience', not from academic abstractions." As the evidence makes clear, Hall consistently opposed this view. See A. R. Wells, *Studies in British Naval Intelligence*, (Ph.D. thesis), University of London, 1972, p128; see also, W. K. Wark, "British Military and Economic Intelligence: Assessments of Nazi Germany before the Second World War", in C. Andrew and D. Dilks (eds), *The Missing Dimension, Governments and Intelligence Communities in the Twentieth Century*, University of Illinois Press, Urbana and Chicago, 1984, pp89–92.

16   The Geographical Work, p1.

17   Ibid., p1. Not all who attempted to get work at the Admiralty were accepted. One who was turned down was A. A. Milne; see Ann Thwaite, *A. A. Milne, His Life*, Faber, London, 1990, p163.

18   See Stuart Wallace, *War and the Image of Germany, British Academics in Wartime Whitehall, 1914–1918*, John Donald Publishers Limited, Edinburgh, 1988, pp237–40, Appendix 5, and also James, *Eyes of the Navy*, pp 129–30. For a discussion of philosophers and the First World War see Thomas Baldwin, "Philosophy and the First World War", in Thomas Baldwin (ed.), *The Cambridge History of Philosophy, 1870–1945*, Cambridge University Press, Cambridge, 2003, pp365–78. E. F. Carritt, who was for a time Collingwood's Oxford tutor, tells the following story about his own wartime service, "During the First Great War I worked for the Ministry of Munitions in a big Charing Cross hotel. One morning the ordinary lift had broken down and we all had to queue up for the Minister's. I happened to look round for some reason and saw that next behind me was Sir Winston Churchill." (See E. F. Carritt, *Fifty Years A Don*, privately printed, 1960.)

19   See Jane Garnett, "Hastings Rashdall 1858–1924", *The New Oxford Dictionary of National Biography*, 2004, 46, p74; see also P. E. Matheson, *The Life of Hastings Rashdall D.D.*, Oxford University Press, London, 1928, pp152ff.

20   See W. H. Walsh, "H. J. Paton 1887–1969", *Proceedings of the British Academy*, 56, 1970, pp293–308, (p293); see also H. J. Paton, "Fifty Years of

Philosophy", in H. D. Lewis (ed.), *Contemporary British Philosophy, Personal Statements*, third series, George Allen and Unwin Ltd, London, 1956, p343.
21   See G. B. Grundy, *Fifty-Five Years at Oxford, An Unconventional Autobiography*, Methuen Limited, London, 1945, p131.
22   See Margaret Leigh, *The Fruit in the Seed*, pp70-71.
23   See Inquiry Document 984, p2.
24   See Heffernan, "Geography, Cartography and Military Intelligence", p517; and also, more generally, Michael Heffernan, "The Politics of the Map in the Early Twentieth Century", *Cartography and Geographic Information Science*, vol. 29, no. 3, 2002, pp207-26.
25   See Heffernan, "Geography, Cartography and Military Intelligence", p517. As we shall discover later Collingwood's school friend and later brother-in-law, E. H. R. Altounyan, was also a friend of Lawrence.
26   See Heffernan, "Geography, Cartography and Military Intelligence", p517; in his discussion of Hogarth's wartime career, Jeremy Wilson sheds further light on the origins of the Geographical Section, "Shortly afterwards, (August 1915), Hogarth returned to England where he joined the new Geographical Section of the Naval Intelligence Division, set up to produce a series of geographical handbooks. Sir Reginald Hall, head of Naval Intelligence, was at that time recruiting a number of experts from the academic world for this Division. The historian H. A. L. Fisher, whose brother was a senior naval officer, later claimed to have been responsible for Hogarth's recruitment. Some writers (e.g. H. V. F. Winstone in *The Illicit Adventure*, Jonathan Cape, London, 1982, p79) have alleged that Hogarth was already working for Naval Intelligence in 1910, but there seems little evidence to support this claim which appears to be inferred from Hogarth's wartime role. In reality the section of Naval Intelligence that Hogarth joined in 1915 was not created until that year. During the war he specialised in geographical, historical and political questions related to his specialist area, the Middle East. Among the reference works he compiled was the secret Naval Intelligence *Handbook to Arabia*, (I. D. 1128 and CB 405), a comprehensive two volume study issued in 1916-17 which ran to more than 1,200 pages. After March 1916 he was responsible, for some months, for coordinating work on these publications at the Geographical Section of Naval Intelligence in London and the Arab Bureau in Cairo." (Jeremy Wilson, *Lawrence of Arabia, The Authorised Biography of T. E. Lawrence*, Heinemann, London, 1989, pp1008-09. Collingwood refers to Hogarth (*An Autobiography*, p82) where he describes him as a "bold revolutionary".
27   See R. N. R. B, "Obituary Dr Henry Newton Dickson, C. B. E", *The Geographical Journal*, vol. 59, no. 6, (June 1922), p479; for further information see the obituary of Dickson by A. S. in *The Scottish Geographical Magazine*, vol. 38, 1922, pp183-4.
28   For a good discussion of the Manuals and Handbooks as works of geography that focuses on their revised use in the Second World War, see

Hugh Clout and Cyril Gosme, "The Naval Intelligence Handbooks: A Monument in Geographical Writing", *Progress in Human Geography*, vol. 27, no. 2, (2003), pp153-73, especially pp154-5, and Cyril Gosme, "The Naval Intelligence Geographical Handbook Series, (Great Britain, 1941-46): A Description and a Call for Comments", *Cybergio, European Journal of Geography*, article 137, 2007, pp1-21. See also T. W. Freeman, *A History of Modern British Geography*, Longman, London, 1980, p103, where the handbooks are described as "somewhat encyclopaedic in character".

29 See Harold Nicolson, *Peacemaking 1919*, revised edition 1943, Methuen, London, 1964, p26; and Margaret Macmillan, *Peacemakers, Six Months That Changed The World*, John Murray, London, 2002, p63 where Winston Churchill is quoted as follows, "What had we to do with peace while we did not know whether we should not be destroyed? Who could think of reconstruction while the whole world was being hammered to pieces, or of demobilisation when the sole aim was to hurl every man and every shell into battle?"

30 Nicolson, *Peacemaking*, p27; for a discussion of the American peace planning arrangements, see *The Intimate Papers of Colonel House*, arranged as a narrative by Charles Seymour, vol. 3, *Into the World War*, April 1917-June 1918, Ernest Benn Ltd., London, 1928, pp174ff and 328ff. "The Inquiry", as the American intelligence gathering unit was called, tended to follow the methods of the British, thus we find on p328, "The Inquiry was able to produce within the space of a few days a complete territorial programme. General propositions were reduced to formulae, the critical territorial issues were isolated, and recommendations drafted in accord with the principles which Wilson was known to approve. In all-day and all-night sessions statistics were gathered and simplified, and illustrative maps constructed, as justifications for the recommendations that were made."

31 See Goldstein, "Hertford House", p85, also *Winning the Peace*, p27; for Amery's decision, see The Rt. Hon. L. S. Amery, C. H. *My Political Life*, vol. 2, *War and Peace 1914-1929*, Hutchinson, London, 1953, p103; also *The Leo Amery Diaries*, vol. 1, *1896-1929*, edited by John Barnes and David Nicholson, Hutchinson, London, 1980, p141.

32 See Inquiry Document 987.

CHAPTER 6

COLLINGWOOD IN I. D. 32

R. G. Collingwood started work in I. D. 32 on 3 January 1916 after completing the lecture course he gave at Oxford in the Michaelmas Term. He had been asked by a friend to join the organisation soon after it was formed in mid-1915, but was at that point unable to accept.[1] Collingwood tells us in his *Autobiography* that "a year or two after the outbreak of the war, I was living in London and working with a section of the Admiralty Intelligence Division in the rooms of the Royal Geographical Society."[2] The Society where the Geographical Section was first based was housed in Lowther Lodge, Kensington Gore. Collingwood's first letter to Macmillan regarding the publication of *Religion and Philosophy*, dated 13 July 1916, was written from there.[3] Later in the war when the expanded section transferred to Hertford House, the home of the Wallace Collection, to cope with increased work for the anticipated Peace Conference Collingwood moved with it, in the process changing his address from 69 Church Street, Kensington, to 30 Bedford Gardens.

Collingwood's early days in the Geographical Section must have had a powerful impact on him. The Royal Geographic Society building itself with its corridors packed full of pictures of mountains, glaciers and yet to be climbed peaks like K2, the glaciers in Karakoram, the summits of the Andes and the famous fifteen feet long panorama of Lhasa, together these must have concentrated his imagination on the task in hand. Family members, however, were not far away for Collingwood's elder sister, Barbara (later Barbara Gnosspelius) also worked in the Geographical Section and she has drawn a vivid picture of their life and work there. In fact, one of the first pieces of evidence for dating Collingwood's service in the Admiralty comes from his sister's memory of their enthusiastically attending a Schumann piano concerto at the Queen's Hall in January 1916 when both worked at the Admiralty Intelligence Division and were sharing a flat above a shop in

Kensington Church Street.[4] It was while Collingwood and his sister worked at the Admiralty that they met Evelyn Underhill and it is in a biography of her that we find Barbara's reminiscence. Barbara writes of Evelyn,

> she was terribly nice with Robin and me, and from the first we were on the easiest and happiest terms. We visited her often at Camden Hill Square, met Nick (Hubert) and had great fun; and they both dined with us in our big basement kitchen, when we moved to 30 Bedford Gardens, and we talked about everything, not so much as I recollect War and Politics, as Philosophy, Psychology and Religion.[5]

Evelyn's first biographer gives us a finely drawn portrait of how their days were spent. She writes,

> In 1916 she began to do war work proper at the Admiralty, translating guide books, where her languages were valuable. In the room where she and her friend Emma Gurney Salter worked, a young brother and sister, Robin and Barbara Collingwood (now Mrs Gnosspelius), were also employed – artistic people with good brains; the sort of company that Evelyn delighted in. Robin Collingwood was already making himself a name as a philosopher. The room where they worked was a gay one, but time sometimes hung on their hands. It was on one of these afternoons when Evelyn invented a country, complete with flora and fauna, and sent it up to the proper authorities – it nearly found its way to the printer. We are not told how the Head of Department dealt with Evelyn.[6]

The emotional impact of the war on those working in Naval Intelligence was sharp, as a later biographer reports. For Evelyn, whose special area of responsibility was Naval Intelligence (Africa), "these were difficult years, she 'went to pieces'."[7]

So what was Collingwood's work in the Geographical Section of Naval Intelligence?

Two matters must be addressed before we can tackle this question directly. Both are concerned with Collingwood's recruitment to Naval Intelligence, the first is to do with his qualifications for the job, the second, much more difficult issue, is with who recruited him. William M. Johnston's early investigation of Collingwood's suitability for intelligence work hits the nail squarely on the head. He writes, "In Admiralty Intelligence, R. G. Collingwood employed his knowledge of French, German, Spanish, and Italian as well as the skill in sifting evidence which he had developed as an archaeologist."[8] Also important are the young Collingwood's skills as a cartographer since the maps and plans in his early archaeological reports he invariably made himself. Collingwood's grasp of the importance of method in obtaining and communicating knowledge together with his sense of the indispensability of historical awareness, admittedly nascent in 1915, also have a clear bearing on his Admiralty employment.

On the issue of who recruited Collingwood, however, we are in the region of conjecture. Two possibilities stand out. The first is W. G. Collingwood, R. G. Collingwood's father, who we know was also employed in intelligence work at the Admiralty. W. M. Johnston suggests that when R. G. Collingwood left Oxford to work at the Admiralty "his father was working in the same office and may have been responsible for securing shore side duty for his twenty-six-year-old son."[9] However, from W. G. Collingwood's letters and diary we can be certain that the opposite is true—it was the son who recruited the father. W. G. Collingwood's established reputation as an historian and archaeologist gave him the skills required, and we also know, as R. G. Collingwood states in one of his obituaries of his father, that "service in the Admiralty Intelligence Division and the privations of wartime life in London left him diminished in strength and looking forward to a shortened span of work",[10] but we now know further that from October 1917 to April 1919 W. G. Collingwood worked at the offices of I. D. 32 at the invitation of his son.[11] The second possibility is the Head of the Geographical Section in which W. G. Collingwood and his son and daughter, Barbara, were employed, H. N. Dickson. Both Dickson and W. G. Collingwood were members of staff at University College, Reading, where Dickson was professor of Geography from 1906 to 1920, and where Collingwood, after starting there in 1903 as Master of Drawing, was from 1907 to 1911 professor of Fine Art. According to Goldstein, Dickson showed great drive and ingenuity in getting the Geographical Section started and in the preparation of maps.[12] We know also from Patrick Beesly's study of Room 40 that Reginald Hall, Director of Naval Intelligence from November 1914, was an independent minded man who realised early in the war that because of the nature and immensity of the work that faced his division it would be both necessary and desirable to recruit from outside strictly defined service personnel.[13] We know also that much of the recruitment from universities was on an informal word of mouth basis, but none of this gives us firm evidence that Collingwood was recruited by H. N. Dickson.[14]

We can now return to the central question, namely, the kind of work that Collingwood did. To a considerable degree this question resolves itself into what kinds of work the Geographical Section was called on to perform since Collingwood was operating as a member of an organisation with its own chain of command and which was moreover required to produce whatever its political and military masters asked of it. In other words, in naval intelligence Collingwood found himself to be as much a part of a bureaucracy as any other academic taking on an administrative role for the state in time of war, and it is worth noting that as his work in I. D. 32 expanded his responsibilities grew. Collingwood's sister, Barbara, refers to his being made "'liaison-officer' between the R. G. S. and the War Office, and will now do most of his work at the W. O."[15] In the light of this we can now make Collingwood's work at Naval Intelligence more intelligible. Two salient facts stand out. The first is that the Geographical Section had a direct role in peace preparations at the earliest only after January 1917, and the second that Collingwood joined I. D. 32 at the beginning of January 1916.

The work that Collingwood did in I. D. 32 was voluntary, unpaid (apart from expenses) and onerous. Moreover, Collingwood never gave up his commitment to Oxford teaching entirely, travelling back once, and later in the war, twice weekly. In his "List of Work Done" Collingwood includes two publications originating from his work in Naval Intelligence—*The Naval Intelligence Manual of Belgium* (with atlas), HMSO, 1918, and *The Naval Intelligence Manual of Alsace-Lorraine* (with atlas), HMSO, June 1919. (Collingwood adds, "These two being the most important of a great quantity of work done in I. D.32 1915–1919.")[16] In *An Autobiography* Collingwood wrote that, "during the latter part of the war I was employed in preparations for the peace conference". (Later we shall need to return to Collingwood's estimate of the peace conference, but for the moment we can focus on his role in preparing for it.)[17] In his *Obituary* of Collingwood R. B. McCallum who knew Collingwood well adds another important piece of information. He writes of Collingwood's work in Naval Intelligence, "As most of this work was secret and much of it no doubt completely transient, little is known about it, but amongst other tasks he wrote a study of the juridical problems concerned with the navigation of the Scheldt up to Antwerp."[18]

When Collingwood arrived in the Royal Geographical Society headquarters as a new member of the Naval Intelligence Division in January 1916 what confronted him was an organisation trying to produce military and political intelligence often against the clock and often in the face of conflicting views as to where the strategic priorities of the war should lie. Further, the cartographic organisation he joined was split between his own section, I. D. 32, and the older established Geographical Section of the General Staff. During 1915 the aim had been to produce a large series of maps covering Europe and the Middle East, which it was hoped would provide the basis for the peace negotiation that would arise after the war. As Michael Heffernan explains, "The explicit objective was to ensure that the new political boundaries of Europe and the Middle East would be shown to an expectant world on a British map designed and produced by British cartographers in London," and, indeed, as it turned out, the British 1:1 million maps were very largely those that were employed at the Paris Peace Conference.[19] Throughout 1915, however, the mapmakers were under pressure from events and the need to develop new strategies to fight the war more effectively. Military stalemate in Europe led many to the view that the Middle East would be a more promising zone of engagement because in it British naval power could be deployed with greater promise of result. Thus, towards the end of 1915, a decision was made, possibly emanating from the Admiralty, to shift, as Heffernan puts it,

> the focus of the NID group strongly towards the Middle East. Detailed research began on the distribution of different tribes and on the territorial jurisdiction and loyalties of various Arab sheiks and warlords. The NID team in the RGS became, in essence, a London branch of the Cairo intelligence office, preparing the way for an Arab revolt and a renewed British campaign in the Middle East.[20]

Further, in January 1916, the time from which we can be sure that Collingwood was a member of the NID group, the supporters of the Middle Eastern strategy gained even more influence. As Michael Heffernan tells the story, Commander William Cozens-Hardy, who was in immediate command of Collingwood's team, aided by Dickson, who was the head of the section, ordered that, as Heffernan puts it, "Work on the 1:1 million sheets was to cease immediately and all other research was to focus on the Middle East."[21] Not, perhaps, unsurprisingly, this was greeted by outrage from those committed to giving the greatest effort towards making maps for the Western Front. At a meeting held on 3 February 1916 it was decided that while help should be given to the European 1:1 million map project the main priority was the Middle East, until the War Office and the Admiralty decided differently.[22] However, through 1916 the balance of power at the RGS was once again affected by events. Cartographic work for the Middle East continued, but once British campaigns in Mesopotamia and Palestine had started in mid-1916 intelligence gathering became the responsibility of Middle East agencies and the NID gradually slipped out of the picture. Additionally, the allied offensives of the spring and summer of 1916, leading to those of 1917, required an intensifying of the provision of maps for the Western Front.

As Heffernan points out, the work of all the cartographic agencies was considerable, "By the end of the war, ninety 1:1 million map sheets had been produced by the RGS cartographers, covering the whole of Europe, the Middle East, and North Africa"; this is in addition to the large number of Handbooks and Manuals that were produced.[23] Moreover, the 1:1 million scale projects were especially significant because they were able to more accurately reflect complex features of a rapidly changing environment and facilitate the raising of new and more demanding questions, in other words, exactly the kind of questions regarding the lines of rivers, railways and language distribution, for example, that were to prove important for the making of boundaries in the peace conference and which later occupied Collingwood in the Manuals on Belgium and on Alsace-Lorraine, and in the atlases that accompanied them.

The two Manuals that we know Collingwood was responsible for (I. D. 1168 and I. D. 1211), as well as the atlases that go with them, were written following a standard format and to satisfy a clear purpose. As a part of an information-gathering team Collingwood would have had some freedom of manoeuvre, but only within an agreed scheme. Just how large the Geographical Section was can be gleaned from Erik Goldstein who writes, "By the Spring of 1918 the Geographical Section had grown to a staff of 120."[24] Collingwood's job was to find out the facts and present them in a comprehensive and intelligible form.

With this judgement in mind we can now turn to the Manuals for which Collingwood was responsible. J. H. Godfrey in the preface to the Geographical Handbook Series (Second World War) tells us a little more about their origin and purpose. He writes,

> In 1915 a Geographical Section was formed in the Naval Intelligence Division of the Admiralty to write Geographical Handbooks on various parts of the world. The purpose of these handbooks was to supply, by scientific research and skilled arrangement, material for the discussion of naval, military and political problems, as distinct from the examination of the problems themselves.[25]

Indeed, from the Note which prefaces the *Manual of Belgium* (I. D. 1168) we can see just how closely Collingwood's team followed this brief. They write,

> This volume together with its companion atlas is, in the first instance, a geographical study of Belgium. The subjects dealt with are those on which geography has had a powerful influence, such as the composition

and distribution of the population, history, agriculture, mining and manufactures, communications and trade. Certain social questions have also been treated in outline, as hardly separable from the subjects above mentioned. In the main, however, the following chapters aim not at solving social and political problems, but at stating economic and geographical facts, apart from which no solution of such questions is possible.[26]

The distinction between the provision of materials for the discussion of problems and the discussion of the problems themselves is important in understanding what is said in the Manuals. *The Manual of Belgium and the Adjoining Territories*, (including Luxemburg and the Rhineland) (I. D. 1168) which involved much of Collingwood's time is a substantial work (of 595 pages). It contains eleven chapters each of which is a highly detailed examination of such subjects as physical geography, population, languages and their distribution, history, including that of the Grand Duchy of Luxemburg, the Rhineland, social conditions in Belgium, the Flemish question, agriculture, mineral resources, industry, communications and commerce. The Manual considers each topic with great care, for example, listing the weaknesses in the Belgian method of poor relief (p271), and it shows every effort to be fair-minded, for example, in its discussion of the different views on the Flemish question (pp294-6). One of the three appendices (Appendix B) consists of a table of the chief treaties governing sovereignty and state boundaries in the region, including the Scheldt and the Rhine (section (d)). Appendix A is a bibliography of works consulted that lists 161 items classified into distinct topics. The atlas which accompanies it, (Manual of Belgium Atlas, I. D. 1168A, February, 1918, Naval Staff, Intelligence Division), then covered by the Official Secrets Act, contains nineteen detailed maps drawn on a 1:1,000,000 scale and ranges over such topics as chemical works, coal-mining, railways and waterways.[27]

The Manual is important, first, because it helps us to date Collingwood's involvement in it more precisely. Since work on the Manual could not have begun before the spring of 1917 when the preparations for the peace were first considered, and since the atlas which accompanies it is dated February 1918, it would seem likely that Collingwood spent most of the intervening period on its production. Further, the bibliography (Appendix A) lists no work after 1916, suggesting not only the extreme difficulty of obtaining contemporary statistics as the war proceeded, but also that 1917 was the year in which the actual research and writing was done. Second, the Manual is of interest because it approaches many of its topics historically. There is an assumption running throughout its discussion of political and social questions that these can be grasped only after their history has been properly displayed and appreciated. Thus, in its examination of the Flemish question, for example, the Manual moves from a history of the problem to the state of contemporary opinion, including the extent to which language divisions bear on political allegiances. So we find in the Manual the following view,

> German pamphleteers, describing the growth of the Flemish Movement, are compelled to admit that in 1914 the Flemings were no more friendly to Germany than the Walloons. The vexed question, 'Is there a Belgian soul?' was at last answered in the affirmative. The old quarrel was dropped and Walloon and Fleming alike took up arms against the Germans. Nor has the course of German occupation done anything to relax the first feeling of hostility.[28]

However, any attempt to forge a direct link between what we read in the Manual and Collingwood's own ideas should be treated with caution for the obvious reason that the Manuals are purpose built artefacts designed to satisfy particular requirements. We should remember, too, that the main purpose of the Manuals was to assist with the preparations for the peace. What was needed and what the Manuals were intended to supply was not only historical and statistical data, but also a reasonably accurate sense of the allegiances of the inhabitants of those territories whose boundaries were likely to be in dispute after the conflict was over. Thus, speaking of the political feelings of the citizens of Luxemburg after 1885 the Manual suggests,

> The commercial element in the population could not but be sensible of the benefits which it derived from the economic connexion with Germany. But the great majority of Luxemburgers had still no political sympathy with the Empire, and Germans of the Empire were on the whole unpopular. Dislike of Prussianism remained strong.[29]

Further, the Manual provides an immensely detailed discussion of Belgian economic resources. Agriculture, minerals, industry including coal mining, metallurgy, weaving, chemical works, the paper industry, the diamond industry of Antwerp, for example, are each extensively examined as well as the history of Belgian commerce, currency regulations and banking, all of which are supported by the most recent statistics regarding production figures and output. There is a meticulous description of communications in Belgium, together with an exhaustive account of Belgian railways that contains intricate descriptions of goods rates, fares and season tickets. In one sense the Manual is no different from a standard academic examination of its topics. The aim, however, is comprehensiveness rather than analysis, and one can readily understand why it is thought of as encyclopaedic in character. It was written, nevertheless, by an academic who used academic methods. Its audience, however, was very far from being academic, since it consisted in the main of politicians who conceived their business not as a neutral exercise in political sociology, but as the advancement of interest in the face of disagreement and rivalry. Even so, we should remember the brief that I. D. 32 was operating with. The purpose is, as the Report to the Inquiry comments,

> to give such a picture of the pre-war conditions of the invaded regions (like Belgium) as will form a basis for computing the damage done by Germany, for assessing the value of natural and other resources transferred by treaty, and for service in other ways to the negotiators at the peace conference.[30]

The *Manual of Belgium* was finally published in 1918, and Major Johnson was so impressed by it as a model of I. D. 32's work that he forwarded it, together with the accompanying atlas, to the "Inquiry" (the American intelligence gathering unit) in Washington because, as he writes, "from them the nature and scope of the undertaking will be evident."[31]

We should now turn to the second of the Manuals which appears in Collingwood's "List of Work Done".[32] This is *A Manual of Alsace-Lorraine*, (I. D. 1211), Naval Staff Intelligence Department June 1919, together with *A Manual of Alsace-Lorraine Atlas* (I. D. 1211A), Prepared by the Geographical Section of the Naval Intelligence Division, Naval Staff, Admiralty. Once again, we should notice that the Manual is a substantial piece of work, (of 422 pages), together with a bibliography (Appendix A) of 236 items. The Atlas contains twenty maps drawn on the scale 1:1,000,000, covering such topics as physical, rainfall, geology, woods and forests, French speakers in German Alsace-Lorraine, minerals, railways and waterways.

What is immediately noteworthy about this Manual is that it is significantly different in tone and content from its companion volume on Belgium. Whereas its predecessor concerned itself in the main with facts rather than opinions, the Manual of Alsace-Lorraine expresses opinions as well as facts. It is, in other words, closer to the problem it addresses and from the internal evidence it is likely that some of it was written after the war was over, but before the Peace Conference that settled Alsace-Lorraine's future. Even so, both Manuals share a common approach. Thus, the Manual to Alsace-Lorraine describes (in Part 1) the physical geography of the region, including river systems, geology and climate; (in Part 2), the population of the region and its history, including the languages and their distribution; and (in Part 3) its economic conditions, including agriculture, mineral resources and waterways. As with the Manual to Belgium, the Manual to Alsace-Lorraine is immensely detailed, descriptions of economic resources are supported by an array of tables and data all carefully prepared and arranged.

It is, however, in the historical sections of the Manual, particularly those concerning Alsace-Lorraine as the German 'Reichland' 1870–1914 (Chapter 11) and under German occupation from 1914, that the tone becomes less restrained. German occupation was "a reign of terror" consisting of mass arrests, deportation, massacre and pillage.[33] In support of these charges the Manual states that "the evidence on this hand is extremely voluminous and comes entirely from German official sources".[34] Reference is made to punishments for speaking French and to atrocities committed by the Germans against those who supported the French. It writes that "villages which had welcomed the French (including an entire suburb of Mulhouse) had to pay for it in some cases by complete extinction, in others by the murder of a greater or less number of inhabitants".[35] Indeed, the Manual specifically identifies the individual German army units that occupied Alsace and who, on receiving orders to behave as if they were in enemy territory, "looted and destroyed at will".[36]

Nor is the Manual nervous about nailing its colours to the mast regarding the political future of the region. We find the following:

> The object of this section is not to describe the conduct of Germany in governing a subject race; we know what these methods are from the cases of Poland and Slesvig. Nor is it to describe the methods by which Germany occupies enemy territory in time of war; we are acquainted with these in the case of Belgium. The whole point of the preceding pages lies in the fact that Alsace-Lorraine is constantly alleged, both in Germany and elsewhere to be—on the whole—a convinced and loyal section of the German Empire. This allegation is of supreme importance, because on it rests the only real argument for Germany's claims to the Reichland.[37]

This argument is, of course, one that the Manual wishes strongly to rebut. Data exist, it claims, for determining the will of the region's population. Such data prove that public opinion in Alsace-Lorraine is bitterly hostile to Germany. It states that "the old myth of its being ethnologically and politically German has been once for all exploded".[38] Even so, the Manual does acknowledge that the people of Alsace-Lorraine are a mixed race, neither wholly German nor wholly French, and that "anti-German feeling is not synonymous with loyalty to France".[39] As Hugh Clout and Cyril Gosme correctly comment, the political message of Alsace-Lorraine (1919) was clear. 'Alsace-Lorraine was indelibly stamped with the mark of France. Such phrases are not rhetoric: they are the only true way of expressing concisely the whole history of the country since 1870. That they are true is well known by all who have studied the country; best known of all by the Germans who have tried to rule it.' (p245)[40]

The History of I. D. 32 written in December 1919 remarks that the Manuals were

> begun early in the work of the Section, when it became apparent that much of the material collected in the course of preparing the Handbooks could not be usefully included in them but would be of value in dealing with problems arising after the war — such as delimitation of frontiers, assessment of damage by enemy action, and readjustment of naval and military dispositions.[41]

The Manuals provide us with tangible evidence of the work Collingwood did. It was intricate work and must have been laborious and time consuming. However, we also know that it was not the only matter that occupied him. In his "List of Work Done" Collingwood refers to "a great quantity of work" that engaged him independently of the Manuals,[42] and while he is not specific we know now that one such topic was the Schleswig-Holstein question, for in the summer of 1916 Collingwood asked that a search be made of the family library so that he could borrow Danish material on the problem.[43] In the light of this it is noteworthy that it is this striving for "accuracy and balance", in Erik Goldstein's words, which the Report to the Inquiry finds relevant. In his Report Major Johnson writes, "in preparing the Schleswig-Holstein Manual Professor Dickson found that English historians had relied largely upon German sources of information because they could not read Danish.[44] He therefore had various Danish documents translated, and says that they put a very different complexion on the whole matter."[45]

Where does this leave the study that Collingwood wrote on the navigation of the Scheldt? Our knowledge of this work comes entirely from R. B. McCallum's Obituary of Collingwood in which we find,

> on the outbreak of war in 1914 Collingwood passed into the service of the Admiralty Intelligence, where his skilful deduction and meticulous and exact method were extremely valuable. As most of this work was secret and much of it no doubt completely transient, little is known about it, but amongst other tasks he wrote a study of the juridical problems concerned with the navigation of the Scheldt up to Antwerp.[46]

We should notice, however, that McCallum's dating is seriously amiss since we know that I. D. 32 was not formed until July 1915 and also that Collingwood did not join it until the start of 1916. Is it possible to reconstruct Collingwood's work on the Scheldt from the kinds of problems it raised and from our knowledge of the period?

Even as early as the first month of the war, British decision-makers were aware of the difficulties of the tactical use of the Scheldt, difficulties which did not lose their force as the war progressed. One recent historian of the war writes of a pre-war meeting held on the 5 August 1914 to decide on the deployment of the B. E. F., in which Sir John French

> revived the Belgian option, suggesting that Antwerp be used as a base and that the B. E. F. operate on the German flank. But the fact that the Royal Navy could not have defended Antwerp without breaching Dutch neutrality as surely as the German army had breached Belgium's worried nobody—least of all Churchill. The First Lord of the Admiralty quashed French's proposal on the grounds of practicality not international law: he announced that the navy could not support operations based on a port so far north.[47]

The Scheldt estuary was a strategically important area for both sides early in conflict and well before it took on the distinctive and disputed role it played in the peace conference. However, the British government took the decision not to infringe Dutch neutrality and as Dutch sovereignty included control of the mouth of the Scheldt then the river and the approaches to Antwerp from the sea were therefore prohibited. The use of British reinforcements certainly prolonged the siege of Antwerp in the autumn of 1914, but it could not prevent its surrender. Thereafter the Scheldt was made impassable because of wrecked shipping and played little further part in the war. As B. H. Liddell Hart comments of the British deployment, "this first and last effort in the west to make use of Britain's amphibious power"[48] blocked German coastal expansion, but it was not to be repeated. Liddell Hart chose his words with care—"the first and last effort in the west"—and so it seems highly unlikely that the navigation of the Scheldt was subject to further investigation for military purposes, although elsewhere in the conflict from 1915 onwards the use of naval forces to sidestep military stalemate on land became an increasingly important issue. Throughout the political history of the Scheldt, questions of law and questions of interest are hard to disentangle. Even so, the work Collingwood did on the Scheldt must surely have been concerned with disputes over its jurisdiction at the peace conference rather than its military significance during the conflict.

Another reason for thinking of Collingwood's work on the Scheldt as being directed at the peace conference is that, as described by McCallum, it concerns the navigation of the Scheldt to Antwerp. In the case of the Scheldt juridical and navigation problems are intertwined since Dutch authority over the lower Scheldt affected Belgian control of its upper reaches. Belgium, therefore, had a clear commercial interest in raising the question of jurisdiction of the Scheldt at the Peace Conference.[49] Even though Holland was a neutral state and so not subject to any decisions made at the Conference Britain had an obvious strategic concern with a geographical area that faced it across the North Sea. It was important, therefore, as a part of the preparations for the Conference, that a British view be ascertained, and, since I. D. 32 was the fact providing body, it is to the Geographical Section in which Collingwood worked that British decision makers turned.[50] It is, therefore, likely that it was Collingwood who was asked to produce such a work because the Manual of Belgium already contained a detailed examination of this question. Consideration of the Manual of 1918 should allow us to establish the difference between the status of the Scheldt as it is described in the Manual and its status after the Peace Conference of 1919.

The first thought that should strike us is just how appropriate the question of the Scheldt was as a subject for Collingwood's investigation. Collingwood's skills as a member of naval intelligence were those of method, of asking the right questions of the problem at hand and of disentangling the many different aspects it might contain. In the case of the Scheldt such a treatment was highly desirable because no single question could unlock its significance. Geographical, historical, political and juridical questions needed to be asked. Thus, the Manual considers the Scheldt as a river formation. Its direction, depth of water and flow are each minutely described. Its individual tributaries are named, the differences between its upper and lower reaches noted and the shape and size of its estuary in the North Sea explained.[51] But the Scheldt is not simply a feature of the physical landscape. So the Manual examines its historical significance as a frontier between two states, and as a waterway of great economic and strategic importance. As the Manual notes, from the sixteenth century onwards the fate of Antwerp and the Scheldt estuary were bound together since whoever controlled the estuary determined whether Antwerp prospered.

In 1917 when the Manual was written it was realised that the status of the Scheldt was an issue that a peace conference would have to address. Who had jurisdiction over the Scheldt estuary was a matter of vital strategic security most obviously for Belgium, but also for the states bordering the North Sea, including Britain. Since the Roman Empire the Scheldt had been recognised as a key route to and from Continental Europe. What the Manual provides, therefore, is a detailed history of the main treaties establishing juridical rights over the Scheldt from 1609 to 1863, including the Treaty of Munster, 1648, which gave the Netherlands control over the estuary, and leading up to the definition of Belgium's northern frontier in 1914.[52] It stresses the importance of the estuary for the navigation of ocean going vessels to Antwerp, but beyond a brief discussion of Dutch intransigence over the extension of the canal system in the area this is the amount of information that the Manual contains.[53]

As we have noted it was not the Manual's job to offer detailed policy advice. Historical and geographical issues are skilfully kept separate, but what is actually provided is background material of a highly non-specific kind. Moreover, the information in the Manual is drawn from public sources. Intelligence questions concerning, for example, the access of military traffic to Antwerp, banned by the Treaty of Paris, 1814, are not discussed.[54] By the same token the implications of the Dutch closure of the estuary in 1914 for the strategic balance of power in that area are beyond the Manual's brief. In fact, both sides in the conflict realised that keeping the Netherlands neutral would be to their advantage since then neither would have access to the Scheldt, and so to Antwerp, to be used for military purposes. As one recent commentator writes,

> The Schelde(t) was, arguably one of the most prized possessions of Dutch neutrality; highly desired by both warring sides for its geo-strategic position since it provided an outlet to the Channel from Belgium as well as an easily navigated route into Antwerp. In fact, one historian went so far as to proclaim that during the Great War both sets of belligerents believed that whichever power controlled the river could control the outcome of the war.[55]

The Manual's silence on intelligence matters concerning military strategy during the war is understandable. What its compilers had been asked to do was provide material for discussion as opposed to participating in the discussion itself. This is even more obviously the case in the matter of British policy regarding Belgian territorial claims to certain areas of the Scheldt after the war was over. By 1919 most of the information contained in the Manual had become out of date or seriously irrelevant to the issues at hand. As Margaret Macmillan remarks of Belgian claims in this area,

The Belgians had hoped that the powers would put pressure on the Dutch to sort out unsatisfactory borders between their two countries especially along the River Scheldt, which flowed out to the sea from the great port of Antwerp through Dutch territory. The Dutch, with their own port in Rotterdam, had done little before the war to improve navigation by, for example, dredging. The Netherlands, which as a neutral power, was not part of the Peace Conference, firmly refused to give up an inch of its soil, even in return for gains elsewhere from Germany. The powers remained silent.[56]

Collingwood's work on the legal status of the Scheldt would have been part of the British preparations for the Peace Conference, specifically the discussion of boundary disputes in Western Europe. In this respect, it is worth noting that, as Erik Goldstein shows, at the close of 1918 it was not always an easy matter to gather together the views of interested government departments in order to put forward a considered point of view.[57] So, in fact, it was E. H. Carr at the Foreign Office who produced the report on *The Question of the Scheldt* because the Admiralty had been dragging their feet.[58] Goldstein writes,

> In the discussion on Carr's report Hardinge suggested that the Admiralty's view should be ascertained, but Tyrrell acidly pointed out in a minute to Crowe, 'I am not hopeful on getting an authoritative answer from the Admiralty having tried for 3 years, but your persuasive powers may be greater. What about trying through D. N. I.?' Eventually Crowe by working through Admiral Hall was able to prise loose the Admiralty's opinion, and it finally concluded that British policy should be to support a return to the status quo ante bellum, with the Scheldt being closed to ships of war.[59]

We are now in a position to provide a summing up of Collingwood's intelligence activities. Overall, what stands out from the story of Collingwood's work in I. D. 32 is just how heavily it was influenced by the strategic and diplomatic priorities in favour at any one time. Further, as preparations for peace gathered pace, with Collingwood taking on responsibility for the two Manuals, an additional feature of the story emerges. British preparations for the Peace Conference were anything but plain sailing. Conflicts of interest, institutional empire-building, jealousies between departments and between academics and civil servants frequently interrupt the flow of information from one section of intelligence to another to the point where work done in one department is deliberately suppressed by another. As we have noticed, even in the early period of I. D. 32's existence disagreements in the Royal Geographical Society surfaced, sometimes reflecting a wider struggle between the War Office and the Admiralty over the broad direction of war strategy. Given

Collingwood's later comment that the war was one "in which statesmanship, even purely selfish statesmanship, was overwhelmed by the meanest and most idiotic passions", it is hard to believe that such conflicts were not familiar to him.[60] Squabbles over the preparations for peace were often as uncompromising as the disagreements which marked the Conference itself. It is to the impact of Collingwood's work that we now turn.

Endnotes

1   Letter from R. G. Collingwood to his father, W. G. Collingwood, dated 5 December 1915 from Pembroke College, Oxford, private possession.

2   R. G. Collingwood, *An Autobiography*, p29; one of the first indications we have of Collingwood's working at the Admiralty occurs in a letter from his father to Arthur Ransome in which he writes, "and Robin, I hear tonight, is going to the War Office", letter dated 6 December 1915 (Ransome Papers, Brotherton Library, University of Leeds); in other letters Collingwood says that he will be returning to London on 1 January 1916 and beginning work at the Admiralty on the 3rd of that month. It seems likely, therefore, that Collingwood was taken on by I. D. 32 some time in early December 1915 and given 3 January as a starting date, possibly to allow him to complete his term's work in Oxford.

3   See R. G. Collingwood, letter to Macmillan, dated 13 July 1916, as listed in Peter Johnson, *Correspondence*, Mli; see also letter dated 8 January 1918, Johnson, *Correspondence*, Mlvi.

4   See, Dick Wakefield, *The Collingwoods at Lanehead*, unpublished manuscript, p44. Collingwood's interest in music was longstanding and never dimmed during the war, on 12 July 1917, for example, he enjoyed dinner in Soho followed by a performance of Figaro (see James Patrick, "Eliot and the New Idealism", *Collingwood and British Idealism Studies*, vol. 7, 2000, p3).

5   As quoted in Margaret Cropper, *Evelyn Underhill*, Longmans, Green and Co., London, 1958, p59; see also Christopher J. Armstrong, *Evelyn Underhill, 1875-1941, An Introduction to her Life and Writings*, Mowbrays, London, 1975.

6   See Cropper, *Evelyn Underhill*, p58, (inventing countries was an enthusiasm of the young Collingwood so it is possible that his influence was not too far away).

7   See "Evelyn Underhill 1875-1941" *New Oxford Dictionary of National Biography*, 2004, 55, pp894-5. The geographer, Hilda Ormsby, (1877-1973), was one of a number of geographers who worked in the Naval Intelligence Division and who also reflected on the importance of her work, "Ormsby worked on maps for the Naval Intelligence Division of the Admiralty during the First and the Second World Wars and was deeply concerned that British soldiers in the First World War suffered at the hands of cartographers more concerned with

aesthetics than accuracy", see the entry by Avril M. C. Maddrell, *New Oxford Dictionary of National Biography*, 2004.

8   Johnston, *Formative Years*, p10; see also McCallum, *Obituary*, p464.

9   Johnston, *Formative Years*, p10.

10   See R. G. Collingwood, "In Memoriam", *Proceedings of the Cumberland and Westmorland Antiquarian and Archaeological Society*, 33, 1933, pp308–12, (p311); and also the obituaries of W. G. Collingwood in *Nature*, vol. 130, 15 October 1932, pp571–2, and *The New Oxford Dictionary of National Biography*, 2004, 12, pp681–3, (by James S. Dearden). In the *Obituary* of his father that R. G. Collingwood wrote for *The Times* (Monday 3 October 1932, p9) he said, "During the War he worked in one of the Government Departments and with characteristic generosity sold the presents which Ruskin had given him for the benefit of The Red Cross."

11   On 8 October 1917 W. G. Collingwood wrote to his son "accepting offer to work for him in London", See W. G. Collingwood, *Diary* (Abbott Hall), 8 October 1917; I am indebted to Matthew Townend for this reference. Inglis, *History Man*, p87 incorrectly follows Johnston.

12   For W. G. Collingwood at Reading, see Dearden, *Obituary*, p682, and Matthew Townend, *The Vikings and Victorian Lakeland: The Norse Medievalism of W. G. Collingwood and His Contemporaries*, Cumberland and Westmorland Antiquarian and Archaeological Society, extra series, vol. 34, Titus Wilson and Son, Kendal, 2009, pp231, 240; for Dickson, see Goldstein, "Hertford House", p87 fn. 4. From Goldstein we learn that Dickson was assistant editor of the *Encyclopaedia Britannica* from 1920 to 1922. Collingwood contributed the article on "Luxemburg" to the 12th edition of the *Encyclopaedia Britannica*, 1920, pp811–12, see R. G. Collingwood, "List of Work Done", Collingwood MS, DEP 22, p23. The "Luxemburg" article is outside our period, but it is not well known. It does, however, contain some interesting remarks on the experience of Luxemburg during the 1914–18 war and on its treatment by the Peace Settlement. As was then the *Encyclopaedia Britannica* practice the initials "R. G. C." follow the article. As this material is hard to obtain I quote the relevant sections below. "On Aug. 2 1914 the capital and the chief railway bridges were seized by German troops, which had already entered the country on the previous day. The protests of the Grand Duchess Marie Adelaide and the Government were ignored, and the country remained in German hands for the remainder of the World War. The native authorities were allowed to conduct the civil administration, but there was a strict German censorship of post, telegraphs and telephones, and for some time the German Emperor resided in the Grand Duchy. There were no allegations of German atrocities, but the openly Francophile attitude of the inhabitants led to a good deal of friction and was probably responsible for such events as the Cabinet crisis of 1915. The American troops which entered the capital after the Armistice, on Nov. 22 1918, were received with the greatest enthusiasm. On the conclusion of the war it

became necessary to reconsider both the position of the Grand Duchy as a member of the German Zollverein and of the Grand Duchess, whose German sympathies were in conflict with the general views of her subjects. She accordingly abdicated in favour of her sister Charlotte Adelgonde early in 1919, and a referendum was held later in the year to decide the political and economic future of the country. The Treaty of Versailles acquitted Luxemburg of her obligations to Germany, and it was known that the Peace Conference would not permit the resumption of the old relation, even if the Luxemburgers had wished it. Voters were therefore asked to choose between economic union with France and with Belgium, and between the existing Grand Duchess, a new ruler, and a republic. They resolved by a large majority upon economic union with France and on the retention of their constitution and of the Grand Duchess Charlotte." (*Encyclopaedia Britannica*, op cit. p812).

13   See Patrick Beesly, *Room 40*, pp125f.

14   For an example (one of many) of the informal contacts which often led to intelligence work (in this case in Room 40), see Margaret Elizabeth Keynes, *A House by the River, Newnham Grange to Darwin College*, Darwin College, Cambridge, 1976, pp196ff. See also Geoffrey Keynes, *The Gates of Memory*, Clarendon Press, Oxford, 1981, p151.

15   Letter from Barbara Collingwood to her sister, Dora, undated but, from internal evidence, probably, late 1916 (WDWGC 4, Letters from Barbara Collingwood to her sister Dora 1903–1919, Cumbria Record Office, Kendal). While Collingwood was not a liaison officer in the field the duties of liaison work in any area were regarded as onerous. Major-General Sir Edward Spears writes in his book *Liaison 1914, A Narrative of the Great Retreat*, second edition, Eyre and Spottiswoode, London, 1968, p331, that "To bring about such understanding and confidence is the problem of liaison, which, nominally concerned with the coordination of operations, is far more important as a method of interpreting commanders to each other. This is a difficult task, in which one generally gets more kicks than halfpence. The liaison officer has to stand up to both sides and defend the thesis of one to the other and vice versa. He deals with all complaints. To one side he is always a foreigner. To his own people he seems to be forever taking the side of the foreigner. His life is spent between the hammer and the anvil." Given the disputes both geographical and political which the agencies involved managed to produce it is likely that Collingwood had his work cut out in keeping them all in hand.

16   R. G. Collingwood, "List of Work Done", Collingwood MS, DEP 22, p16. Since Collingwood specifically includes the atlases in his List we should assume that these were his responsibility in addition to the Manuals. *The Manual of Belgium* (p574) refers to a number of different scale maps for use with the volume, including the 1: 1,000,000 maps. For Collingwood's expertise in this area see his "Review of Map of Roman Britain, Second Edition, Southampton,

Ordinance Survey of the United Kingdom, 1928", in *The Geographical Journal*, vol. 72, July to December 1928, pp565-6.
17   R. Collingwood, *An Autobiography*, p89.
18   McCallum, *Obituary*, p464.
19   See Michael Heffernan, "The Politics of the Map", *Cartography and Geographic Information Science*, vol. 29, no. 3, 215, p17.
20   Michael Heffernan, "Geography, Cartography and Military Intelligence", p517.
21   Ibid., p517.
22   Ibid., p518.
23   Ibid., p518.
24   Goldstein, "Hertford House", p85.
25   From the Preface to Geographical Handbooks, 1944, p viii.
26   *Manual of Belgium And The Adjoining Territories*, Prepared by the Geographical Section of the Naval Intelligence Division, Naval Staff, Admiralty, His Majesty's Stationary Office, London, 1918, p5.
27   For discussion of the significance of the 1:1 million scale map see Michael Heffernan, "Geography, Cartography and Military Intelligence", pp508-11.
28   Manual of Belgium, pp295-6.
29   Ibid., p198.
30   Inquiry Document 987, p12.
31   Ibid., p12.
32   R. G. Collingwood, "List of Work Done", Collingwood MS, DEP 22, p16.
33   *A Manual of Alsace-Lorraine*, Naval Staff, Intelligence Department, June 1919, p236; for detailed discussion see John Horne and Alan Kramer, *German Atrocities 1914 A History of Denial*, Yale University Press, New Haven and London, 2001, pp22-3ff, and, more broadly, Alan Kramer, *Dynamic of Destruction, Culture and Mass Killing in the First World War*, Oxford University Press, Oxford, 2007.
34   Ibid., p237.
35   Ibid., p237.
36   Ibid., p236, The Manual lists the German army units in footnote 1.
37   Ibid., p242.
38   Ibid., p243.
39   Ibid., p244.
40   See Clout and Gosme, "The Naval Intelligence Handbooks", p155.
41   See The Geographical Work, p1.
42   R. G. Collingwood, "List of Work Done", Collingwood MS, DEP 22, p16
43   Collingwood's work on the Slesvig-Holstein question involved him and others in acquiring a working knowledge of Danish so that they could master the original sources. What was required was the most recent information on population and language use in disputed areas. The Geographical Section's

Manual on the Question of Slesvig-Holstein (I. D.1133) was eventually completed. However, there was a great deal of duplication with no less than three organisations producing memoranda on the same subject, in this case, I. D. 32, the Political Intelligence Department, and M. I. 2(e), the section of Military Intelligence concerned with historical and population matters. While there was agreement about the best policy, the return of Danish populated areas to Denmark, with a plebiscite for disputed territory, there was considerable overlap with three organisations working on the same material. As published (April 1919) the *Handbook on Slesvig-Holstein* (Handbooks published under the direction of the Foreign Office, no. 27) did contain in its bibliography many of the Danish works on questions of population and language use that Collingwood was inquiring about. In the end, however, most of the work for the final document was completed by K. W. M. Pickthorn, a member of M. I. 2(e). (See Goldstein, *Winning the Peace*, pp127–8).

44 See Goldstein, *Winning the Peace*, p27.
45 Inquiry Document 987, p12.
46 McCallum, *Obituary*, p464; Inglis, *History Man*, p96 appears to follow McCallum in his discussion of Collingwood's work on the Scheldt.
47 See Hew Strachan, *The First World War*, vol. 1, *To Arms*, Oxford University Press, Oxford, 2001, p204, and also p272.
48 B. H. Liddell-Hart, *The Real War 1914–1918*, Faber and Faber Ltd, London, 1930, p81.
49 For discussion of Belgian claims regarding the Scheldt see R. H. Lord, *Some Problems of the Peace Conference*, Harvard University Press, Cambridge, Mass. 1920, pp61–9.
50 See Goldstein, *Winning the Peace*, p127.
51 *Manual of Belgium*, pp19–23, 537.
52 Ibid., p175–8.
53 Ibid., p178.
54 For a discussion of these, see H. W. V. Temperley (ed.), *A History of the Peace Conference of Paris*, vol. 2, *The Settlement with Germany*, Oxford University Press, London, 1920, pp194–5.
55 See Maartje Abbenhuis, "Caught between the Devil and the Deep Blue Sea: Some Problems with Dutch Neutrality in the Great War, 1914–1918", Paper presented to the Inaugural European Studies Conference, National Centre for Research on Europe, Christchurch, New Zealand, May–June 2002, p2.
56 Margaret Macdonald, *Peacemakers*, p286; the difficulty raised by the status of the Scheldt and Antwerp was one of a number of territorial questions with a naval aspect that the Peace Conference had to try to settle. The problems involved are well stated as follows: "The principal remaining issue in regard to the status of Belgium was that of the channel and estuary of the Scheldt below Antwerp. This problem arose from fact that part, at least, of these were in

Dutch territorial waters, whereas the commercial use of the waterway was almost wholly a Belgian interest, since these Dutch waters, from the economic point of view, were simply the entrance to Belgium's principal port. The conservancy of this waterway had been placed, and still remained, in the hands of a mixed Dutch-Belgian commission, and it was thought, in Belgium, that the efficiency of the commission (on which the prosperity of Antwerp ultimately depended) was impaired by the supineness of Dutch members". See Arnold J. Toynbee, *Survey of International Affairs 1920–1923*, Oxford University Press, London, 1925, pp66-7; for further discussion both of the origins of the dispute and its course after 1919, see C. A. Macartney, *Survey of International Affairs 1925*, Oxford University Press, London, 1928, pp166-72; and L. P. Mair, "The Scheldt Controversy", *Economica*, vol. 24, 1928, pp351-69. Regarding the Belgian territorial claims over its northern border Temperley (p196), comments "Belgian prosperity is not bound up with an increase of territory at the expense of her neighbour."

57 See Goldstein, *Winning the Peace*, pp127-8.

58 See *The Question of the Scheldt*, Handbooks prepared under the Direction of the Historical Section of the Foreign Office, no. 25, December 1918, especially pp12-13 where it is advised that satisfying Belgian grievances is neither practicable nor justifiable; for Carr's work on the Scheldt in the Foreign Office, see Jonathan Haslam, *The Vices of Integrity, E. H. Carr 1892–1982*, Verso, London, 1999, p22.

59 See Goldstein, *Winning the Peace*, p128, and also footnote 21, p128, where the document in which the Admiralty's views were expressed is cited: "Notes on Matters Affecting Naval Interests Connected with the Peace Settlement", Jan. 1919, (3rd revise), ADM 167/57.

60 See R. G. Collingwood, *An Autobiography*, p89.

CHAPTER 7

PREPARATIONS FOR PEACE

British preparations for the Peace Conference were not haphazard, but neither did they evolve organically from a single centrally directed plan. Different departments jostled with each other to put their views across, duplication and sometimes triplication of effort were not uncommon and lack of co-ordination often meant the arbitrary suppression of one case at the expense of another. For I. D. 32 the struggle for influence began early. Tensions over accommodation between the new arrivals from the Admiralty and the resident geographers in the Royal Geographical Society soon surfaced. The academics working for the Naval Intelligence Division quickly found themselves in conflict with the Geographical Section of the General Staff over new developments in cartography and, as Michael Heffernan has shown, almost open warfare broke out between the different groups over the role of the new 1:1 million scale maps in settling the peace.[1] Heffernan quotes a letter written in early 1916 in which the writer calls the Admiralty Geographical Section an "an amateur organisation", and it was some time before ruffled feathers were calmed.[2]

After I. D. 32 moved to Hertford House it was the Peace Conference which dominated its agenda, but even though throughout 1917 the volume of completed work and the industry of the Geographical Section both increased this was the time when, as Erik Goldstein comments, "the focus of peace preparations slowly drifted away from Naval Intelligence".[3] Foreign Office determination to keep the planning for the peace firmly in its own hands is one important reason for this, but the downgrading of Admiralty influence was also accompanied by some sharp criticism of I. D. 32's work which cannot be explained solely in terms of the need for co-ordination and control. Major Douglas Johnson who talked freely to the main participants in British planning and reproduced much of the information he obtained in his

Report to the Inquiry is clear both about the opposition to I. D. 32 and about the methods used to minimise its influence in any future settlements. Reading Johnson's Report it is impossible not to be aware of the gap between Dickson's own high opinion of his work and that of the Foreign Office officials who were making the arrangements for the Conference. The Manuals and Handbooks produced by I. D. 32 are described as impractical and verbose, and the Report quotes Alwyn Parker, whose job it was to organise peace planning under the auspices of the Foreign Office, as saying that Dickson was

> an impractical professor, prolix, and incapable of getting down to important facts; that he had been told to reduce his reports by 75%, that none of his volumes would be used at the conference (although a set might be taken along) and that Dickson himself would not go if he (Parker) could help it.[4]

The result was that the Handbooks and Manuals were filleted; the geographical information substantially cut and edited so as to produce the short manageable volumes the Foreign Office required.[5] Valuable though its work was I.D. 32 was fated only to play an indirect role in the run-up to the Peace Conference, so much so that the Head of the section, H.N.Dickson, alone among the section heads, was not invited to attend. No doubt, inter-departmental rivalries and suspicions of "head in the clouds" academics were at work in this, but the overriding reason was that Naval Intelligence was being told to keep off the Foreign Office grass. Erik Goldstein writes,

> By early 1918 Hall had recognised that too many government officials were opposed to what they considered as Naval Intelligence meddling in a matter that was properly the concern of the Foreign Office, and he effectively withdrew N.I.D. from such work. The Historical Section under George Protheroe was transferred to the Foreign Office in February 1918, while Dickson's section was retained in Naval Intelligence as its general work was still of military importance. The Geographical Section, however, did play an indirect role in the final preparations by providing background information and maps to those departments that became responsible for the final arrangements.[6]

There is a clear sense in which the restriction of the role of I. D. 32 derived from the nature of the intelligence it provided. What I. D. 32 dealt in came largely from public information. It was concerned with what has become known as "open source intelligence", and its brief was to act as the geographical reference section of naval intelligence producing data on a given area or topic which was accurate, comprehensive and succinctly expressed, remaining impartial and avoiding tendentiousness.[7] It is noticeable that Collingwood's work in

I. D. 32 was as much concerned with winning the peace as with prosecuting the war. In this respect, as Michael Heffernan has pointed out, the cartographers played their part in preparing for the Peace Conference because the peace meant a redrawing of boundaries and this meant maps.[8] Furthermore, the ideals of self-determination and national autonomy which the Conference attempted to apply, often inadequately and certainly with great difficulty, to frequently intransigent political subject matter, required a clear understanding of just where the boundaries of statehood rested, where on nationality, where on language and where on tradition, or, indeed, on the contingent nature of political events. Often, as in the case of Alsace-Lorraine, the maps that resulted from these criteria did not produce a completely harmonious picture. This is one of the reasons why the *Manual of Alsace-Lorraine* spends a great deal of time on language, including such apparently arcane matters as the distribution of different languages within a given region and the differences between native and acquired dialects. Thus, we find that the Manual states in regard to shifts in linguistic frontiers,

> During the war (the Franco-Prussian war of 1871) Alsace-Lorraine was flooded with Germans and depleted of patriotic natives. But dialects are not easily eradicated; nor does the use of a Teutonic dialect by a majority of the population imply adherence to the cause of the German Empire in Alsace-Lorraine any more than in Switzerland or Holland or England.[9]

Policy matters were not the I. D. 32's concern. Thus, when the *Manual of Alsace-Lorraine* states that "anti-German feeling is not synonymous with loyalty to France",[10] it could be understood as suggesting that the will of its inhabitants should actually be canvassed as opposed to what everyone knew to be the case, namely, that after the hostilities had finished Alsace-Lorraine would be returned to France because of French insistence on not holding a plebiscite.[11] Margaret Macmillan makes the point well,

> Everyone agreed that the two provinces of Alsace and Lorraine which France had lost to Germany in 1871, must be French again. And by a tacit understanding no one raised the awkward issue of self-determination; there was no question of consulting the locals, many of whom might have disobligingly preferred to remain German.[12]

What the Manual emphasises is the extent of the opposition in the region to German occupation and the weaknesses in the historical arguments used by the apologists for it.[13] But what it does not do, and, indeed, could not do given its brief, is to engage with the policy questions themselves. Where to hold fast to the principle of self-determination and where to negotiate a compromise on the basis of national interests were questions that had to be left to the Conference participants themselves.

If I. D. 32's role in the preparations for the Peace Conference was limited to that of information provision then we might ask how much influence it actually had in the specific cases that we know Collingwood was concerned with. It needs to be clearly recognised in tackling this question that government intelligence gathering operates at different levels. Largely factual material, a great deal of which is in the public domain, such as statistics and government reports, including the representation of this material in the form of maps, is of a different order from intelligence regarding the intentions of other states. Nor should we ignore the fact that while playing only an indirect role in the preparations for peace I. D. 32 nevertheless played it to the full. Indeed, it was Harold Nicolson's view that "the trouble about the Paris Conference was not that there was too little information, but that there was far too much. The fault was not lack of preparation, but lack of coordination".[14] Co-ordination was, of course, well outside the administrative aegis of I. D. 32, but when we realise the amount of detail that the Manuals contained, especially on peripheral matters, it is not difficult to understand Nicolson's point.

What we have been aiming to do in this study is not simply to identify the work that Collingwood did at the Admiralty, but also to discover its significance. From a close examination of the Manuals we now have a better grasp of the kind of intelligence they provided. We also know at what level I. D. 32 operated and we have seen something of its distance from the formulation of policy and the making of political decisions. The preparations for the Peace Conference which the Manuals were designed to assist were, however, highly fluid. Not only did the kind of peace the parties wanted vary with their aims, but also the issues that the parties were called upon to settle varied both in terms of seriousness and intractability. Thus, when the political need arose individual academic specialists in particular intelligence sections often found themselves at the centre of the creation of policy. Was the question of the Scheldt on which Collingwood worked this kind of problem?

The short answer is no for the obvious reason that at least in 1919 the major powers had no intention of permitting Belgian territorial expansion in this area. Furthermore, the question of the Scheldt was not an issue of war reparation nor was it one to be settled by recourse to plebiscite. It was not, in other words, an issue which tested the principle of self-determination, even though security considerations and commercial interests were heavily involved. By contrast, the matter of the boundaries of Poland, to take just one example, was geographically and politically complex since it involved precisely those factors of nationality, language and ethnography which made the whole idea of a post-war settlement so challenging. If this was not enough, the ambitious nature of Polish demands threatened the very coherence of the criteria that the parties to the Peace Conference were using. The Polish Commission had awarded Poland large territorial gains at Germany's expense, but in doing so it had given the politicians a dilemma. How was Germany expected to make war reparations if, for instance, wealth creating areas such as Upper Silesia were handed to Poland? Additionally, the German delegation had condemned ceding Upper Silesia to Poland as an abandonment of the principle of self-determination. On this charge, and it was a serious one, the Conference was accused of contradicting its own principles. But if there was a case for a plebiscite then in what area should it take place? On what line on the map should the frontiers be drawn? A similar problem existed in the case of Danzig where the attempt to redraw the boundaries on ethnographic, commercial and strategic lines was felt by some of the parties in the Conference to risk leaving Germany with a justified sense of grievance because it did not fully take into account the need to offer plebiscites in those areas with a clear majority of German speakers.

In constructing the boundary in accordance with the Commission's priorities it was the job of the experts, as Macmillan describes it, to try to "keep rivers and lakes in one country, to make sure that railways did not wander back and forth across international borders, and to leave as few Poles and Germans as possible on the wrong sides."[15] Collingwood's friend and Oxford colleague, H. J. Paton, was one such expert. Two years older than Collingwood and also beginning his career as an Oxford philosopher at the start of the war, Paton served from 1914 to 1918 in the Naval Intelligence Division of the Admiralty. During this time he had accumulated a vast amount of statistical data on precisely the questions that mattered when consideration was given to redrawing the Polish frontiers. In February 1919 Paton was summoned to Paris to act as advisor on Polish Affairs and it was, therefore, his specialist knowledge that was sought when the Polish settlement ran into difficulties. Sir James Headlam Morley in his memoir of the Conference takes up the story,

> The Prime Minister was much disturbed about the Polish frontier and Paton was explaining the details, pointing out that in some cases they had perhaps been pressed against Germany too far. The Prime Minister

said that he was very disturbed by the situation supposing the Germans refused to sign, and wanted to deprive them of any just reason for this. Paton explained several detailed points in which concessions might be made, especially those in which the frontier had been advanced too far west either for strategical reasons or because of railways.[16]

The Manuals produced by the Geographical Section like those on Belgium and on Alsace-Lorraine were aimed at the provision of material for discussion as opposed to the discussions themselves. Of course, this did not categorically rule out the participation of experts from the Geographical Section, or any other, in the examination of specific questions when the needs of policy making required it. However, we may suggest two factors as separating Paton's work on Poland from that of Collingwood on the Scheldt. First, in 1919 Paton was a government advisor and, therefore, expected to urge specific courses of action on his political masters and to ask for justifications for the policy proposals under review. Furthermore, even though Paton had the statistical data on the ethnographic distribution of population in his area at his fingertips this was general material of the kind that we find in all the Manuals. What was asked of him as an advisor involved something more than the ability to compile factual material. The powers of persuasion, judgement and sensitivity to the views of others were also required.[17] Obviously, the final decision on any given issue was a matter for the politicians, but in reaching it there was still a great deal to be said.[18] Second, the problem of navigation on the Scheldt while important to Belgium and the Netherlands was not a major concern for the parties in the Peace Conference. As a neutral power in the war the Netherlands did not attend the Conference and the Scheldt became an issue mainly because the Belgians insisted on making it one. Indeed, the Scheldt dispute could be thought of in the same terms as the many minor territorial disagreements which distracted the parties to the Conference when they wished to focus on the aims that mattered to them such as German disarmament, war reparations and self-determination.[19] In other words, from the British perspective in 1919 the Scheldt was important only because Belgium and the Low Countries were important and these, of course, Britain considered a vital strategic interest because they gave Germany a corridor into France and to the western coast. In hoping to annex Luxemburg and to take territory from the Netherlands, the Belgians looked to Britain for support, but, as David Stevenson explains, "The British, however, stuck to a commitment to restore the pre-war status quo, rather than see Belgium either expanded or realigned as a French satellite."[20] So when, in late 1918 and early 1919, Belgian plans for Luxemburg and their territorial ambitions for the left bank of the Scheldt and for South

Limburg were at their most vociferous, the British saw no necessity to revise their view.[21]

There is one question on which the Manual provides much more than simply factual information. In its discussion of ill-treatment of civilians in Alsace-Lorraine under German occupation the Manual identifies the German units involved, the places in which it alleges criminal behaviour towards civilians occurred, and it also itemises the available evidence.[22] Here the Manual does adopt the tone of a guide to those contemplating bringing charges for war crimes rather than a neutral statement of statistical data. We have seen how material submitted by I. D. 32 was edited by a body responsible to the Foreign Office. This is what happened to the *Manual of Belgium and the Adjoining Territories*, but the *Manual of Alsace Lorraine* is different. In this case, there is evidence for concluding that the Manual was not finished in time for use at the Conference. The history of the Geographical Section written in December 1919 lists the Manual as in preparation, and the published work itself is dated June 1919, so well behind the point where it could have been utilised in Paris. Furthermore, the Handbook which was prepared for the Peace Conference is dated February 1919, was produced under the aegis of the Foreign Office, and, while stressing the wishes of the majority of Alsace-Lorraine to remain French, is silent on the question of German atrocities, although it does discuss the suppression of the French language and the treatment of deserters under German occupation.[23] Matters of much more interest to the *Handbook* include the strategic considerations which attend the return of Alsace-Lorraine to France.[24] In other words, the Handbook was tailored to meet the requirements of the Conference as the Foreign Office saw it. It is worth adding that, whether or not the Manual recommended the prosecution of German war crimes, actual moves in this direction in the period immediately following the signing of the Treaty were very largely unsuccessful. While the British government demanded the right to bring to trial those charged with crimes against civilians, for many different legal and political reasons the results in practice were meagre.[25]

It is not difficult to reconstruct the views on the first war that Collingwood held at the time he was working at the Admiralty. Collingwood was a critic of both pacifism and conscientious objection.[26] He had no uncertainty about supporting the League of Nations and about the need to guard against the revival of German power after the war. In an Address given in May 1919, coincidentally written on the very day that the German delegation was given the peace terms by the Allies, Collingwood spoke to a conference of Belgian students. His title was "The Spiritual Basis of Reconstruction" and in his talk Collingwood made out a case for the British Empire as an instrument of peace and for the League of Nations as a unifying institution that would promote co-operation and trust. He supported the idea that the League of Nations would be a defence against "a revival of the Prussian spirit",[27] defended the right of national self-determination and was in favour of returning the disputed territory of Alsace-Lorraine to France.[28] Collingwood was no more nervous about identifying the causes of the war and its catastrophic course. He concluded his address with the following appeal,

> One alternative before us is mutual service and devotion, abnegation of self, of class, of race, nation, and language in the service of civilization and of the world; the other is to see Europe a desert, silent, unpeopled, uncultivated; riddled with the craters of shells and scorched black with the fumes of poisonous gases. There is no third alternative.[29]

Collingwood saw the war as the expression of a spiritual disease. The League of Nations and national reconstruction on the basis of a liberalism inspired by Christianity were, Collingwood felt at the time, the only remedies. Even so, Collingwood was in no doubt that the war had to be fought, not only to stem the advance of "the Prussian spirit", as he termed it, but also because victory would further the course of civilisation.

Endnotes

1 Heffernan, "Politics of the Map", pp217–18.

2 Heffernan, "Geography, Cartography and Military Intelligence", p518. A sense of the difficulties faced by the Society is provided by some remarks by Douglas Freshfield in his Address at the Anniversary General Meeting: "During the course of last summer we were able to give some help to the Intelligence Division of the Admiralty War Staff, whose quick appreciation of the resources of our library and map collection led in a short time to an urgent request that we should give room in our house for the establishment there of a special branch of this division. Under the charge of Dr. Dickson, a member of our Council, the work done by this branch has greatly increased, and the encroachments made upon our accommodation have been limited only by our refusal to deprive our Fellows of the one remaining room upon the first floor." Douglas W. Freshfield, "Address at the Anniversary Meeting 21 May 1917", *The Geographical Journal*, vol. 48, 1917, pp2–3. For contemporary accounts of the work of the Society during the war and in the Conference which followed see B. B. Cubitt, "War Work of the Society", *The Geographical Journal*, vol. 53, no. 5,

May 1919, pp336-39, and Anon, "Geography at the Congress of Paris 1919", *The Geographical Journal*, vol. 55, no. 4, April 1920, pp309-12.

3 Goldstein, "Hertford House", p86.

4 Inquiry Document 987, p16.

5 Erik Goldstein tells the story of how the editing process took place. "The basic information for each of the handbook's three sections was provided by three offices. The War Trade Intelligence Department was responsible for the first two sections of the handbooks. The material for the geographical section was based on information abstracted from Hertford House's handbooks and manuals, so Dickson's labours were not altogether lost. Information was also provided by Military Intelligence's geographical section. The WTID furnished the information for the economic section from data supplied by the War Trade Statistical Department. Prothero himself directly supervised the historical and political portions of the work, but the actual narrative was done by outside experts." (Goldstein, *Winning the Peace*, p42; see also Erik Goldstein, "Historians Outside the Academy: G. W. Prothero and the Experience of the Foreign Office Historical Section 1917-1920", *Historical Research*, vol. 63, 1990, pp195-211). A substantial amount of material from I. D. 32's original Manuals was discarded. The *Manual of Belgium and the Adjoining Territories* (1918) in its original form consisted of a volume of 595 pages, approximately 185,000 words, together with three appendices, including a lengthy bibliography, index and separate atlas. After editing this was reduced to the *Handbook to Belgium* (April 1919), a volume of 220 pages, approximately 67,000 words, together with one appendix and a list of authorities and a fold out map inserted. Some of the discussion in the *Handbook*, for example, that on the Dialects of Flemish (pp197-8) is taken word for word from the *Manual* (see pp298-9) but, overall, the editor's aim was brevity and compactness, and so a large quantity of background information was removed. The *Manual of Alsace-Lorraine* (June 1919) was completed after the *Handbook* (February 1919) and so seems not to have been edited, but the same point applies. The *Manual* is a volume of 422 pages, approximately 148,000 words, together with two appendices, including a substantial bibliography, index and separate atlas compared with the *Handbook* which is a volume of 121 pages, approximately 42,000 words, together with one appendix and a list of authorities, and a fold out map inserted. Of course, much information from the Manuals did find its way into the thinned down Handbooks to be used at the Conference, but, even so, it is clear that Parker's policy of severe pruning was very largely followed.

6 Goldstein, "Hertford House", p86.

7 See Matthew S. Seligmann, Spies in Uniform, British Military and Naval Intelligence on the Eve of the First World War, Oxford University Press, Oxford, 2006, p113.

8   Heffernan, "Geography, Cartography and Military Intelligence", p522-3.
9   Manual of Alsace-Lorraine, p152.
10   Ibid., p244.
11   See David Stevenson, *1914–1918 The History of the First World War*, p521. The link between principle and expediency in the application of self-determination was strong, see V. H. Rothwell, *British War Aims and Peace Diplomacy 1914–1918*, Oxford University Press, London, 1971, Appendix 1.
12   See Margaret Macmillan, *Peacemakers*, pp170-1.
13   See the *Manual of Alsace-Lorraine*, for example, pp233-43 where a number of pamphlets on the subject are discussed; for a contemporary account there is Ernest Barker, *Linguistic Oppression in the German Empire*, Longmans, Green and Co., London, 1918, especially Part 3.
14   Harold Nicolson, *Peacemaking*, p25.
15   Margaret Macmillan, *Peacemakers*, p227.
16   See Sir James Headlam Morley, *A Memoir of the Paris Peace Conference 1919*, edited by Agnes Headlam Morley, Russell Bryant, Anna Cienciala, Methuen, London, 1972, p135. Headlam Morley's memoir testifies to the major role played by Paton in drafting and redrafting the Polish frontiers. It is worth noting that Paton had originally supported the handing of Danzig to Poland, see his memorandum dated 27 February 1919, "The Polish Claims to Danzig and West Prussia", FO 608/66/20216, cited and summarised in Headlam Morley, pp39-40n2; for detailed discussion of Paton's role, especially that of drawing up Poland's eastern boundary along the so-called 'Curzon' line, see Headlam Morley, pp33, 53, 55, 64, 134, 150, 170. Collingwood was a friend of Paton, see R. G. Collingwood, letter to G. de Ruggiero, dated 22 November 1921, cited in Johnson, *Correspondence*, D1ix, p53.
17   See Headlam Morley, *A Memoir*, p55. "The Polish Commission has now got on to the eastern frontiers of Poland; Paton is very sensible on the matter and I think we may be assured that he will do his best to get a just result; it is rather a serious responsibility to put on someone with so little experience. I am of the opinion, however, that things will be better in his hands than in those of anyone who is not equally honest and scientific in spirit." See also Headlam Morley's comment on p170, "Paton, who came out from Oxford, and brought very great knowledge and persistence."
18   Ibid., p170 where Headlam Morley speaks of the "strong pressure" brought on him by experts on the Polish Committee to persuade the prime minister to adopt a particular proposal.
19   See Harold Nicolson, *Peacemaking*, p147. "Apart from the divergence of opinion upon such central problems as French Security, the Rhineland, Reparation, the Saar Valley, the disposal of the German Fleet, the Blockade, Conscription, and the Polish Frontier, the energies of the Supreme Council were incessantly being tapped and wasted by petty problems arising from

disagreements between the smaller Powers." Arnold Toynbee records in his *Experiences*, p102, that Headlam Morley had said to him in 1919 that when starting to write history he should choose a topic that was small and not very important, suggesting "that I should begin by writing the history of the post-war dispute between the Netherlands and Belgium over the navigation of the Scheldt". As we have seen, Toynbee wrote a study of the course of the dispute from 1920 to 1923 that was published in 1925. In 1920 the dispute had not lost its capacity to raise the temperatures of each side, see C. A. Macartney, *Survey 1925*, pp168–70; on p168 we find, "Both sides, however, preferred to stand on their assumed rights with the result that situations sometimes arose which an outsider might have difficulty in treating seriously." Nevertheless, the treaty of 8 January 1925 did produce some new measure of agreement.

20 See David Stevenson, 1914–1918 The History of the First World War, p147

21 See D. Stevenson, "Belgium, Luxemburg, and the Defence of Western Europe, 1914–1920", *International History Review*, vol. 4, 1982, pp504–23, especially p513 where Stevenson writes, "The Lloyd George government did not reply to a new memorandum about Luxemburg, and Arthur Balfour, the Foreign Secretary, saw no need to define a standpoint over Limburg and the Scheldt before the conference began." The *Manual of Belgium* points strongly towards the preservation of Luxemburg independence, "as regards the attitude of the Luxemburgers towards their neighbours, the wish to be left as they were still prevailed" (p198). Further, even though closer relations with Germany possessed economic benefits, "the great majority of the Luxemburgers had still no political sympathy with the Empire, and Germans of the Empire were on the whole unpopular. Dislike of Prussianism remained strong" (p198). Disputes over the Luxemburg problem lumbered on during 1919, see Sally Marks, "The Luxemburg Question at the Paris Peace Conference and After", available at www.flwi.ugent.1970, accessed 1/6/2009.

22 Manual of Alsace-Lorraine, pp237–43.

23 *Alsace-Lorraine*, Handbooks prepared under the direction of the Historical Section of the Foreign Office, no. 28. February 1919, pp51–2.

24 Ibid., pp56–7.

25 For discussion see John Horne and Alan Kramer, *German Atrocities*, pp329–55; Geoffrey Best, *Humanity in Warfare*, Weidenfeld and Nicolson, London, 1980, pp224–37 and James F. Willis, *Prologue to Nuremburg The Politics and Diplomacy of Punishing War Criminals of the First World War*, Greenwood Press, West Port, Connecticut, 1982.

26 For Collingwood's argument against pacifism, see R. G. Collingwood, "War in its Relation to Christian Ethics", 1930, Paper read to the Group, 17 November, 1932, pp2–4, Collingwood Manuscripts, Bodleian Library, Dep. 1/8; and for his views on conscientious objection, see R. G. Collingwood, *Speculum*

Mentis, Clarendon Press, Oxford, 1924, p305, and also *The New Leviathan*, 29.9–29.98 where Collingwood specifically refers to Russell's pacifism in the first war and his retraction of it in the second. For discussion and the historical context of Collingwood's views, see James Connelly, *Metaphysics, Method and Politics, The Political Philosophy of R. G. Collingwood*, Imprint Academic, Exeter, 2003, pp179–81, and David Boucher, *Editor's Introduction* to R. G. Collingwood, *The New Leviathan*, revised edition, Clarendon Press, Oxford, 1992, especially pplv–lvii.

27   See R. G. Collingwood, "The Prussian Philosophy", in *Essays in Political Philosophy, R. G. Collingwood*, p204.

28   Ibid., p201, as we have seen it was at this time that Collingwood was working on the *Manual of Alsace-Lorraine*.

29   Ibid., p206.

CHAPTER 8

FRIENDSHIPS IN WARTIME

R. G. Collingwood's relationship with his father was close, devoted and respectful on both sides. In the famous dedication to *Speculum Mentis* W. G. Collingwood is described affectionately as "My first and best teacher of art, religion, science, history and philosophy."[1] Comradeship between father and son was enduring, and so it is, perhaps, no surprise to learn that for a time they served alongside each other in I. D. 32.[2] Indeed, there is good reason for treating them together because for long periods of their lives that is exactly how they thought of themselves. W. G. Collingwood was in Coniston when he received his son's invitation to join him in Naval Intelligence and towards the end of October 1917 he travelled to London to start work at Hertford House where his duties, like those of his son, concerned the British preparations for peace.[3] Collingwood had earlier written revealingly of his response to the war to his friend Arthur Simpson,

> We have lost so many, relations and friends and there is so much going on, that one can only hope and wait...it is the day of the young, and I really think there is a good side to it all, in the stimulus and self-sacrifice. But it is hard on parents and such-like: one can only try to hold on.[4]

Another of the many at the time who were trying to "hold on" was Wilfred Owen, then in Craiglockhart House recovering from shellshock suffered in the devastating battles of 1916 and 1917. It was while he was at Craiglockhart that Owen in September 1917 wrote "Anthem for Doomed Youth", one of his most admired war poems and a work which perfectly expresses the mixture of sentiments that Collingwood communicates in his letter. Had Collingwood read this poem on its publication some two years after Owen was killed he must surely have remembered the occasion in the summer of 1912 when the young poet cycled the long forty miles from Keswick to Coniston to visit him.[5]

Owen had deliberately gone missing from attendance at an evangelical convention, to speak to the man who had been Ruskin's friend and secretary. The evening was a success, Collingwood's hospitality generous and the ride back to Keswick speedy, since Owen had been fortified by plentiful supplies of his host's whisky.

While literary reputation had not yet touched Owen in 1917, Collingwood was already well known as a writer, antiquary and historian. He was also a painter of repute and something of an archaeologist and draughtsman. In fact, his skills were exactly the ones required for work in the Geographical Section of Naval Intelligence. When W. G. Collingwood joined the organisation in October 1917 British preparations for peace were gathering pace. As 1917 came to a close with hardly any reward for the human cost of the war, "there was a groundswell of liberal and radical opinion, identifying itself with Wilsonian idealism, in favour of a British declaration in support of an 'idealistic' peace."[6] After Lloyd George's address to the Trades Union Congress in January 1918, followed a little later by Woodrow Wilson's announcement of his famous "Fourteen Points", a liberal consensus gradually emerged that outlined British peace aims. Subject to the military situation British peace policy was to be grounded in support for the basic principle of self-determination, underpinned by the strategic demands of national interest and security. In the light of these concerns, some of the issues to be settled, such as the re-statement of Belgian sovereignty and the return of Alsace-Lorraine to France, were relatively straightforward. As we have seen, these were topics that concerned the young Collingwood. But it seems that his father was presented with work on much more contentious matters. Collingwood worked first on the *Manual of European Russia*, a vast project in geographical and political terms, which was abandoned after the Armistice, possibly because of the difficulty of obtaining reliable information, but also because of the volatile situation in Russia after the Revolution.[7] As one senior British diplomat remarked, "there is little positive to be said when one is dealing with something which is today hardly a geographical expression."[8] Similar comments were made about Persia, Collingwood's next assignment on which he started working towards the end of January 1918.[9] Persia was a vital British interest because of its strategic position regarding India and also because of its massive reserves of oil. The traditional Russian threat southwards was seen to be receding and, yet, chaotic conditions in Persia discouraged any thoughts of it being the subject of direct discussion at the Peace Conference, the British government's preference being for bilateral negotiations.[10] Lord Curzon, in discussion in the Eastern Committee, famously described the Persian issue as, "one of the most puzzling, and in some respects one of the most discouraging with which we have to deal".[11] Geographical information, particularly regarding communications in the region, was important, however, and, given that no Manual (or Handbook) of Persia is listed in the History of I. D. 32, it seems likely that Collingwood's work was used to support the various memoranda that were produced by Foreign Office staff to aid political decision-making in this area.[12]

In fact, W. G. Collingwood spent two periods working in the Geographical Section, the first from 24 October 1917 to 25 April 1918, the second, with the Armistice fast approaching, from 22 October 1918 to 19 April 1919.[13] Living in wartime London took a serious toll on Collingwood's already fragile health. It was an experience that, as his son tells us, "diminished his strength".[14] He saw German air attacks on London at first hand; encounters which must surely have had a serious effect, since the psychological impact of German aircraft-based bombing towards the end of the war was at the time a cause for concern.[15] When Collingwood returned to Coniston on 21 April 1919 events at the Peace Conference in Paris were slowly inching their way towards a conclusion, although it would be two months after that before the signing of the Treaty and another month again before I. D. 32 was demobilised. As we have seen, neither father nor son was called to Paris, but Dr A. A. Altounyan, a figure who would become well known to the Collingwood family, was.[16] It is a story that we should tell in a little more detail since it gives us a record of a family and its friends in time of war.

R. G. Collingwood's life as an archaeologist was not unaffected by the war. The death of Francis Haverfield in 1919, together with many students of his who did not survive the war, left Collingwood, as he writes himself, "the only man resident in Oxford whom he had trained as a Romano-British specialist."[17] So, feeling under an obligation to Haverfield, his first mentor and example in archaeology, Collingwood turned down all offers of employment elsewhere, decisions that would, in effect, make Oxford the academic centre of his world for the next two decades. But in 1916 the war touched Collingwood's life more directly, for in that year in the July offensive that we know as the Battle of the Somme the friend from Collingwood's school days, Ernest Altounyan, was seriously wounded while serving with the Royal Army Medical Corps.

Collingwood and Altounyan were both born in 1889. They had got to know one another well at Rugby School between 1903 and 1908 where they became close friends, Altounyan often visiting the Collingwood family home at Lanehead, Coniston, in the Lake District where he met and later married Collingwood's elder sister Dora.[18] After 1908 their ways parted, Collingwood to University College, Oxford, Altounyan to Cambridge to study medicine. At the start of the war, Altounyan was working at the Middlesex Hospital as part of the process of qualifying to be a doctor. Dora and he married in September 1915, Altounyan volunteering for the RAMC in 1916. He was badly wounded during the Battle of the Somme when he was half buried by a shell that burst near him as he was picking up the wounded. We should let his daughter take up the story, "He told us often how his life had been saved by a doctor who noticed a foot sticking out of a heap of rubble."[19] Altounyan's injuries were so severe that his active war service was over, he and his wife and daughter remaining in England until the autumn of 1919 when they travelled to Aleppo in Syria for Ernest to work in the hospital run by his father.

Mention of Altounyan's father takes us from the war to the peace because Dr A. A. Altounyan was the representative of the Armenians of western Asia at the Peace Conference in July 1919.[20] Just as Ernest Altounyan's experience during the Battle of the Somme must have brought the risks and dangers of war home to Collingwood personally so would the experience of Altounyan's father of having political hopes dashed in a fraudulent Peace. For in Paris the fine liberal sentiments regarding the atrocities suffered by the Armenians at the hands of the Turks came to nothing. A mandated Armenia held little attraction for the Allies and even if it had it would not have been a practicable policy. For, as Margaret Macmillan explains, Armenia was a distant land, surrounded by enemies who were not prepared to countenance its independence and in any case Allied forces were too much occupied elsewhere to undertake a campaign in a remote and inhospitable region.[21] Taqui Altounyan remembers the spring and summer of 1919 as a time of much activity for the Collingwood family, with both R. G. Collingwood and his father completing their work at the Admiralty, and Ernest Altounyan in London along with his father, who was preparing for the Peace Conference.[22] With his sister about to embark on a journey involving an uncertain future contemporary political events were at the forefront of Collingwood's concerns at the time.

It is from another close friend of the Collingwood family, one who became in some respects the more well known, that we learn further about their responses to the new political world that was forming around them. Arthur Ransome, the author of the *Swallows and Amazons* tales, thought of W. G. Collingwood almost as a second father.[23] Ransome helped to arrange accommodation for the Collingwood family when they stayed for a time in London in 1904 and in the formative period of his literary career Ransome regularly turned to W. G. Collingwood for advice about his writing, thinking of him as a mentor, a counsellor and friend. In early 1913 R. G. Collingwood wrote to Ransome to exchange family news and to tell him of the progress he was making in translating Croce's book on Vico.[24] In Russia for most of the early years of the war, Ransome nevertheless managed to keep in touch with Collingwood's published work in philosophy, even arranging for a copy of *Religion and Philosophy* to be sent out to him in the diplomatic bag.[25] So in 1915 when Ransome spoke from Russia of his feelings at not having enlisted, as his brother, Geoffrey, had done, Collingwood replied, saying that "good minds were required to promote understanding between Russia and Britain, to keep the Alliance strong".[26] And, as his letters indicate, his closeness with W. G. Collingwood never diminished, even though they were forced to disagree over the new regime in Russia. In a letter to his mother, Ransome gives us a clear picture of how political differences were dealt with in the Collingwood household. He writes,

> Mr. Collingwood was sweet. He knew I knew of his violent anti-bolshevism, and I think he thought I was rather avoiding discussion. Well, one day he just walked round the table after dinner and collared my right hand secretly with his left one, and said it was very nice to see me again or something like that...the words didn't matter. But the whole incident nearly made me weep. Also something has happened which has made him see that I was a great deal nearer the truth about our policy than he supposed. A quite independent source has informed him of our annexation plans for Turkestan, which of course corroborates all I have been saying.[27]

Ransome's views are not difficult to reconstruct. As an apologist for Bolshevik aspirations it galled him in the summer of 1919 to see a British government taking every possible measure to isolate the new regime in Russia, even if that meant suppressing local autonomy and adopting a policy of intervention to try to bring about its defeat. Thus, for Ransome, what liberals like W. G. Collingwood failed to see was how the British government paid lip service to the principle of self-determination while strictly following the protection of British interests as it perceived them. In the event political realities ruled the day and the populations of the new states of Central Asia were left to their own devices. Ransome's pro-Bolshevik stance went far beyond promoting understanding between two sovereign states, certainly too far for some of the Collingwood family, even though it is doubtful if they were aware of his more covert activities. As Ransome's latest biographer comments,

Most of Ransome's friends were violently opposed to Bolshevism. Robin Collingwood was working for naval intelligence. W. G. Collingwood, the ancient Skald of the Lakes, anticipated a showdown the moment Ransome set foot back in the country, while Barbara Collingwood implored him in her letters to give up dabbling in politics, which he was clearly no good at, and return as soon as possible to romances.[28]

The Armenians were not the only people who felt betrayed by the Conference since the Arabs, too, were to have their hopes for independence set aside in the face of competitiveness between the Allies and their often brutal sense of political realism. Both Altounyans were present at the Conference, with Ernest leaving a remarkable memoir of T. E. Lawrence who he had first met at Carchemish in 1911.[29] Talking of Lawrence, Altounyan writes,

> A day or two later as we were lunching in the vast dining room that contained most of the British Peace Delegation, he came in to speak to my father. As he stood by our table the room stopped eating and under the impact of that silence, as his eyes swept over their heads, I could almost hear him say, 'How-jolly-and-how-foolish'. I only once saw him really moved by a personality. Waiting to see him in his bedroom at the Carlton (Feisal's London headquarters), he arrived in uniform and flinging his cap on the bed exclaimed, flushing with pride, 'I've just had half an hour with Curzon'. I feel positively that though by this time he must have known that his Arab policy was going west he was never troubled by remorse.[30]

The presence of both Altounyans at the Peace Conference and Ernest's intimacy with the Collingwood family, is an encouragement to bring Collingwood's work in the Admiralty closer to the public events of the time.[31] In May 1919 Collingwood gave an address to Belgian students on the need for spiritual reconstruction after the war, but at least three years earlier during one of the war's gravest periods Collingwood was concerned enough about the importance of his ideas to find the time to speak out about them.[32] Even when Admiralty work is at its most taxing Collingwood never put philosophy aside. Thus, in 1916 Collingwood wrote to Macmillan about his final revisions to *Religion and Philosophy*, "I have put it through with all possible speed, but delay is inevitable when one can hardly reckon on three hours in the week free from office work."[33] Similar sentiments can be found in the Preface to Collingwood's book, where he writes, "The claims of a 'temporary' occupation, very different from that in which I began to write, leave no opportunity for the rewriting and careful revision which such a work demands, and I had set it aside to await a greater period of leisure."[34] But Collingwood tells us further that his work is a study of religion from an intellectual rather than a devotional point of view and that since this is a topic that excites strong interest he is publishing his book as it stands to make a contribution to this debate. It was about this time, too, when Collingwood had his famous encounter with the Albert Memorial. Once more it was an intellectual problem that preoccupied him, in this case, how an architect could have created something so obviously and patently bad, a puzzle which led him to the series of day-to-day reflections that eventually produced the logic of question and answer.[35] As we have seen, one of the ways the war impinged on Collingwood's life was through its impact on his feelings for those closest to him, but his main response was intellectual.[36] How could philosophical reflection on the nature and origins of war contribute to its avoidance in the future? At the Admiralty the habits of thought that Collingwood needed were orderliness and precision. For Collingwood the philosopher an intelligent response to the war also required these habits, possibly as much as the worker in Naval Intelligence, but as a philosopher Collingwood was compelled to ask for more.

Endnotes

1   R. G. Collingwood, *Speculum Mentis*, Clarendon Press, Oxford, 1924, Dedication.

2   Matthew Townend, *Vikings and Victorian Lakeland*, p244, (citing W. G. Collingwood's *Diary*, 8 October 1917).

3   W. G. Collingwood, *Diary*, 23 October 1917 (Abbott Hall).

4   As cited in Townend, p243.

5   See Dominic Hibberd, *Wilfred Owen, A New Biography*, Phoenix, London, 2003, p108. It seems that Owen had been given a letter of introduction to Collingwood from a Miss Rayner who Collingwood knew while teaching at the University of Reading, see also Wilfred Owen, *Collected Letters*, edited by Harold Owen and John Bell, Oxford University Press, London, 1967, pp129 and 149.

6   Michael L. Dockrill and J. Douglas Goold, *Peace without Promise, Britain and the Peace Conferences 1919–1923*, Batsford Academic and Educational Ltd, London, 1981, p18

7   The Geographical Work, p3.

8   As cited in Goldstein, *Winning the Peace*, p141.

9   W. G. Collingwood, *Diary*, 22 January 1919, " Dickson took me off 'Russia' and turned me on 'Persia'" (Abbott Hall).

10   See Margaret Macmillan, *Peacemakers*, p50

11   As cited in Goldstein, *Winning the Peace*, p177

12   The Geographical Work, pp1–3

13   See W. G. Collingwood, *Diary*, 24 October 1917, 25 April 1918, 21 October 1918 and 19 April 1919 (Abbott Hall); for *Obituaries* of W. G. Collingwood which mention his war service, see *The Times*, 3 October 1932, (by R. G. Collingwood); *Transactions of the Cumberland and Westmorland Antiquarian and Archaeological Society*, vol. 3, new series, 1933, pp310-11, (by R. G. Collingwood); *Yorkshire Archaeological Journal*, vol. 31, 1934, pp192-3, (by H. B. McCall), and the "Memoir" by R. B. Graham, *Journal of the Fell and Rock Climbing Club of the English Lake District*, volume 9, 1932, pp194-6; see also James S. Dearden, "Collingwood, William Gershom 1854-1932", in the *New Oxford Dictionary of National Biography*, online edition, Oxford University Press, 2004.

14   Transactions, p311.

15   See Matthew Townend, *Vikings and Victorian Lakeland*, p244, n. 8.

16   For discussion of the arrangements for attendance by British experts at the Peace Conference, see Sally Marks, "Behind the Scenes at the Paris Peace Conference of 1919", *Journal of British Studies*, vol. 9, no. 2, 1970, pp154-89; some individuals from I. D. 32 apparently did attend, see W. G. Collingwood, *Diary*, 3 April, 1919, (Abbott Hall).

17   R. G. Collingwood, *An Autobiography*, p120

18   Ernest Haig Riddell Altounyan (1889-1962) was born of an Armenian father and an Irish mother. Educated in England at Rugby and Emmanuel College, Cambridge Altounyan was a close friend of both the Collingwood family and, among others, T. E. Lawrence. Among his other English friends he counted E. M. Forster, (see P. N. Furbank, *E. M. Forster: A Life*, vol. 2, Oxford University Press, Oxford, 1979, p206, n. 3: Altounyan "was a doctor and poet and published a sequence of poems *Ornament of Honour* (1937) in memory of Lawrence. Forster was very friendly with him round about 1915 but they were later estranged."), as well as Leonard and Virginia Woolf. Virginia Woolf was not wholly entranced by Altounyan, see her characteristic letter to Lady Ottoline Morrell, dated 21 May 1919, "I've see an Armenian called Altounyan who wants us to print his novel. The poor man's mouth is fixed open, like that of some large fish, in hope of praise; it is positively alarming. Compared with him, I merely flicker a long thin tongue. But the attitude is not ungraceful; and God knows what we're to say to his novel; and how can we advise him, as he wishes, to throw up his career, desert his father on the edge of the grave, and devote himself to fiction?" (see Nigel Nicolson (ed.), *The Letters of Virginia Woolf*, vol. 2, *1912-1922*, The Hogarth Press, London, 1976, p360). In another letter this time to Vanessa Bell, dated 17 July 1919, Virginia expressed her opinion of Altounyan less circumspectly, "Altounyan and his sister (Norah) have been dining here. I'm afraid he is a great bore—Why will people talk so much nonsense about their writing? After having made me read his manuscript, he told me that he didn't care what I thought of it, but only wished to see how much I was capable of understanding. There's the cloven hoof of

Cambridge in all this, — rather like Hom (Meredith) I mean; the honest sort. How I detest them!" (ibid., p377). Altounyan dined with the Woolfs on a number of occasions. The editor of Virginia Woolf's *Diary*, Anne Olivier Bell, points out, that Altounyan had been recommended to Leonard Woolf by E. M. Forster "in May 1915 on the grounds that he had once been mad and might be of help to VW, who was then in the throes of madness; LW had then invited him once or twice to Hogarth House" (see *The Diary of Virginia Woolf*, vol. 1, *1915-1919*, The Hogarth Press, London, 1977, p275, n. 13) Altounyan appointed the Woolfs his literary executors, (see *Diary*, p276, entry dated Thursday 22 May 1919), and also visited the Woolfs soon after his marriage accompanied by Dora (see *Diary*, p296, entry dated Sunday 7 September 1919). Altounyan owned at least one of Virginia's novels since a copy exists of her first book, *The Voyage Out* (1915) signed and dated "E. H. R. Altounyan/1915" in black ink. Leonard Woolf first invited him in May 1915 and it is possible that this copy was given to him on one of his visits. Nothing came of the publication of Altounyan's novel by the Woolfs, possibly because of E. M. Forster's low opinion of it; in her *Diary*, p291, entry dated Saturday 12 July 1919, Virginia reports Forster as saying "He did not at all care for it; no form, no character; no one figure dominating the others." The unpublished novel seems to have been about his life with the Collingwood family at Lanehead. In her memoir Taqui Altounyan writes that "The novel, which does not seem to have had a title, was finished in 1917" (see Taqui Altounyan, *Chimes*, p57), and she gives a brief description of a passage in which the author, her father, takes a boat alone across Coniston Water to Peel Island where the Collingwood children habitually played. When Altounyan published his poem *Ornament of Honour* in 1937 Collingwood wrote to him saying that his old friend "had achieved a real poem" (*Chimes*, p122). For Altounyan's early life with the Collingwood family see also *The Autobiography of Arthur Ransome*, prologue and epilogue by Rupert Hart-Davis, Jonathan Cape, London, 1976, *Signalling From Mars, The Letters of Arthur Ransome*, selected and introduced by Hugh Brogan, Jonathan Cape, London, 1977; Hugh Brogan, *The Life of Arthur Ransome*, Jonathan Cape, London, 1984; Roger Wardale, *Nancy Blackett, Under Sail With Arthur Ransome*, Jonathan Cape, London, 1991; Christina Hardyment, *Arthur Ransome and Captain Flint's Trunk*, Jonathan Cape, London, 1984. The memoirs of Altounyan's daughter Taqui, are, however, the primary source, see *Chimes*, along with her first book of memoirs, *In Aleppo Once*, John Murray, London, 1969.

19   See *Chimes*, p64.
20   Ibid., p66.
21   Margaret Macmillan, *Peacemakers*, pp389-91.
22   See, for example, *Chimes*, pp66ff.

23   See the books listed at the end of note 18 for details of Ransome's friendship with the Collingwood family.
24   See R. G. Collingwood to Arthur Ransome, letter dated 26 January 1913, (Ransome Papers, Brotherton Collection, University of Leeds, Peter Johnson, *Correspondence*, R1i).
25   See Arthur Ransome to Edith R. Ransome, letter dated 1 May 1917, in Arthur Ransome, *Signalling from Mars*, p43. The use of the diplomatic bag was facilitated by the liberal MP, Sir Francis Acland.
26   See Roland Chambers, *The Last Englishman, The Double Life of Arthur Ransome*, Faber and Faber, London, 2009, p105.
27   See Arthur Ransome to Edith R. Ransome, letter dated 13 June 1919, in Arthur Ransome, *Signalling from Mars*, p97. Ransome also mentions this occasion in his *Autobiography* (p270), "I went to Coniston and W. G. Collingwood did not allow his disapproval of all revolutions to cloud for a moment his friendship for me."
28   Roland Chambers, *The Last Englishman*, p244.
29   Michael Asher, Lawrence, *The Uncrowned King of Arabia*, Penguin Books, London, 1999, p84; for further detail on Altounyan's friendship with Lawrence, see *The Letters of T. E. Lawrence*, edited by David Garnett, Jonathan Cape, London, 1938, p760.
30   See *T. E. Lawrence by his Friends*, edited by A. W. Lawrence, Jonathan Cape, London, 1937, p117.
31   See *Chimes*, and *In Aleppo Once*, for much detail concerning this.
32   See "The Spiritual Basis of Reconstruction", Address to the Belgian Students' Conference at Fladbury, 10 May 1919; Collingwood MS, DEP 24, partially reprinted in *R. G. Collingwood, Essays in Political Philosophy*, pp201–06. Collingwood was responding to the needs of Belgian students who found themselves refugees in Britain during the war; for two impressions of the refugees' lives and experiences, see *Arthur Lionel Smith, 1916–1924*, p202 and *The Letters of Dorothy L. Sayers, 1899–1936*, chosen and edited by Barbara Reynolds, Hodder and Stoughton, London, 1995, p103.
33   Letter to Macmillan dated 19 November 1916, Peter Johnson, *Correspondence*, M1v.
34   R. G. Collingwood, *Religion and Philosophy*, pv.
35   R. G. Collingwood, *An Autobiography*, p29ff.
36   Collingwood's marriage in 1918 to Ethel Winifred Graham also brought him into close contact with those who had personal experience of the war. Ethel Graham's brother, Angus (with whom Collingwood was to collaborate on a number of archaeological investigations, see "Skipness Castle" by Angus Graham and R. G. Collingwood, *Proceedings of the Society of Antiquaries of Scotland*, vol. 5, no. 9, 1922–3, pp266–87), served with the Highland Light Infantry and was wounded at Gallipoli, see Angus Graham, *Skipness, Memories of a Highland Estate*, Canongate Academic, Edinburgh, 1993, pxiii; Joanna

Gordon, "The Objects Themselves: A Short Note on the Life and Ideas of Angus Graham", *Review of Scottish Culture*, no. 6, 1990, pp1-6, and J. G. Dunbar, "Angus Graham", *Proceedings of the Society of Antiquaries of Scotland*, 111, 1981, pp1-6. It is likely that it was through the Graham family that Collingwood encountered and later corresponded with Mary Dolling Sanders (later known as the novelist, Ann Bridge) who in 1913 married Owen O'Malley, a cousin of the Grahams. She had met her husband through her friendship with Ethel Graham when they both worked for the Charity Organisation Society in London in 1913. Mary O'Malley as she became, (later Lady O'Malley) worked for Admiralty Intelligence during the war deciphering German codebooks and radio messages, so it is likely that she was employed in Room 40 or one of the rooms associated with it, for this information, see Ann Bridge, *Portrait of My Mother*, Chatto and Windus, London, 1955, p230 and also her *Moments of Knowing, Some Personal Experiences Beyond Normal Knowledge*, Hodder and Stoughton, London, 1970, pp19-24.

CHAPTER 9

THE WAR'S CRITIC

In *An Autobiography* Collingwood presents himself as a severe critic of the war of 1914–18, saying that he sided with Norman Angell's belief, expressed in his book *The Great Illusion*, that there could be no victors in modern warfare. Not only was the war an immense human catastrophe it was representative of the all-consuming power of technology and behind that the almost irresistible reach of natural science. Thus, Collingwood writes, "I seemed to see the reign of natural science, within no very long time, converting Europe into a wilderness of Yahoos."[1] Scientific rule over nature totally outmatched its capacity to control human affairs. The combatants in the war, Collingwood asserts, were engaged in a dreadful and uncontrollable conflict, but they did not know why. Further, the victors did not know what their victory meant. They knew only what was common to both sides, namely, just how much human suffering the struggle had cost them. In philosophical terms, Collingwood associates the war with positivism, but he supplements this by referring to disdain for metaphysics as one of the intellectual forces that brought the conflict about and which also prevented the rivals from finding a solution to it. Collingwood writes,

> A war of unprecedented violence broke out: and when the belligerents tried to discover what they were fighting for, nobody knew. The analytic thinking which ought for half a century or more to have been clarifying the issues had not been done, and such thinking cannot be done in a hurry.[2]

Rational thought, Collingwood continues, was replaced by propaganda and cliché. As the war took its predictable course towards stalemate, for Collingwood, a blind faith in technology replaced historical judgement and trust in the power of reason.

In the context of a world rushing headlong towards another global conflict, Collingwood's later views about the causes of the war of 1914–18 are understandable. It is also true that in *An Autobiography* Collingwood was not concerned to join up all the dots either in his explanation of the course of his thought or of his life. Nevertheless, some unconnected biographical dots are significant because they refer back to Collingwood's experience of the war, and so they help us to see why he found the unity of thought and action elusive at that time. It is helpful to consider the following quotations from *An Autobiography*:

> I knew that for sheer ineptitude the Versailles treaty surpassed previous treaties as much as for sheer technical excellence the equipment of twentieth century armies surpassed those of previous armies.[3]

> I write as one who during the latter part of the war was employed in preparations for the peace conference.[4]

What is Collingwood saying here? What does he want us to believe? Our most obvious response is that he wants us to accept his view that the Versailles Treaty was an act of folly because his is the testimony of someone who was actually there, one who played a part in its preparations. But, as we have seen, many academics worked on the peace conference preparations and some who were closer to the making of decisions than Collingwood, for example, H. J. Paton, did not share his view. Moreover, the technical capacities and innovations which Collingwood condemns in his criticism of the war were also in operation in naval intelligence, playing a major role in trying to prosecute the British war effort more efficiently. The most obvious line of thought is not, therefore, the most successful. We should try a different tack. Consider the possibility that the two quotations can be given a more compelling meaning if we think of them as evidence of the way Collingwood viewed his life. In Collingwood's philosophical work during his service at the Admiralty his growing belief in the unity of thought and action stands out. But this belief was not reflected in his life. He lived as if the belief was false, and so the work he did in preparing handbooks and drawing maps of regions to assist the peacemakers was the work of a specialist, unconnected both with his philosophy and with his low view, to be repeated more emphatically later, of the decisions the politicians made.

The unity of thought and action that Collingwood was drawn towards is a philosophical idea. Collingwood is saying is that we can no more construe thought independently of action than we can action independently of thought. This is the force of his early opposition to realism. So, when, in *Religion and Philosophy*, Collingwood writes that "it is no longer possible to uphold the familiar distinction between a life of thought and a life of action" he is making a conceptual claim rather than agreeing with the pragmatist that ideas are tested only in life or the utilitarian that ideas are valueless unless their practical consequences can be established.[5] This is what thought and action mean. However, if we do interpret Collingwood in this way, as making a philosophical claim and nothing more, then this seriously dilutes what he actually says. For Collingwood insists in *An Autobiography* that what he means by "a theoretical rapprochement between theory and practice"[6] is one in which "I still conducted my daily life as if I thought that the business of that life was theoretical and not practical."[7] In other words, on Collingwood's own account of his life, it would be false to picture that life as a philosophical one with a merely personal existence tacked on.

To this we should add another complication. When Collingwood says that he lived as though he disbelieved his own philosophy he is not saying only that what was true in his theory was false in his life. If that was all he was saying then the description of the early Collingwood as someone who was unable to live up to his ideal of the unity of thought and action would fit. By not living in a way that was faithful to his philosophy Collingwood was indicating just how much of realism needed to be erased. What Collingwood is saying is not that what was true in his ideals was false in his life, but that what was false in his life came about because he had the wrong ideals. Theory can be related to practice in different ways. Collingwood had an important motive for writing *An Autobiography*. He wanted to tell us how he came to realise that any rapprochement between theory and practice would fail if it followed a single axis. So without an equally satisfactory rapprochement between philosophy and history any reconciliation between theory and practice would remain incomplete.

In *An Autobiography* Collingwood presents himself as a fierce critic of the First World War and the Peace Settlement that followed it. In 1942 he launched an equally fierce assault on the League of Nations, not simply against its practical incompetence, but the principles on which it was based and the attitudes of its founders. He writes, "They thought of the League as a kind of heaven on earth. They ought to have known that if you aim at a heaven on earth you are certain of getting a hell on earth."[8] However, what Collingwood thought of as wholly inadequate at the start of the Second World War, he considered very differently during and after the First. The point here is not to do with the consistency of Collingwood's thinking about politics. Political institutions are tested by changes of events and any attitude taken towards them that wishes to be counted realistic needs to reflect this. What concerns us is how we are to understand Collingwood's response to the First World War at the time, assuming that his autobiographical description is true. For Collingwood not only served his country in the war and was actively involved in the preparations for the peace, his views at the time were anything but fiercely critical. While Collingwood was not at the time one of those who aimed for "a heaven on earth", he could nevertheless be counted as both a patriot and an internationalist. When Collingwood says in his *Autobiography* that there was a time when he acted as if he disbelieved his own philosophy he is, in effect, giving his former self a serious rebuke.

At this point we should be clear about the problem that faces us. In 1919 Collingwood gave the idea of a League of Nations his strong support. But from the perspective of his *Autobiography* in 1939 Collingwood says that in 1919 he regarded the peace settlement as an act of "unprecedented folly",[9] and the statesmen who concluded it as "a mob of imbeciles, capable only of throwing away all the opportunities their soldiers had won for them".[10] Collingwood is here reporting views he claims he held at the time. Indeed, if this were not the case what he says would make little sense because it was the failure of the peace settlement that gave Collingwood one of his most important reasons for turning his attention to history. Collingwood says that in 1919 he had little choice but to investigate the philosophical problems of history because "he wished to do his share in laying the foundations of the future."[11] But the significance of this choice would be lost if Collingwood's dating of his criticism of the peace settlement was mistaken. We should notice, too, that we cannot eradicate this problem simply by saying that throughout the 1930s Collingwood came to see that the League of Nations was weak and ineffectual. He certainly did come to see this, but in itself this change of heart has no bearing on the views he held during the war. Equally, we cannot remove the problem by distinguishing between the peace settlement and the League because the principles at the heart of the settlement were precisely those that the League wished to enshrine. Many liberals who supported the League in 1919 were given good reasons to alter their views as political events developed. But our problem concerns Collingwood's self-understanding in the formative stage of his life, for if his autobiographical account is true then it is at odds with the principles that we know he supported at the time.

It is impossible to miss the depth of Collingwood's later disillusion with the League and with the Peace Settlement itself. As a second war with Germany looked increasingly unavoidable during the 1930s a willingness to blame the peacemakers became widespread. Whether this mood was either widespread or justifiable is not our main concern here. Even so, it is worth mentioning that Collingwood's later indictment of the Settlement is less a matter of argument than an expression of despair. Little by way of a detailed justification is to be found for his arguments, and he often speaks as if 1919 was merely a prelude to 1939, in other words, that nothing else happened in the period between the wars which could have explained the rise of Hitler.[12] Collingwood's liberal disillusion is a complex and unsettling state. An object of belief, once strongly held, is turned into a fallen idol, something to be denied, possibly thought of scornfully. It is not only in the stridency of Collingwood's language that we notice this; we find it in his later willingness to make sweeping judgements of government actions during the First World War that at the time he was a party to himself.

Consider the issue of German atrocities as a relevant example. One of the main features of Collingwood's later criticism of the First World War and the Peace Settlement that followed it was his claim that both resulted from a long neglect of analytical thought. So, Collingwood writes, as a consequence of this,

> the propaganda-literature of the belligerents, instead of stating what the fundamental principles at stake were, confined itself to irrelevancies (e.g. each side accusing each other of 'atrocities', as if war had ever been conducted without 'atrocities' on both sides, and as if 'atrocities' had anything to do with the question which side had the better cause).[13]

But, as we have already noticed, in the *Manual of Alsace-Lorraine* which was published in June 1919, Collingwood refers to wholesale arrests without trial, deportations, closure of newspapers, political murders, destruction of property, massacres, burnings, pillage and spoliation, all committed during the German occupation. Collingwood comments that "the evidence on this hand is extremely voluminous and comes entirely from German official sources".[14] In other words, at the time actual proof of atrocities was anything but off the point. It had everything to do with which side had the better cause and, in relation to the Peace Settlement, which side had the better claim to disputed territory. To put this slightly differently, Allied war aims were expressed in the Settlement that followed, and the *Manual of Alsace-Lorraine* that Collingwood wrote in 1918–19, was intended to reflect and support this.

If Collingwood was later disillusioned by the Peace Settlement then this can only be because he had ideals with which he became disillusioned. But Collingwood says that he knew at the time that the Settlement was a disaster, one that would succeed only in laying up problems for the future. Further, what Collingwood claims he knew at the time was not just that the implementation of the Settlement's principles was incompetent, but that the principles themselves were empty. When we bear in mind that Woodrow Wilson's Fourteen Points, as the rules which in theory at least governed the Settlement's conclusions, were written by someone who was a Christian and a liberal then Collingwood's claim seems extremely curious, since what Collingwood most obviously was at that time was a Christian and a liberal.[15] Now it would be open to us to divide the Settlement into those parts that invited Collingwood's approval and those which did not, but this move simply drives us back to the original difficulty while taking away the interest of the problem. In other words, and this is worth emphasising, we are not concerned with the consistency of Collingwood's thought. The issue that faces us is how, apparently, Collingwood can be both a supporter of the League and an opponent. The solution lies, perhaps, in not trying to dispel the contradiction. It lies in accepting Collingwood's explanation of it, namely, that at that time he lived as though his life and thought were in separate compartments. He lived as though he disbelieved his own philosophy.

One response to this way of thinking is that if we take Collingwood's autobiographical account to be true then what follows is this: it was not that he lived then as though he disbelieved his own philosophy, but rather that he *did* disbelieve it. To live as though you disbelieve your philosophy is to say that something is lacking in your life that we should expect to be present. By contrast, simply to disbelieve your philosophy is to have no such expectation. We should make a little more of this response. Collingwood says that he lived as if "the vulgar division of men into thinkers and men of action" was true.[16] But that claim would be true quite independently of Collingwood's views on the Peace Settlement. All that we are licensed to say on the basis of that claim is that whether he was a supporter of the Settlement or a critic, Collingwood lived as though his thought was irrelevant to his life. His thinking about the Peace Settlement either for it or against it had no bearing on his life. In other words, from Collingwood's recognition that he lived as though his thought had no bearing on his life it could follow either, that his thinking about the Peace Settlement was contradictory, but that this had no practical importance to him, or, that while a supporter of it in theory, in his life he behaved as if he was not, including the possibility that he did not believe a word.

It should be clear that we have to answer this response. One way is to reduce the force of the dilemma that faces us. We could say, for example, that in the public pronouncements he made during the war Collingwood was an internationalist in name only. Now we can be certain that Collingwood was not the kind of internationalist who believed that military conflict could be completely eradicated. Further, we can be sure that Collingwood was not the kind of internationalist who believed in world government.[17] But this merely assumes that the Peace Settlement was, in fact, wholly distant from the ideals that Collingwood did wish to defend and this is far from being the case. The Manuals on Belgium and on Alsace-Lorraine were tailored to meet the requirements of a government that was very well aware that peacemaking would be a complicated, delicate and often imperfect exercise, one that could not be advanced by abstract principles alone and would require hard day-to-day negotiations in which the good intentions of the parties involved could not always be counted on. Equally, the Manuals provided empirical information on, for example, language distribution, that was vitally necessary for a government that had realised the problems it would face in attempting to apply the principle of national self-determination to complex realities. Similarly, the inclusion of statistics regarding racial and linguistic minorities was aimed at satisfying the need for the Settlement to set out principles for the permissible treatment of minorities, rules prohibiting their forced exclusion or assimilation and the degree of toleration that they had a right to expect. Of course, no peace settlement could reach its decisions without leaving some kind of ambiguous legacy for the future. The Peace Settlement of 1919 was no exception. It is true, as Collingwood says himself, that many of its conclusions were based on national self-interest, especially the self-interest of the major powers. And, yet, it is not true that there were no good reasons for this. As the *Manual of Belgium* notes, the security of the Low Countries was a vital British interest.[18] It was not something that could be uncritically set aside to satisfy the aspirations of Belgium nationalism, for example. It is also true, as Margaret Macmillan has demonstrated, that the Peace Settlement left a number of loose ends, both large and small.[19] Not all the states involved in the dispute over the navigation on the Scheldt, to take a relatively small loose end, but one, as we have seen, on which Collingwood worked, were content with the arbitration that was arrived at and, in fact, it took many years for a workable compromise to be reached. Some issues were simply too intractable to permit an immediate solution. Equally, some solutions simply stored up problems for the future. Even so, it is hard to disagree with Macmillan's conclusion that the peacemakers attempted to imbue international relations with a new spirit, but for Collingwood in 1919 it was the future and its relation to present and past that required investigation.[20]

The peacemakers assumed that the future was something they could not control. But, as Collingwood was to realise with increasing clarity throughout 1919 and the early 1920s this view was based on a false philosophy of history. Collingwood knew that history understood as the knowledge of a dead past would achieve little by way of helping human beings to act in the present, but at this time he also came to see that if the past "was incapsulated in the present and constituted a part of it not at once obvious to the untrained eye, then history stood in the closest possible relation to practical life."[21]

Collingwood's progress in understanding the nature of historical thinking was clearly a move towards a rapprochement between theory and practice, but in 1919 a full transition still remained opaque. It did so because, as Collingwood tells us in *An Autobiography*, he still lived "as a professional thinker whose college gate symbolized his aloofness from the affairs of practical life".[22] Actions appropriate in one area of his life were segregated from all others. Thus, Collingwood's service at the Admiralty had no bearing on his philosophy and his philosophy had no bearing on his life. It is not whether Collingwood held contradictory beliefs about the Peace Settlement or the League of Nations that is important, but the terms he used to think about himself. And in *An Autobiography* he tells us exactly that at one time in his life he lived as if his life consisted in a series of unrelated specialised activities. The Official Secrets Act applied to all the publications with which Collingwood was concerned at the Admiralty and, in terms of the track we have been following, it might also have seemed to him to segregate each area of his life. Even though Collingwood was not able to formulate a full philosophical exposition of his belief in the unity of experience until *Speculum Mentis* in 1924, the doctrine was sufficiently embedded in his thought in 1919 for him to know that he was living as if it had no claim on him.

Endnotes

1   R. G. Collingwood, *An Autobiography*, p91. For a modern discussion of the effect of technology on warfare in the First World War see John Terraine, *White Heat, The New Warfare 1914-18*, Guild Publishing, London, 1982. Collingwood's broad-brush account of technology in the First War is not wholly convincing, but it is worth noting that not all attempts to involve science in the application of technology to military operations were successful, see for discussion of one example, the Board of Invention and Research, Jack K. Gusewelle, "Science and the Admiralty during World War 1: The Case of the BIR", in Gerald Gordon (ed.), *Naval Warfare in the Twentieth Century, Essays in Honour of Arthur Marder*, Croom Helm, London, 1977, pp105-17.

2   R. G. Collingwood, "The Function of Metaphysics in Civilization", in R. G. Collingwood, *An Essay on Metaphysics*, revised edition, edited with an

introduction by Rex Martin, Clarendon Press, Oxford, 1998, p382, pp380–83 are also relevant.

3   R. G. Collingwood, *An Autobiography*, p91; see also "The Function of Metaphysics in Civilization", p382–83 where Collingwood writes, "The peace treaty, which ought to have laid down the principles governing the policy of the party that dictated it, and to have worked out their practical consequences, laid down no principles whatever, and is of importance in history only as a declaration of intellectual bankruptcy. That bankruptcy was the direct and inevitable consequence of the intellectual history of the nineteenth century."

4   R. G. Collingwood, *An Autobiography*, p89.

5   R. G. Collingwood, *Speculum Mentis*, p15.

6   R. G. Collingwood, *An Autobiography*, p150.

7   Ibid., p150.

8   See R. G. Collingwood, *The New Leviathan*, 21.47 and 29.69. For an account of the rise and decline of Collingwood's support for the League, see David Boucher, *The Social and Political Thought of R. G. Collingwood*, pp190–93, 284.

9   R. G. Collingwood, *An Autobiography*, p89.

10   Ibid., p89–90.

11   Ibid., p88.

12   See Margaret Macmillan, *Peacemakers*, p499–500. Collingwood's main grounds for his later rejection of the League seem to be, first, its determination to punish the aggressor through the policy of war reparations and punitive sanctions, (see *The New Leviathan*, 29.85) and, second, the belief that economic sanctions could replace war, (see *The New Leviathan*, 29.69). That the 1919 Peace Settlement was a combination of idealism and harshness seems clear (exactly how harsh is a matter of some dispute), but at the time Collingwood was more robust on the first issue than he was later, and the difficulties in the League's sanction policy became apparent only as the 1920s and 1930s took their course.

13   See R. G. Collingwood, "The Function of Metaphysics in Civilisation", p382.

14   See Manual of Alsace-Lorraine, p237–8.

15   R. G. Collingwood, *The New Leviathan*, 21.46. It may be that the turning point in Collingwood's support for the League came in 1936 for in his essay "Man Goes Mad", started August 1936, Collingwood, addressing the problem of how weak states can be protected in a world increasingly dominated by force, argued that, "A League of Nations cannot solve the problem without facing the alternative of either itself becoming a belligerent, using armaments of its own or the forces put at its disposal by its constituent members, or else confining itself to diplomatic weapons and expressions of disapproval against aggressors." See R. G. Collingwood, "Man Goes Mad", in David Boucher, Wendy James and Philip Smallwood (eds), *R. G. Collingwood, The Philosophy of Enchantment*, Clarendon Press, Oxford, 2005, p309.

16 R. G. Collingwood, *An Autobiography*, p150.
17 See David Boucher, *The Social and Political Thought of R. G. Collingwood*, p191. In 1935 Collingwood spoke about the abolition of war as being at least an intellectual possibility, see W. H. Dray and W. J. van der Dussen (eds), R. G. Collingwood, *The Principles of History*, Oxford University Press, Oxford, 1999, p194, later, however, he took a different view, see *The New Leviathan*, 30.8.
18 See Manual of Belgium, p193.
19 Margaret Macmillan, p495.
20 Ibid., p499.
21 See R. G. Collingwood, *An Autobiography*, p106.
22 Ibid., p151.

CHAPTER 10

THE CHRISTIAN PHILOSOPHER

It is hard to ignore the role of Collingwood's intellectual inheritance and upbringing in helping to shape his Christian commitment.[1] Similarly, the move from theory to practice in philosophy had a history in the nineteenth and early twentieth century with which Collingwood was more than familiar.[2] But the problem that faced Collingwood in his formative years was not one that he could solve by retracing his steps. Collingwood was looking for a voice that expressed in his life the meaning that his religious commitment demanded. To live as if his life occupied one compartment and his philosophy another would be in Collingwood's understanding to live a segregated and, hence, a deficient life. But in this early period Collingwood wrote as a Christian philosopher and by a Christian philosopher Collingwood did not mean a philosopher who just happened to be a Christian. Nor did he mean by a Christian someone who just happened to live a Christian way of life. A Christian who just happened to live a Christian way of life might well be considered an odd sort of Christian, but a philosopher who happened to be a Christian some might not consider odd at all. And, yet, Collingwood's commitment to the unity of the life of the mind asked him to think precisely that. So, in Collingwood's picture a Christian philosopher is not just someone for whom a compelling philosophical account of their Christianity is an advantage. It is mandatory. But Collingwood, in the period prior to the publication of *Speculum Mentis*, had not yet developed a systematic account of the relations between philosophy and religion which means that the nature of religious belief and its relation to other kinds of belief were issues that Collingwood had not fully addressed. Thus, for Collingwood, identifying a philosophical voice meant in large part discovering how philosophy can play a role in vindicating religion.

Collingwood understood the war as a spiritual disease. From this it should follow that there is a spiritual cure or, at least, that whatever alleviates the condition represents a transformation of ideas. For some this serves only to reveal Collingwood's tendency to treat "bombers and Panzer divisions" (we might equally say barbed wire and machine guns), as epiphenomena, significant only as ideas.[3] However, this is an error Collingwood did not make and it is a relatively easy matter to defend him from resources within his own philosophy. So, when Collingwood, in *Religion and Philosophy*, remarks that "A boot is more adequately understood in terms of mind — by saying who made it and what he made it for — than in terms of matter", he is, in fact, pointing out what is true in materialism, not simply what is false in it.[4]

The idea that as an intellectual Collingwood had in some sense automatically debarred himself from practical matters should also be resisted. For Collingwood was a member of a group formed to reassert precisely the unity of though and life that was important to him in these early years. The Cumnor Circle was formed in 1911 and its meetings continued until 1923. The dominant influence was the theologian and writer, Lily Dougall, and it was at her house, Cutt's End, in Cumnor, near Oxford, that the group met. The meetings were informal and the membership at any given time fluctuating.[5] Even before the war started the members of the Cumnor Circle were aware of the dilemma that faced them,

> Victorian optimism had been sapped by a 'cosmic' uneasiness, by a philosophy of moral relativity, by a realisation of the indifference of nature to the individual, by the sickness of an industrial order built on a false political economy, by an increased sensitiveness to the evil and cruelty in the world.[6]

In other words, the threat posed by the war came not from the force of arms alone, but from the mentality that produced it. The aim of the Circle was to bring about a change in attitude. One of their guiding members writes, "The assumption with which we all set out in these group-books was that there can be no real opposition between true religion and true science and true art. All truth, all beauty, all goodness, must ultimately be of God. If there appears to be opposition between science or art and religion, it is because the human beings who are interested in these things partially misconceive or misunderstand their real nature."[7] By the same token, members of the Circle were well aware of the difficulties that faced the implementation of their programme of national reconstruction. They write,

> The conclusion of Peace will leave Europe for many years face to face with economic, political and social problems of unexampled difficulty; and a solution of these will have to be attempted by nations financially

THE CHRISTIAN PHILOSOPHER

exhausted, vitally weakened and depressed by the acute moral and psychological reaction which, humanly speaking, must follow an epoch of intense strain. Nothing but the sober determination, the quickened insight and the disinterested devotion, due to the permeation of society by some great and creative spiritual force, can avail to meet the situation.[8]

At this point, perhaps, we should re-trace our steps a little to note what Collingwood is not saying in his remark that he lived as if he disbelieved his own philosophy. He is not saying that at one time he defended the view that philosophy is one thing, life something totally different. Everything we know about Collingwood's writing during the war years points to his asserting exactly the opposite. So, in *Religion and Philosophy*, for example, we find him commenting,

> While fully agreeing that there is a difference between the work of a statesman and that of a philosopher, for instance, we should not admit that this difference is of such a kind that the former can be correctly described as a man of action and the latter as a man of thought.[9]

What Collingwood is actually saying in his *Autobiography* is that although this is the position he had reached in his philosophy he lived as though it was false. What was true in his philosophy was false in Collingwood's life.

But Collingwood also claims that he "philosophized as if I had not been the professional thinker that in fact I was".[10] Here Collingwood's meaning is a little less clear. What he certainly is not saying is that his engagement with philosophy was slipshod or amateur. It is true that when Collingwood looked back on the philosophical work of the early period he criticised some of it for being juvenile and confused, but this is precisely what we should expect a "professional thinker" to be doing. A more compelling interpretation is that Collingwood is referring to a tendency to present his personal beliefs as if they were philosophy. So what is true of Collingwood's beliefs in his early life, say, his Christianity or his patriotism, he also assumed to be true in philosophy. This is what he thought unprofessional about it.

With these considerations in mind we can obtain a tighter grip on the kind of life that Collingwood aspired to live. It is also by his own account a life that eluded him. It should be a life that is informed by his philosophy, but not one in which his philosophy is directed by his life. Collingwood, in other words, needed to believe in his own philosophy in order to live, so what, then, kept such a life closed to him? A comment that Ray Monk makes on the differences between Wittgenstein's values and those of Russell allows us to explore the question further. Monk writes,

> If I were asked to summarize in a sentence the difference between their respective values, I would say that Wittgenstein sought to improve himself, while Russell sought to improve the world, and that therefore Wittgenstein's values were essentially religious and Russell's essentially political.[11]

As Monk is right to imply, there is something slightly forced about this contrast, but it provides, nevertheless, a useful tool for teasing out what makes Collingwood's position different.

We should notice from the start how little space Collingwood makes in his writings for discussion of his inner life. He begins the Preface to *An Autobiography* with the famous sentence, "The autobiography of a man whose business is thinking should be the story of his thought."[12] Quite obviously, it is not that Collingwood had no personal life. It is rather that he did not judge it relevant to telling the story of his thinking. But making a judgement about what is relevant to the story of your life is one thing. Collingwood's claim that there was a time when he lived his life as if he disbelieved his philosophy is different again. We can bring this difference out in the following way. Someone who analyses moral statements as akin to expressions of taste and yet lives a life of great earnestness might be described as disbelieving their own philosophy. But we should describe this as a judgement of relevance only if there were already compelling grounds for separating philosophy from life. And it is, of course, the absence of such compelling grounds that Collingwood doubts. It would be an odd conclusion indeed, if we were to think that living your life as if you disbelieved your philosophy meant exactly the same as living it in the belief that your philosophy was irrelevant. The result of this would be that we would have to think of Collingwood as a member of Russell's camp, a state of affairs that is some distance from being the case.

Even so, it has to be said that Collingwood's focus on the world as opposed to (although not necessarily at the expense of) the inner life is characteristic of his thought. In an essay that Collingwood wrote in 1936 we can see just how far Collingwood was prepared to separate the personal and the public realms. He writes,

> A man who asks himself whether he ought to take voluntary part in his country's war is not struggling with personal fear; he is involved in a conflict between the moral forces embodied in the institution of the State, and those embodied not merely in the ideal, but in the equally actual reality of international peace and intercourse.[13]

Whereas Wittgenstein thinks of the struggle with personal fear as taking priority for him, for Collingwood it is less an individual than an historical issue that needs to be faced. In other words, for Collingwood, war comes about through the imperfections of social and political institutions. Military service undertaken for reasons to do with integrity might elevate the state of one's soul, but the result is confusion between the personal and the public which could well lead to a misunderstanding of what is at stake.

Collingwood's remark that were times when he lived as if he disbelieved his philosophy should not be taken to mean that he thought his philosophy must always be reflected in life. Indeed, it can be argued that there were occasions in Collingwood's life when his philosophical views either foreclosed on life or were difficult, and sometimes impossible, to live up to. To put this point another way. We have noticed already that bridging the gap between philosophy and life is as much a matter of getting the philosophy right as it is of finding a meaning in one's life. This is the reason why Wittgenstein was so demanding of himself both in his philosophy and his life. But more important than avoiding the separation of philosophy from life is discovering a philosophy in which it is possible to believe. So when Collingwood says that there were times when he lived as if he disbelieved his philosophy he must mean a philosophy that he thought worthy of belief. There is a distinction, in other words, between disbelieving a philosophy because it is simply unliveable — to put this in Wittgenstein's terms, a philosophy that consisted in continually asking for the wrong thing or for a kind of justification which it is not possible to give — and disbelieving it because in life either through evasion or distraction the philosopher fails to accommodate the meaning that his philosophy has found. Living as if you disbelieve your philosophy is different from a life in which there is no philosophy to believe.

During his service at the Admiralty Collingwood was not only working alongside geographers, he was to a considerable extent doing the work of a geographer. Now we might think of compiling statistics, amassing historical facts and representing these by means of maps as activities that embody the realist theory of knowledge. The acquisition of facts regarding, say, language use within a given territory is, therefore, quite independent of its effect both on the knower and the known. While Collingwood's work in intelligence occupied one compartment of his life, the use that was made of the results took place in another. Similarly, his activities as a geographer are remote from his thought as a philosopher, almost, but not quite as his work in I. D. 32 was utilised in ways over which he had little control. Now if we were to think of Collingwood as like Russell nothing in this state of affairs would matter too much. Collingwood would simply set his philosophy aside on entering the Admiralty buildings where he worked. But it is clear that Collingwood did not believe that philosophy could be set aside. Later Collingwood came to think of geography as one of the natural sciences.[14] Geography, as a natural science, lacked the self-critical character of history, but this manoeuvre was not available to him at the time he was at the Admiralty. At that time, too, his philosophy of history was in the early stages of its development and, even if his criticism of positivism was secure, the implications of this for his life were far from incomplete. The gap between life and philosophy still had to be bridged.

With this context in mind we can look again at the distinction between improving oneself and improving the world. For in the light of Collingwood's pursuit of the unity of experience what seemed a sound way of separating Wittgenstein and Russell now looks to have less relevance. Collingwood aimed for a perspective that would not leave the religious and the political segregated from each other. Indeed, the whole tone of Collingwood's contribution to the spiritual reconstruction of life during and in the immediate aftermath of the war emphasises harmony and the need to reconcile apparently conflicting activities and modes of thought. Indeed, what is distinctive about Collingwood's Christian apologetics in this period is just how closely he identifies philosophy and religion and just how all-inclusive is his account of religious belief.[15] If the Christian religion is to be vindicated at all then in the first instance this must be by its appeal to the intellect rather than the character of its rituals. There is no doubting the capacity of religion to draw on our emotions or even to inspire our conduct, but these would remain unfocused if religion went uninformed by thought.

While there is certainly a sense in which *Religion and Philosophy* is a pre-war book (Collingwood had started it in 1912, and completed it in draft by 1914, adding the chapter on Evil in 1915), it is also a work of anticipation.[16] Its keynote is interdependence, of philosophy with religion, and of history with philosophy. As a work of anticipation, however, it is also incomplete for in it the dialectic that Collingwood developed in *Speculum Mentis* to account for the relations between different modes of understanding is largely absent. In *Religion and Philosophy* and in other writings and addresses in this period Collingwood saw Christianity as a solution to a philosophical problem.[17] Reflection and faith are not opposites, but mutual requirements. Thus, Collingwood can speak of the importance of argument in religious justification and of trust in the world. Christian values, in other words, are not closed to critical attention. In this respect, Collingwood philosophised in order to live because the ideals that he wished to articulate and defend were precisely those that the war seemed to him to overturn. Christianity was not remote from life, but at the heart of thought and civilisation. As against divisive explanations of religion derived from psychology, Collingwood argued that, as W. M. Johnston writes, "Philosophy can help religion to restate its basic doctrines by making it aware of the nature of language as symbol."[18] A Christian doctrine such as that of the Trinity, for example, can be restated in philosophical terms so as to avoid literalness and, hence, misunderstanding.

Collingwood's Christianity is at the heart of his response to the war, but it is a Christianity shaped by his philosophy. The ideals he defended were Christian ideals, but they were grounded in argument and tested by rational enquiry. Thus, Collingwood's re-affirmation of the human capacity to challenge evil rests on the arguments he gives to support the notion of a transcendent God. On this view, the devil is not God's converse, but a false idol whose power over human beings comes not from irreversible forces, but choice. Collingwood's assertion of the freedom of the will is radical, but it needs to be understood alongside his belief that "truth, reality, God are real things existing quite independently of our individual life and private opinions".[19] Thus, Collingwood rejects the possibility of someone knowing the good, but acting badly;[20] certainly, a substantial reading of Hegel is reflected in this conclusion, one he arrived at in 1916, but also Plato and T. H. Green,

> Man's life is a becoming; and not only becoming, but self-creation. He does not grow under the direction of irresistible forces. The force that shapes him is his own will. All his life is an effort to attain to real human nature. But human nature, since man is at bottom spirit, is only exemplified in the absolute spirit of God. Hence, man must shape himself in God's image, or he ceases to be even human and becomes diabolical.[21]

Collingwood wished a philosophy that was also a philosophy of life. To live the life of a Christian philosopher it is not sufficient to live as a Christian. The Christian beliefs that inform life must also be sanctioned by philosophy. In *Religion and Philosophy* Collingwood thought that he had said enough to show why a Christian life could be made philosophically compelling, but by the time he wrote *Speculum Mentis* he could see faults in his argument.[22] In *Religion and Philosophy* Collingwood had argued for the identity of theology, religion and philosophy, but in doing so he had overlooked the distinction between the implicit and explicit, so he modified his original argument by saying that "theology makes explicit what in religion as such is always implicit, and so with philosophy and theology".[23] Collingwood acknowledged that he had earlier given too intellectual an account of religious belief and that this had led him to understate the significance of symbolism in religion and the importance of "the uniqueness of Christ, of miracle, and of worship".[24] *Speculum Mentis* superseded *Religion and Philosophy* in many important ways. It took up challenges regarding the nature of experience with which Collingwood in 1916 was not equipped to deal.[25] But what is often not noticed is that in both works it is philosophy that calls the tune. If in 1924 Collingwood gave religion a greater degree of autonomy it still remained the case that it was through philosophy that its boundaries were established.

While Collingwood in 1916 was capable of speaking admiringly of unreflective religious faith he was also conscious of its uncertainties, and so was equally sure that religion had to be construed as a matter of doctrine as opposed to myth, of creed as opposed to symbol. Since doctrinal truth must be a public matter it is tempting to say that Collingwood's emphasis on it leaves little room in religion for the inner life. Thus, Collingwood's picture of Christianity as the solution to a philosophical problem is at one with his view of its role in national reconstruction. Here contrasts between Collingwood and Wittgenstein are readily apparent. To be sure, neither Collingwood nor Wittgenstein saw religious beliefs as amenable to scientific proof, but one important difference between them is that Wittgenstein did not understand religion to be a matter of doctrine at all. Indeed, we might say that a simple religious faith is exactly what Wittgenstein aspired to. So, we find Wittgenstein writing,

> Christianity is not a doctrine, not, I mean, a theory about what has happened and will happen to the human soul, but a description of something that actually takes place in human life. For 'recognition of sin' is an actual occurrence & so is despair & so is redemption through faith. Those who speak of it (like Bunyan), are simply describing what has happened to them; whatever gloss someone may want to put on it![26]

In this way Wittgenstein's realisation during the war that his life, as Brian McGuinness comments, "was in God's hands" was not the result of any kind of theoretical reflection on the nature of fate, but the way he expressed the meaning he saw in his life at that time.[27] And, so, for Wittgenstein, the only way the philosopher can get to grips with religious concepts is by seeing them in the context of the religious life. Further, this is not something that can be arrived at through reasoning either independently of the beliefs involved or by viewing them as a solution to a philosophical problem.

Collingwood certainly did not think that it is possible to understand religious beliefs independently of religious experience but, equally, experience is not by itself sufficient to establish a belief as true. Thus, empirical reports of miracles, say, or visions, would not by themselves confirm their claim to truth. In this Collingwood does have something in common with Wittgenstein who also resisted the idea that visions can give us a picture of God, "as a sense experience does an object" but, Wittgenstein continues, neither can such experiences be thought of as conjectures.[28] Rather, they derive their sense from the context of human life in which they arise.

For Wittgenstein the truth or falsity of religious beliefs shows itself in the manner of the religious person's life. What mattered was not whether Christianity was true in any abstract sense, but living in a way that was true to its ideals. Thus, the philosopher whose Christianity belonged wholly to the intellect would miss the struggle against falseness that is essential to the Christian life. To see Christian doctrine as prior to Christian practice is to play down the importance of the inner life and, hence, to weaken what is for the Christian a necessary source of scrutiny and self-criticism. It was a feature of Wittgenstein's life that he took these precepts extremely seriously. They gave him the basis for his own life. They explain his earnestness in the judgements he makes of himself and, incidentally, they account for his otherwise surprising support for Nietzsche's view that if Christianity is to have a value then this will come not from the reasons for believing it to be true, but the example it sets to life.[29] Collingwood, too, read Nietzsche for the first time during the war, but in doing so he expresses a view that is, in important respects, notably different from that of Wittgenstein.[30] Collingwood distinguishes the Nietzsche that was held responsible for the war—"the Euro-Nietzschean War", as Collingwood says one Piccadilly bookseller described it—from the Nietzsche of his own writings. When we actually read his work what we discover is not a denial of Christianity, except for its altruism. Nietzsche when we read his words is not the savage critic of Christianity that he is commonly thought to be. For Collingwood, Nietzsche actually re-affirms Christian values in its conception of the tragic nature of human life, and in its opposition to utilitarianism and "code-morality", so concluding that "much of his polemic against Christianity is a championing of real Christianity against the false Christianity of his 'respectable relatives at Naumberg'".[31] All this we might imagine Wittgenstein agreeing with, but where he would surely part company with Collingwood is over his asking that Nietzsche's re-affirmed Christianity be made to exhibit a unity well beyond that which Wittgenstein thinks it needs. Christianity, for Wittgenstein and Nietzsche, is not a set of beliefs, but a way of life, one that in being lived shows how suffering might be borne. Further, to think about Christianity as a set of beliefs is to damage the insight that it offers about life. Thus, when Collingwood attempts to link the Christian life with the answer to a philosophical problem he is led to miss the very feature of religion that Wittgenstein illuminates.

We can bring this point out in a slightly different way. *Speculum Mentis* went a great deal further than *Religion and Philosophy* in distinguishing religion from both theology and philosophy. Even so, Collingwood remained committed to a distinction between the expression of religious belief and its meaning. The business of philosophy was the eliciting of meaning (in *Speculum Mentis* not simply with the identity of religion as a form of experience, but also with how it relates to the other forms, and with philosophy itself). However, this move leaves the meaning that religion has for the believer somewhat undervalued since, as Maurice Cowling perceptively indicates,

> Collingwood was distinguishing worship from the eliciting of meaning. Religion certainly had a meaning that had to be elicited. But eliciting was not the centre of religion, which always supposed that it had expressed its meaning before the eliciting had begun.[32]

Collingwood, in other words, was unable to allow religious beliefs to speak for themselves. This is because the programme of reconstructing the unity of experience that Collingwood set himself to complete during the years of the war had its own rationale, and although it took note of what others say about themselves and their activities it was with its own special vocabulary that it was primarily concerned.

It is worth emphasising that Collingwood's concern with spiritual unity in his early work serves to separate his thought from both Wittgenstein's and Russell's. It is different from Wittgenstein because for him neither religion nor philosophy can be understood as bodies of doctrine. If, as Wittgenstein thought, philosophy is not a theory, but an activity then living as though you disbelieve your own philosophy is not like disbelieving a theory. After the war Collingwood, like Russell, tended to support organisations that wished to make the world a safer place but, unlike Russell, who thought Christianity an insuperable obstacle to the achievement of this, for Collingwood, Christianity was at the heart of civilisation. Collingwood, as much as Wittgenstein, was distant from Russell's unbelief but, unlike Wittgenstein, he wished a religion whose boundaries were the result of intellectual conviction rather than from the utterances of an inner voice.

According to F. R. Leavis, Wittgenstein retreated into the inner life after the war.[33] Russell, by contrast, became preoccupied with the improvement of the world. Collingwood reveals little about his inner life—how he thought of himself and how he gave his life meaning—save ruling it out as a source of moral philosophy, but, as much as Russell, although with a very different focus, he urgently sought a rapprochement between theory and practice. Such a rapprochement is important because it concerns the nature of philosophy and the role it might play in telling us how to live. But could we imagine anyone living like *Religion and Philosophy*, or, to stretch the imagination to its limits, like *Speculum Mentis*? If we could, then living like *Speculum Mentis* would require not simply that we believe its philosophy, but that we live a life in which specialisation was wholly absent. Or, to put the same point another way, to live as though you disbelieved the philosophy of *Speculum Mentis* would mean a life which concentrated exclusively on one activity, say, science, when you believed that all activities made up a unified whole.

Endnotes

1   Collingwood was baptised a Christian late and by his own choice at Rugby where he took George as his middle name. For Collingwood's family background, see Teresa Smith, " R. G. Collingwood: 'This Ring of Thought': Notes on Early Influences", *Collingwood Studies*, vol. 1, 1994, pp27-43; Fred Inglis, *History Man*, Chapter 1; Peter Johnson, *R. G. Collingwood: An Introduction*, Thoemmes Press, Bristol, 1998, Chapter 1; James Patrick, *The Magdalen Metaphysicals*, especially Chapter 4; see also James Patrick, "Eliot and the New Idealism: Poetry and History at Oxford 1914-1915", *Collingwood Studies*, vol. 7, 2000, pp1-31; and James Connelly, "Collingwood and his Contemporaries: responses to critics 1918-1928", *Collingwood Studies*, vol. 7, 2000, pp72-93.

2   For the historical background to Collingwood's treatment of the theory/practice problem in the period as well as its immediate context, see James Patrick, *The Magdalen Metaphysicals*, pp77-92. Rightly, Patrick picks out T. H. Green and, of Collingwood's contemporaries, J. A. Smith, as important influences. For broader contextual matters regarding the philosophy of religion and philosophical idealism in this period, see Alan P. F. Sell, *The Philosophy of Religion 1875-1980*, Thoemmes Press, Bristol, 1988, and also his *Philosophical Idealism and Christian Belief*, University of Wales Press, Cardiff, 1995. Also relevant and useful are D. M. Mackinnon, "Some Aspects of the Treatment of Christianity by the British Idealists", *Religious Studies*, 20, 1984, pp133-44, and Rev. J. S. Boys Smith, "The Interpretation of Christianity in Idealistic Philosophy in Great Britain in the Nineteenth Century", *The Modern Churchman*, vol. 21, 1941, pp251-73.

3   See, for example, Stefan Collini, *Absent Minds, Intellectuals in Britain*, Oxford University Press, Oxford, 2006, p346.

4   R. G. Collingwood, *Religion and Philosophy*, p93.

5   Information on the Cumnor Circle is scanty (see Johnston, p52, for this view). However, for Lily Dougall, (1858–1923), see the Obituaries in *The Christian World*, 18 October 1923, and *The Times*, 13 October 1923, and B. H. Streeter's biographical note in Lily Dougall, *God's Way With Man*, SCM Press, London, 1924. The members of the Circle were Lilly Dougall, B. H. Streeter, C. W. Emmet, A. Clutton-Brock, C. H. Dodd, J. A. Hadfield, Edwyn Bevan, R. G. Collingwood, A. S. Pringle-Pattison and J. L. Hodgson. The main publications resulting from the Circle's method of group discussion were *Foundations*, Macmillan, London, 1913, *Concerning Prayer*, Macmillan, London, 1916, *Immortality*, Macmillan, London, 1917, *The Spirit*, Macmillan, London, 1919, and the following published after the Circle was wound up, *Reality*, Macmillan, London, 1926, and *Adventure*, Macmillan, London, 1927, all edited by B. H. Streeter; see also James Connelly, "Natural Science, History and Christianity", *Collingwood Studies*, vol. 4, 1997, especially pp102–03. In a private letter to the author (dated 30 January 1973) C. H. Dodd, a member of the group, testified to Collingwood's regular attendance at meetings. The Cumnor Circle is to be distinguished from The Group, another religious discussion group that Collingwood belonged to in Oxford, see James Patrick, *The Magdalen Metaphysicals*, ppxxvii and 87. For an interesting discussion of the importance of spiritual and theological matters in Collingwood's philosophy overall, see David Bates, "Rediscovering Collingwood's Spiritual History (In and Out of Context)", *History and Theory*, vol. 35, February 1996, pp29–55, especially pp44–7, where the context of Collingwood's early examinations of the philosophical and historical aspects of religion is discussed, including his membership of the Streeter group. As Bates points out, (p46, n. 85,) Streeter was a consultant to Macmillan when they published Collingwood's early work.

6   B. H. Streeter (ed.), *Foundations*, Macmillan, London, 1913, pp6–7; for discussion of Streeter see Peter Hinchcliff, *God and History, Aspects of British Theology 1875–1914*, Clarendon Press, Oxford, Chapter 10.

7   B. H. Streeter, Biographical Note, in Dougall, p17; the need for a spiritual basis in any reunified national life was also a theme in the work of the Woodbrooke Settlement, a Quaker organisation founded in 1903 whose publications J. A. Smith was a contributor to, see James Patrick, *The Magdalen Metaphysicals*, p178 Bibliography, items 4 and 6, and whose guiding ideal was "that the common features in civilised life outweigh the differences, that mankind tends more and more towards the unity of life and thought, and that there is a common fabric of civilisation which will survive even the most injurious assaults", (in *The Woodbrooke Council, Eighth Annual Report*, Birmingham, October 1915, p15).

8 B. H. Streeter, Introduction, *Concerning Prayer*, pix; for discussion of Christian views of the Peace Settlement, see Alan Wilkinson, *The Church of England and the First World War*, SPCK, London, 1978, Chapter 11.

9 R. G. Collingwood, *Religion and Philosophy*, p35.

10 R. G. Collingwood, *An Autobiography*, p106.

11 Ray Monk, Philosophical Biography, p13.

12 R. G. Collingwood, *An Autobiography*, Preface.

13 R. G. Collingwood, *The Idea of History*, Clarendon Press, Oxford, 1946, p331.

14 Ibid., p79.

15 See *Religion and Philosophy*, pxv, where Collingwood writes that "religion is undoubtedly an affair of the intellect, a philosophical activity. Its very centre and foundation is creed, and every creed is a view of the universe, a theory of man and the world, a theory of God". On the inclusiveness of religion, see *Religion and Philosophy*, p35, where we find, " As every life includes, and indeed is, both thought and action, so every life is essentially religious; and the secular life, if that means a life negatively defined by the mere absence of religion, does not exist at all." See also R. G. Collingwood, "Christianity in Partibus", *The Challenge*, vol. 9, no. 232, 4 October 1918, p323, where Collingwood writes, "The spirit of prophetic Judaism was more faithfully served by the Jesus who was indicted for irreligion than by the priests who condemned Him; and there is a very real danger that the 'non-religious man' may prove a more faithful trustee of the spirit of Christianity than many of those who call Jesus Lord." (See the introduction to the reprint of Collingwood's essay by James Connelly and Peter Johnson, "R. G. Collingwood's 'Christianity in Partibus'", *Collingwood Studies*, vol. 6, 1999, pp166-71.

16 See R. G. Collingwood, "List of Work Done", Collingwood MS, DEP 22, p15

17 See the great deal of material by Collingwood on the philosophy of religion in the early period, much of it unpublished. It is listed in Van Der Dussen, *History as a Science*, Bibliography 1, pp445-6; see also Burchnall, p1.

18 W. M. Johnston, *Formative Years*, p47 and also Part 2, Chapters 5 and 6 where Johnston's discussion is highly relevant to this point.

19 R. G. Collingwood, "The Devil", p474.

20 Ibid., p 474, see also R. G. Collingwood, "Lectures on the Philosophy of St. Paul", Somerville College, Oxford, 1918, Collingwood MS, DEP 1/3.

21 R. G. Collingwood, "The Devil", p474.

22 R. G. Collingwood, *Speculum Mentis*, p108 n. 1.

23 Ibid., p108 n. 1.

24 Ibid., p108 n. 1.

25   See the valuable discussion in Lionel Rubinoff, *Collingwood and the Reform of Metaphysics, A Study in the Philosophy of Mind*, University of Toronto Press, Toronto, 1970, pp50–55.

26   Ludwig Wittgenstein, *Culture and Value*, 32e.

27   See Brian McGuinness, *Young Ludwig*, p256.

28   Ludwig Wittgenstein, *Culture and Value*, 97e.

29   See Ray Monk, Ludwig Wittgenstein, The Duty of Genius, pp121–3.

30   See R. G. Collingwood, "Review of J. N. Figgis, The Will to Freedom: or the Gospel of Nietzsche and the Gospel of Christ", in *The Oxford Magazine*, 31 May 1918, p299.

31   Ibid., p299.

32   See Maurice Cowling, *Religion and Public Doctrine in Modern England*, Cambridge University Press, Cambridge, 1980, p171.

33   See Brian McGuinness, *Young Ludwig*, pp273–4.

CHAPTER 11

A VISION OF LIFE

Collingwood is not long into his address on *Ruskin's Philosophy* before he embarks on a discussion intriguingly entitled, "On the Philosophy of Non-Philosophers".[1] Here Collingwood argues that there is in the life of every individual what he calls "a ring of solid thought"[2] consisting of ideas, convictions and principles which that individual holds on to unquestioningly. This moral nucleus makes up the individual's character. It is rarely called upon to be put into words, and when it is the reaction is usually silent astonishment. So Collingwood states, "It may seem strange that our deepest and most important convictions should habitually go unexpressed."[3] And, yet, it is not uncommon for human beings to behave in ways that run contrary to the basic beliefs that make up their inner lives. It is the philosopher's job, Collingwood continues, to uncover the nature of such basic beliefs, even, or especially, where "the attempt to discover a man's philosophy often reveals facts very startling to the man himself—facts which he will regard less as truisms than as paradoxes".[4] Now what should we make of this? Unlike Ruskin, who in Collingwood's view was not a philosopher and was, therefore, unable to "dissect his own mind to find out what his philosophy was", Collingwood felt himself required to do precisely that.[5] What should be immediately apparent is just how distinctive Collingwood judges the philosopher's self-understanding to be by comparison with that of the non-philosopher. Self-examination, in other words, is an essential part of the philosopher's job. So whereas non-philosophers need not put their fundamental beliefs into words, but can still remain true to them, this is what, on Collingwood's account, the philosopher cannot do. The philosopher makes explicit in his own life what in the lives of others is often left unsaid.

Throughout his life Collingwood saw philosophy as a moral task as much as an intellectual one. He pursued interconnections between different ways of thinking where others may well have held back. Philosophy in this account is treated as an historical discipline in such a way as to produce genuine philosophical enlightenment. The distinction between thought and action is rejected, so encouraging exploration of how the intellect informs the active life. There are occasions nevertheless where it is the disjunction that is illuminating. Collingwood's philosophy told him that thought and actions are linked, but he behaved as if he disbelieved it. This is not to say that what Collingwood did in his life can be understood independently of his intentions, motives or purposes, but it is to say that there was a time when a part of his life was closed to philosophy. We should remember, perhaps, that it was as a "professorial goose" that Collingwood wished to cackle.[6] We are surely being led to understand that not any kind of goose will do and that in the past the goose had not always cackled to order.

So we can say that for Collingwood, as for Socrates, the unexamined life is not worth living, but does this corroborate the role in life that Collingwood saw for philosophy? For if it does then on Collingwood's own account at one time his life was not worth living. Well, not quite, because Collingwood was not short of belief. He lived only as if he disbelieved his own philosophy. What he knew in philosophy to be true was false in his life. Even so, what remains still gives philosophy a large claim on life. Moreover, this surely rests on the assumption that philosophy is able to deliver a life that is actually liveable. Surely, this must be what being a "professorial goose" means. But what is it to live a philosophically embodied life? In Collingwood's case what it most obviously means is the attempt to live a Christian life, but Collingwood was not just a Christian who happened to be a philosopher. He was a Christian who believed that Christianity needed to be philosophically informed. Did this belief give him a life that he could live?

Ruskin's Philosophy comes at an intermediate stage between Collingwood's *Religion and Philosophy* and his *Speculum Mentis* in 1924. It looks forward to the dialectical enfranchisement of religion that Collingwood aimed to provide in the latter work and back to his attempt to reveal the inherent rationality of Christianity in 1916; both texts indicate Collingwood's distinctive brand of Christian apologetics hard at work.[7] In both texts, too, we encounter Collingwood's belief that Christianity needs to be philosophically informed. What does this belief amount to? And, further, what are the consequences for Collingwood's Christianity if it fails?

One commentator on Collingwood's work who sheds light on these questions is Alan Donagan, and I would like to spend some time considering the implications of what he says.[8] For Donagan one argument stands out in Collingwood's philosophically informed Christianity. It is a position he first formulated in 1916, and never gave up. In his essay "The Devil" Collingwood writes, "The type of all false religion is to believe what we will to believe, instead of what we have ascertained to be true; supposing that reality must be such as to satisfy our desires, and, if not, go to, let us alter it."[9] Collingwood's philosophy of religion, then, is characterised by a single, persistent theme. Christianity is to be seen as "a critical solution to a philosophical problem", but, as Donagan points out, if this is true then it can never be accepted on its own terms.[10] The conclusions of Christianity have to coincide with the conclusions of philosophy because it is not as symbols that Christians take their beliefs to be true. The rituals and practices of the Christian religion are inspirational not because of the emotional effects they produce in the private inner states of religious believers, but because they convince. Collingwood could have chosen to renounce his Christianity or to disconnect it from the intellect, but he chose neither, preferring instead to ground Christianity in a system of rational belief. It is at this point that Collingwood's strategy encounters a fatal flaw. For as soon as religious believers become intellectuals they cease to be believers. What the rationalist thinks of as superstitions the simple believer regards as essential to the faith. Adapting F. H. Bradley's criticism of Matthew Arnold, Donagan applies it to Collingwood with great effect. He writes,

> 'Is there a God?' asks the reader. 'Oh, yes', replies Collingwood, 'and his existence is a presupposition of natural science and practical living.' 'And what is he then?' cries the reader. 'The fact that the universe as a whole is rational; that the world into which we have unwillingly been thrust is a world that contains scope for action and will give us a fair chance of showing what we are made of', is the answer. 'Well, and God?' 'That is God', says Collingwood, 'there is no deception, and what more do you want?'[11]

In *Speculum Mentis* Collingwood makes his commitment to Christianity perfectly plain. It is, he says, "the only religion which gives the soul peace", but the meaning of this statement is anything but plain since, as we have seen, Collingwood is also committed to the idea that the soul cannot obtain peace unless the Christianity in which it believes is true.[12] Donagan's criticism now appears to be directed less at Collingwood's arguments and more at the basis they provide for a Christian life. We are not surprised, therefore, when Donagan argues as follows,

> Confronted with the claims of a religion, a philosopher can do no other than stand with the sceptical disciple, and demand evidence. A Christian must retort that although to believe having seen is well, blessed are they who have not seen, and yet have believed. Collingwood

was at least inclined to accept this reproof. Like the penitents in Ash Wednesday, he was of those 'who will not go away and cannot pray'. It is as though he divined in Christianity something which compelled his veneration, while eluding his ardent attempts to define it.[13]

Seen in this perspective Collingwood's statement that there was a time in his life when he lived as if he disbelieved his own philosophy appears in a new light. As a Christian Collingwood was committed to live a Christian life, but as a philosopher he was equally committed to the apprehension of his life in thought. So, for Collingwood living as if he disbelieved his own philosophy means living the life of a plain Christian, but it was not plain Christianity that gave Collingwood grounds for belief.

It is a feature of Donagan's commentary that it pays close attention to Collingwood's awareness of the difficulties that his own vision of life contained. But, in 1916, Collingwood's understanding of religion was so thoroughly imbued with his own philosophy that it is hard to separate them. In *Religion and Philosophy* Collingwood writes that,

> if there is such a thing as the religious life, it must be one which, like any other, involves both thinking and acting; and the religious life, so conceived, is not any more than a philosopher's life or a statesman's the mere sum of two different lives. For of the two ingredients neither can exist by itself. It must exist in union with the other or not at all. Any real life must contain both elements, each playing as important a part as the other.[14]

We must surely see this picture of the unity of experience as marking one very early point in Collingwood's search for a rapprochement between theory and practice. If this is true then the philosophy he disbelieved in his life must have been as much a philosophy of religion as of epistemology or politics. Moreover, a life that is false to philosophy is one in which the philosophical, the religious and the political are disunited, and a disunited life in Collingwood's terminology is one that has no existence at all.

Collingwood gave his address on Ruskin some ten months after the war ended. In it he does not refer to the conflict directly, but his way of speaking about Ruskin's thought—"its resolute envisagement of the spirit as a single and indivisible whole"—brings Collingwood's view of modern war close to Ruskin's.[15] Both saw war as a symptom of an underlying disease and both were unafraid to associate this with materialism and the uncritical advance of science. So when Ruskin writes that

> Nowadays, persons who quarrel fight at a distance, with mechanical apparatus, for the manufacture of which they have taxed the public, and which will kill anybody who happens to be in the way; gathering at the same time, to put into the way of them, as large a quantity of senseless and innocent mob as can be beguiled, or compelled, to the slaughter, [16]

it is not hard, even with important qualifications, to see Collingwood agreeing, for in his lecture to the Belgian students given just a few months before his Ruskin address Collingwood expresses his complete unwillingness to speak of the war in anything other than spiritual terms.

Indeed, the talk to the Conference of Belgian Students, entitled "The Spiritual Basis of Reconstruction", was one of a number of pronouncements on matters of public policy that Collingwood made in 1919.[17] In this Collingwood diagnoses the immediate cause of the war as being a "false and evil imperialism", in which Germany attempted to impose her own way of life on that of her neighbours.[18] Interestingly, in light of the fact that work on the *Manual of Alsace-Lorraine* was taking up much of his time at the Admiralty during 1918 and 1919, Collingwood in his talk gives German repression of French speech and habits in Alsace-Lorraine as an example of the kind of "false imperialism" he has in mind. German state worship may well be the expression of deeper philosophical failings. It may lead to a philosophy of pessimism that paralyses the spirit and undermines freedom of action. But its first effect was on the lives of those who were forcibly made subjects of it, and, as we have seen, the Manual provides evidence of this and, additionally, arguments to show that German claims were false, not only historically, but also when assessed in terms of the speech habits and allegiances of the local population.

The war of 1914–18 was a global war in terms of its scope, its effects and the voracious demands it made on human resources. In Britain's case the direction of military policy was determined as much by the need to preserve the empire as it was by the requirement of security in Western Europe. Collingwood gave his 1919 talk as a defender of imperialism, the true imperialism as he understood it, the imperialism that represented the progress of civilization, which was a force for good. At this time in his life Collingwood can be counted a liberal imperialist. Later, his liberalism would supplant his imperialism, and later still, his liberalism would give way to his Christianity, his belief that a specifically Christian civilization is both historically manifest and a philosophically defensible way of life. Collingwood's religious opinions are closely entwined with his political views. It is true that the contrast between optimism and pessimism had little appeal for him but, as a liberal, he was surely inclined more to the former than the latter. Collingwood's orthodox Anglicanism supported this. There was evil in the world, but its existence does not threaten the omnipotence of God, for God is not quiescent in the face of evil, "He conquers it", through repentance and faith.[19]

Collingwood's patriotism in time of war and his defence of the ideals of empire were derived from liberal principles. These in turn flowed from a philosophy of the spirit in which philosophy, religion and history were seen as mutually supporting. Collingwood's political views were not merely clothed in his philosophy, but they were views that were often defended at the time quite independently of philosophy of any kind. Not all patriots were liberals and many imperialists were not liberals at all. It is a curious feature of liberalism that it can turn against the political conclusions it leads to. In other words, liberal policies are conditional on liberal principles, and this means that patriotism and imperialism are very much secondary sets of beliefs to be dropped if they fall foul of the principles themselves. So, for example, the imperialist who is not a liberal at all will stick to their imperialism through thick and thin whereas the liberal imperialist will discard the belief in empire should a liberal principle such as self-government require it.

When Collingwood looked back on his life he said that there was a time when he lived as if he disbelieved his own philosophy. We can now look again at this statement from the perspective of Collingwood's political beliefs. Collingwood clearly did not live as if he disbelieved his own patriotism. His service at the Admiralty quickly eliminates that possibility. Nor can we say that he lived as if he disbelieved his own liberalism. For it is in the nature of liberalism that its commitments are conditional on its principles, a point that Collingwood recognised in his address when he said that true imperialism cannot be pursued without defeating the false. The passage runs as follows,

> We must remember that we civilized nations have still to exercise our function of true imperialism: to bring light to the dark places of the earth. If we can do that, our civilization will be justified in the eyes of history as the civilization of Rome has been justified. But we can only do it if we conquer the false imperialism of enslaving our fellows.[20]

There is ambiguity in these remarks since Collingwood can be read either as a Christian imperialist bringing light where there was darkness or as a liberal imperialist committed to bringing self-government quite independently of what the governed believe. So if we are unable to say that Collingwood lived as if he disbelieved his own political beliefs, we can say that he was uncertain about where his liberalism and his Christianity might lead him.

Uncertainty about what you believe is usually erased by finding grounds for belief or disbelief, but in some cases it arises because beliefs are in conflict or it is unclear which has priority. Collingwood's uncertainty comes about because at that time in his life he was unable to see how his liberalism related to his growing sense of the importance of history. When Collingwood is read in this light the key remark in the above passage is his reference to justification "in the eyes of history". Why should a philosopher who was also a Christian find this convincing? Collingwood gave his answer about the role of history in the growth of religious understanding in *Religion and Philosophy*, but in 1919 what still remained to be solved was the major problem of finding a rapprochement between philosophy and history and also between theory and practice. Collingwood argues that Roman civilisation is absolved by history, but if the eyes of history are blind then the aspiring liberal who is looking to reconcile philosophy and practice is likely to remain dissatisfied. Clearly, Collingwood's philosophy of history would need a great deal more refinement before he was able to answer that question.

Collingwood wrote as an intellectual, but he was also one who knew that in many human activities it was practical experience that counted more than ideas. One of the most important insights that Collingwood gained from Ruskin was the belief that artistic appreciation is impossible without trust. We appreciate what the artist is doing by noticing his skills not by reading a handbook on how to acquire them. Equally, Collingwood knew from his own musical experience and from attending to his parent's work as artists that the day to day effort at finding the right effect is of greater moment to the artist than any theory. In Collingwood's aesthetics the sculptor's skill in moulding the clay or the painter's craft in finding the right mix of colour are deliberately emphasised, often to diminish the role in art of advance planning or to play down the belief that the work of art can be understood as spun entirely from the artist's imagination. In politics and history, however, the material is human and, as Collingwood never ceased to stress, self-conscious and expressive of rational freedom. To think of politics aesthetically, therefore, is to think of a political society as malleable in much the same way as a potter approaches his wheel or a theatre director the production of a play. But to adopt such a stance is to deny precisely the rational freedom that Collingwood thought was inextricably involved in being human. Thus, if philosophy was to be brought into close conjunction with life it would fail if life was thought of on the model of art. To put this point another way, if philosophy was to have a bearing on politics it needed a rapprochement with history. This is, perhaps, the most important reason why, for Collingwood, the rapprochements between philosophy and history and between theory and practice must go hand in hand.

Endnotes

1 R. G. Collingwood, *Ruskin's Philosophy*, pp9–12.
2 Ibid., p10.
3 Ibid., p11.
4 Ibid., p11.
5 Ibid., p11.
6 See R. G. Collingwood, *An Essay on Metaphysics*, p343.
7 Lionel Rubinoff attempts to link Collingwood's discussion of Christianity in *Religion and Philosophy* with what he says about presuppositions in *An Essay on Metaphysics*. So in both texts Collingwood's aim is, as Rubinoff writes, "to explain what it means to believe in a God whose existence is not the conclusion of an argument but an absolute presupposition of the form of life which such a belief makes possible", see Rubinoff, *Review*, p178. But even if we were to grant Rubinoff the truth of this claim in terms of Collingwood's intellectual biography, Collingwood's actual argument would still remain firmly impaled on Donagan's hook since Donagan's point is that what Christian believers worship is not the presupposition God, but God.
8 For Donagan's discussion, see his *The Later Philosophy of R.G. Collingwood*, Clarendon Press, Oxford, 1962, pp297–307; and also his "Collingwood and Philosophical Method", in Michael Krausz (ed.), *Critical Essays on the Philosophy of R. G. Collingwood*, Clarendon Press, Oxford, 1972, pp1–19, especially, pp18–19.
9 See R. G. Collingwood, "The Devil", p474, quoted in Alan Donagan, *Later Philosophy*, pp304–5.
10 R. G. Collingwood, *Religion and Philosophy*, pxiii.
11 Alan Donagan, *Later Philosophy*, p304.
12 R. G. Collingwood, *Speculum Mentis*, p145.
13 Donagan, *Later Philosophy*, p307.
14 R. G. Collingwood, *Religion and Philosophy*, pp31–2.
15 R. G. Collingwood, *Ruskin's Philosophy*, p41.
16 John Ruskin, "Modern Warfare" (*Frazer's Magazine*, July 1876), see *Complete Works of John Ruskin*, library edition, edited by E. T. Cook and Alexander Wedderburn, George Allen, London, 1908, vol. 34, p523.
17 Collingwood's address is dated 10 May 1919.
18 R. G. Collingwood, *Essays in Political Philosophy*, p201.

19 R. G. Collingwood, *Religion and Philosophy*, p144.
20 R. G. Collingwood, *Essays in Political Philosophy*, p205.

CHAPTER 12

RETURN TO OXFORD

I. D. 32 was demobilised on 28 July 1919, almost a month after the Treaty of Versailles was signed with Germany (Collingwood, in fact, closed his desk a little earlier, on 3rd June 1919).[1] Of the territories on which Collingwood worked neither Belgium nor Alsace-Lorraine raised difficult issues for the Peace Conference to settle and although the Scheldt problem rumbled on this was largely to do with the sheer intransigence of the geographical and juridical questions it involved. Along with the Political Intelligence Department and the Historical Section (I. D. 27), I. D. 32 was one of the main components of British preparations for the Peace Conference. As the information-providing arm of naval intelligence it produced material in such quantity that it came close to being a geographical encyclopaedia. Manuals and Handbooks of that size and detail were not, however, what the diplomats and politicians wanted and much was edited out in the interests of compression and usefulness. Other more political interests were also at work in minimising I. D. 32's influence. The Foreign Office wished to retain its traditional control of policy matters and to this end ensured that the role of the Geographical Section was indirect. Indeed, neither Admiral Hall as Head of Naval Intelligence nor H. N. Dickson as Head of the Geographical Section attended in Paris.

With the disbandment of I. D. 32 the academics it employed were free to return to their universities, the classicists as likely to start research on Attic red-figure vases as the geographers to silting in the Amazon basin and so on. Collingwood was among them, going back to the philosophy of history and archaeological excavations, but in his case there is a difference, for in his *Autobiography* Collingwood explicitly links his own war service with his condemnation not only of the war but also the peace which followed. Collingwood's words are worth quoting in full. He writes,

> A war had just ended in which the destruction of life, the annihilation of property, and the disappointment of hopes for a peaceable and well-ordered international society had surpassed all previous standards.

What was worse, the intensity of the struggle seemed to have undermined, as if by the sheer force of the explosives it consumed, the moral energies of all the combatants; so that (I write as one who during the latter part of the war was employed in preparations for the peace conference) a war of unprecedented ferocity closed in a peace-settlement of unprecedented folly, in which statesmanship, even purely selfish statesmanship, was overwhelmed by the meanest and most idiotic passions.[2]

Collingwood expresses his criticism in general terms. He says nothing about his own participation beyond mentioning it and, yet, it is an indication that is important because we have already seen how administrative squabbling led to the curtailing of influence, how, in the build up to the Conference, decision makers kept the experts at arms length, and how, at the Conference itself, political pragmatism ensured that the gap between theory and practice remained wide. It is absolutely clear from Collingwood's *Autobiography* that his response to the war shaped much of the work on philosophy and history that occupied him for the rest of his life. "What was needed" Collingwood wrote "was not more goodwill and human affection, but more understanding of human affairs and more knowledge of how to handle them."[3] Collingwood did not attend the Conference nor was his Section directly involved in it, but, even so, it is hard to see his urging as wholly derived from the facts of the situation as he saw them and not at all from his personal experience of how the preparations for the Conference actually worked.

When Collingwood returned to Oxford the world had changed. It had changed for him personally because, since his marriage in June 1918, he had bought a house at 5 Fyfield Road in Oxford and so needed permission to reside outside his College. With this being speedily granted, Collingwood becoming the first married fellow in the history of Pembroke College, his life as a university teacher seemed to have resumed its course.[4] And in some respects it had. Lectures still had to be prepared and delivered, tutorials held, essays marked, meetings attended, books, reviews and articles written. So in December 1919 we find Collingwood writing lectures on the Ontological Proof, to be given in the Hilary Term, 1920. Collingwood's work in archaeology, too, had not been unaffected by the war, for the death of Francis Haverfield's pupil, G. L. Cheeseman, during the Dardanelles Campaign in 1915 left Collingwood one of the few in Oxford capable of assisting Haverfield in his work on the Roman Inscriptions of Britain. When Haverfield himself died in October 1919 Collingwood assumed the main responsibility for the project, and this was to be one of his most demanding occupations in archaeology through the following decade and beyond.[5]

Collingwood was resuming the habits and routines that had begun some eight years before. However, there were other respects in which his life could not simply continue as it had prior to the war. For the war had given Collingwood an intellectual problem to solve. We see from a short essay written in October 1919 just how closely Collingwood linked the results of the war with his conception of the philosopher's task and with his diagnosis of contemporary ills. Moreover, this essay is one of the first in which the concept of history receives independent examination. Collingwood argues that the modern fragmentation of mind will lead to catastrophe. He writes,

> Unless history moves faster in these days, it may not come for another nine centuries: our present conflicts, like the agonies of the expiring Roman Republic, are but a ripple on the surface of history. But it must come: and as surely as it comes, so surely it will be followed by the revival of humanity into a new life.[6]

Concerns like these needed resolution. For Collingwood at this time all work was work in progress. And so his worries anticipate his attempts to resolve them; they look forward to his writings of the 1920s, most importantly to *Speculum Mentis*.

In 1938 Collingwood saw himself as a "professorial goose" whose job was to cackle at impending danger. It was a picture of the philosopher's task that had gripped him for most of his life. In 1916 the enemy had already been engaged and Collingwood was fully occupied in the effort to counter aggression and with making preparations for what he hoped would be a lasting peace. The Manuals that Collingwood worked on at Naval Intelligence are not wholly technical guides and so we should not be surprised to find some degree of overlap with his political beliefs of the time. A liberal state at war needed to convince itself not only that the cause it was fighting for was just, but also that at the close of hostilities it would bring about a just peace. To liberals there is no justice in victory alone. Thus, the principles that were implicit in the Manuals, most noticeably in the Manual of Alsace-Lorraine, were the same ideals of self-government and consent that animated the official view of the Peace Conference. For Collingwood, as a liberal, they were his principles, too. We should not exaggerate this overlap, however. The Manuals had a standard format and those involved in their production were largely expected to toe the departmental line. While there is a little internal evidence of

Collingwood straining at the leash, in general he follows the instructions of his intelligence masters closely.

In typical Civil Service manner the Manuals were intended as briefing documents for politicians to use in making decisions. How far any politician, as opposed to their administrative assistants, actually read them is difficult to ascertain, but a detailed line by line scrutiny is doubtful, and it appears as if the Manuals were consulted on a pragmatic basis and were delved into if and when necessity arose.[7] They were clearly more important than simply background material because their design focused on exactly the issues of nationality and language use that were thought valuable to those who were engaged in redrawing political boundaries. Further, while liberal political principles are not hard to detect in the Manuals, the necessity to furnish information relevant to political interests is rarely ignored. So, for example, the historical discussions in the *Manual of Belgium and the Adjoining Territories* stress the British security interest in maintaining a belt of independent states in Western Europe. Similar points could be made regarding British economic interests. Even so, it has to be said that the basic role of the Manuals was to provide information leading to advice. After that the hard realities of political negotiation took precedence.

The search for connections between Collingwood the philosopher and Collingwood the Temporary Clerk in Naval Intelligence is a tempting one to undertake. Affinities of content and method, possibly even webs of influence between his philosophical work and his experience at the Admiralty, might be sought for and traced. When Collingwood's thought and his life are considered together, however, the bearing one has for the other is less direct. It is right to say that the period of Collingwood's war service was part of the process of thought that led to *Speculum Mentis*. Collingwood described his thinking as involving a long and difficult gestation. In the case of *Speculum Mentis* the image is apt since the book was born not only from Collingwood's dissatisfaction with the modern world, but also from an intellectual inheritance that lay deep in his upbringing and in his family's assumptions about how life should be lived. In this respect, the book's remarkable Prologue in which Collingwood sets out his version of medievalism and embarks on an explicitly Christian campaign to reunite the warring factions of the mind is clearly his solution to problems that had long troubled him. In the medieval period, Collingwood wrote in 1919 that "speculation and authority were at one", clearly hinting at the kind of ideal he had in mind for modernity to follow.[8] But Collingwood knew the dangers of revivalism from his aesthetics and he was keen to avoid a standpoint in which the past was simply transplanted to the present.

Collingwood also knew the misunderstanding that can result if a single image is allowed to dominate the argument. Thus, the idea of a map as a representation of the world bears little relation to the unity of thinking and experience as it is explained in *Speculum Mentis*. If order can be brought to a piece of terrain by picking out the features that we wish to identify, geology, say, or land use, then why should the same purpose not be achieved with the life of the mind? Just as a map of Europe, say, marks the boundaries of the states it contains so will a map of the mind mark the different ways by which the mind apprehends the world. This was Collingwood's project in the years leading up to 1924, to reassert the unity of the mind through the ordered elucidation of its constituent forms—art, religion, science, history and philosophy itself. However, the main interest in the notion of mapping the mind lies largely in Collingwood's rejection of it. *Speculum Mentis* is a post-war book, a call to order after the war, but this goal will not be reached by portraying the mind as a region to be mapped. Indeed, Collingwood's final chapter contains two powerful reasons why human understanding cannot be grasped by mapping it as if it were an unexplored country. First, each form of experience is very far from being autonomous and none is content to limit its activities to a specific terrain. So, Collingwood writes, "the scientist does not want a map of the forms of knowledge. There is for him only one legitimate form, science; and that is its own map. All other forms are not other territories, but false maps of the same territory."[9] A point it is worth remembering that is equally true of the artist and the religious. And this means that what we are faced with is not a map of knowledge in which different vocabularies co-exist peaceably because their boundaries have been settled by a kind of epistemological boundary commission, but a battleground in which each form of experience fights for supremacy with every other. Second, if the countries of the mind turn out to be distorted versions of the same country then what is this country? Might this be organised and presented as a map? Collingwood thinks of this one country as "the world of historical fact, seen as the mind's knowledge of itself", but it, too, is closed to representation as a map.[10] So Collingwood argues, "There is and can be no map of knowledge, for a map means an abstract of the main features of a country, laid before the traveller in advance of his experience of the country itself."[11] For Collingwood, there is no "map of knowledge distinct from knowledge itself".[12]

By the time Collingwood's war service ended he had become convinced that history needed to be brought into a much closer relation with practice. He realised also that such a move would be impossible if history was understood on the model of realism. Rescuing history from realism is, therefore, the first move in the project of linking history with life. In 1919, however, Collingwood's thinking was in its early stages. The essential notion of the living past was germinating in his mind, as was the idea that historical and practical knowledge were in some important way intimately connected. But none of this had been fully worked out and, indeed, it would not be for another ten years or so before Collingwood was able to reach a considered position. Now there is one obvious sense in which history and politics merge. Historians were heavily involved both in the preparations for peace and in the Peace Conference itself. Some were in influential positions offering expert advice on how to solve pressing and often intransigent problems. Others played key roles in editing the information accumulated by the different intelligence agencies including Collingwood's own Geographical Section. One such historian was H. W. V. Temperley who was a government expert on Easter European affairs, particularly Serbia, and who later edited the standard history of the Peace Conference. Temperley shared Collingwood's ambitions for history, stating in a lecture that

> we are working as students of history have never done before, with the actual living fabric of things. The more these problems are pondered the more we shall have the occasion and opportunity for influencing the world at large.[13]

Liberal optimism was also cautioned by scepticism. Another historian George Prothero who was responsible for editing the material for the final Peace Handbooks to be used in the Conference was under no illusions about their impact.

> 'Even if the books are ready our negotiators will never look at them', Prothero wrote gloomily in his diary, and although he did attend in Paris he was barely consulted, writing a couple of pieces of policy guidance the conclusions of which 'were not adopted, perhaps not even read'.[14]

It was not that the historians had not furnished the politicians with information. The facts were available in abundance. As Prothero confided to his diary on his leaving Paris, "I felt I was a fifth wheel in the coach."[15]

The war acted as the immediate instigator of Collingwood's practical aspirations for history, but it also challenged them by testing the arguments that were brought in their defence. So, as Collingwood's philosophy of history developed and matured, key difficulties concerning action, meaning and intentionality were often best illustrated and, in something of a paradox, severely challenged by the war as an historical event. Collingwood did not expect history to bear on life as an oracle speaks to an expectant world, but he did come to think of history as essential to self-knowledge in morality and politics as much as in the life of a single individual. In 1919 Collingwood's ideas were in their early formative period. The Peace Conference made many academics aware of the gulf between theory and practice. As the conclusion of one global conflict gradually became the forerunner of another both Collingwood's arguments and his hopes would be made to stand trial.

There is a difference between a life lived as though you disbelieved your own philosophy and having a philosophy that is unworthy of belief. Collingwood wished to live a life that reflected his beliefs. Even though there were times when he felt unable to live such a life, his conviction that there could be one remained secure. But what does this security depend on? Clearly, it cannot be the force of Collingwood's personality or his strength of will because that would set up exactly the disjunction he wished to overcome. In other words, the move from philosophy to life is not practical, but philosophical in character. Collingwood needed a picture of the unity of thought and action that was philosophically compelling. There is a sense in which Collingwood needed a philosophy in order to live. A life unsanctioned by philosophy would be an incomplete life or one lived in the shadows, as Plato might think of it. It is not that Collingwood thought that philosophy could tell him what to do, but rather that without the authority of philosophy, links between thought and action would be too easily broken. But Collingwood also knew that an additional and possibly more demanding requirement had to be met. He knew that no rapprochement between philosophy and life would be convincing unless it could be expressed in his own voice. The voices of those like-minded philosophers who Collingwood looked to in his quest — of Hegel, Croce and de Ruggiero, of Ruskin — these voices gave him encouragement through the knowledge that others had taken this road before him, but they could not tell him how to find his own.[16] It is how Collingwood speaks about the quest himself that is significant rather than the views of the philosophers who influenced him, even those who were most sympathetic. If this is true then, for Collingwood, speaking about the unity of thought and action in the wrong voice will not be like making a technical mistake, say, the kind of howler in logic that he thought the realists had made, but is more a sign of failure. This is what a commitment to the unity of the life of the mind means.

Even so, we need to read Collingwood's aspirations for the unity of thought and life alongside his autobiographical account of his thinking at that time. Once we do that we arrive at a picture of Collingwood's early life in which relations between thought and action are a little less harmonious. In 1919, Collingwood wrote later, "I still conducted my daily life as if I thought that the business of that life was theoretical and not practical."[17] The Collingwood who returned to Oxford in 1919 content for his college gate to shut tight behind him was also the Collingwood who had spent the last three years in the service of his country. But, on his own analysis, he could make no connection between them. Was Collingwood, then, the unhappy man of modernity? If so, he would be the man who, as Collingwood describes him in *Speculum Mentis*, "wishes to be an artist, but there is nothing for him to do as an artist except to paint pictures that nobody wants", the man who "wishes to devote his life to religion or philosophy, and he can only preach sermons to which no one will listen or write books that no one will buy".[18] Well, no not quite, for if Collingwood's autobiographical account is to be trusted (and we have no reason not to trust it) he was equally aware from his philosophy that writing books would not be enough. The point was to write books that would change people's thinking. And it is hard to believe that Collingwood's experience of the war played no part in his realisation of that.

Endnotes

1 The Geographical Work, p3.
2 R. G. Collingwood, *An Autobiography*, p89.
3 Ibid., p92.
4 See R. B. McCallum, "Obituary, R. G. Collingwood (1889–1942)", *The Oxford Magazine*, 4 February 1943, p160; see also Collingwood's letter to the Master of Pembroke dated 21 October 1919, see Peter Johnson, *Correspondence*, 1998, D2i.
5 See R. P. Wright, Preface to R. G. Collingwood and R. P. Wright, *The Roman Inscriptions of Britain*, Clarendon Press, Oxford, 1965, pv–vi, where Wright refers to Haverfield's choice of Collingwood to execute the drawings – "This was R. G. Collingwood whose superb draughtsmanship, combined with excellent archaeological judgement, enabled him to draw each inscription after detailed critical examination" (pvi). Clearly, Collingwood possessed the map making skills needed for the Geographical Section of Naval Intelligence, see the *Manual of Belgium Atlas* (I. D. 1168A) Naval Staff Intelligence Division, February

1918 and the *Manual of Alsace Lorraine Atlas* (I. D. 1211A), Prepared by the Geographical Section of the Naval Intelligence Division, Naval Staff, Admiralty, HMSO, London, both of which Collingwood was responsible for; for further information, see R. G. Collingwood, "Note to the Second Edition", in *Catalogue of the Roman Inscribed and Sculptured Stones in the Carlisle Museum*, Tullie House, by the Late F. Haverfield, second edition, Public Library and Museum Committee, Titus Wilson and Son, Kendal, 1922, piii (not in Richmond, Dreisbach or Taylor); see also R. G. Collingwood, *An Autobiography*, p145; Sheppard Frere, *Roman Britain Since Haverfield and Richmond*, A Lecture delivered in All Souls College, 23 October 1987, pp1–3; Van Der Dussen, *History as a Science*, p221, and W. M. Johnston, *Formative Years*, p38. For memories of G. L. Cheeseman, see Arnold Toynbee, *Experiences*, pp10, 105, 114, and 387.

6   R. G. Collingwood, "A Footnote to Future History", Collingwood MS, DEP 12/1, as quoted in Van Der Dussen, *History as a Science*, p130. Van Der Dussen is surely right to point out that Collingwood's thinking at this time was at a transitional stage. What is implicit in his mind in 1919 is made explicit in *Speculum Mentis* in 1924.

7   On the question of the influence of the manuals and handbooks on the delegates to the Conference Erik Goldstein is instructive, arguing that they were used mostly by junior officials as a reference source for writing reports on specific policy questions as they arose. Goldstein concludes, "While the Historical Section did not directly influence the outcome of the Paris Peace Conference, it did provide a firm underpinning of fact for the British negotiating position at Paris, in turn allowing the British delegation to speak with greater accuracy, and therefore with greater force." (Erik Goldstein, *Winning the Peace*, pp45-6; E. L. Woodward who worked in the Historical Section came to be realistic about the influence of the published material on politicians themselves, writing that "As far as I could gather, Balfour alone among ministers of state read our books. I also suspect that, in his queer way, he already knew most of the facts. On the other hand, Mr. Lloyd George never showed any sign of knowing much about the background of the problems with which he was dealing." (E. L. Woodward, *Short Journey*, Faber and Faber Ltd. London, 1942, p102).

8   R. G. Collingwood, *Speculum Mentis*, p307.
9   Ibid., p309.
10   Ibid., p309.
11   Ibid., p310.
12   Ibid., p310.
13   See John D. Fair, *Harold Temperley, A Scholar and Romantic in the Public Realm*, University of Delaware Press, Newark, 1992, p298.
14   As quoted in C. W. Crawley, "Sir George Prothero and His Circle", *Transactions of the Royal Historical Society*, Fifth Series, 20, 1970, p124.

15   Ibid., p125.
16   For a recent discussion of the influence of Hegel on Collingwood's thought generally, see Gary K. Browning, *Rethinking R. G. Collingwood, Philosophy, Politics and the Unity of Theory and Practice*; for discussion of Collingwood and Italian philosophy, see James Connelly, "Art Thou the Man: Croce, Gentile or de Ruggiero?" in David Boucher, James Connelly and Tariq Modood (eds), *Philosophy, History and Civilization, Interdisciplinary Perspectives on R. G. Collingwood*, University of Wales Press, Cardiff, 1995, pp92–114, and Rik Peters, "Collingwood's Logic of Question and Answer, its Relation to Absolute Presuppositions: Another Brief History", *Collingwood Studies*, vol. 6, 1999, pp1–28, especially, pp6–10; for the influence of Ruskin generally, see W. M. Johnston, *Formative Years*, especially Chapter 2.
17   R. G. Collingwood, *An Autobiography*, p150.
18   R. G. Collingwood, *Speculum Mentis*, p26.

AFTERWORD

The Geographical Section of Naval Intelligence concluded its business, or, to be more precise, had its business concluded for it, at the end of July 1919. A year or so later those Manuals whose confidentiality was now deemed irrelevant were offered for sale to the general public. Even in 2010 it is still possible to find the occasional volume in a second-hand bookshop, one covering the Danube, perhaps, or more exotically, Portuguese Nyasaland, its For Official Use Only stamp cancelled and, invariably, a discarded library ticket hanging from its dusty cover. The work of the Geographical Section revealed a slowly gathered recognition of the global character of the conflict the opposing empires fought. It expressed, too, the realisation that if the peace that followed the war was to be stable then it had also to be global. By around 1921 the Manuals, so urgently required for the preparation of the Peace Conference, had served their purpose. And, yet, even in 1919 it was doubtful if the purposes of those who prepared the Manuals were shared by the politicians for whom they were intended. In the main, the politicians had their own agendas, and book learning was conspicuously not one of them. During the inter-war period, years which played havoc with most of the good intentions behind the Peace Settlement, the Naval Intelligence Division became itself something of a backwater, that is until the start of the Second World War when it became indispensable once again, and it was realised that geographical intelligence was just as powerful an imperative as it had been in the First War. Norway in 1940, as much as Gallipoli in 1915, indicated the priority that should be given to good topographical intelligence. And so, under the direction of Rear-Admiral John Godfrey, the new Head of Naval Intelligence, who had, in fact, served in Intelligence under "Blinker" Hall in the First World War, I. D. 32 was, early in 1941, reconstituted as N. I. D. 5, and an entirely new series of Manuals, this time more directly concerned with naval matters, was set in train.

Oxford geographers had been preparing confidential reports for military operations since 1940 but, as in 1914, recruitment was in this early stage neither extensive nor organised. The need to find experts amongst academics, was, however, equally pressing. In the light of this, Collingwood's remark to his friend and student, T. M. Knox, is revealing. For in a letter dated 6 January 1940 Collingwood wrote of the lectures on moral philosophy he was then delivering in Oxford, that it was "more important to do this than to obtain any alternative employment in the service of the government".[1] We do not know what was in Collingwood's mind when he made this comment. However, it is likely that he was thinking of his ill health that would have ruled out any severely demanding occupation. It is also likely that he was thinking of his duty as he saw it, as a teacher and a public intellectual, to re-invigorate the democratic ideals his country was fighting for. And so it was more important to complete *The New Leviathan*, the book Collingwood thought of as his major work in political philosophy, than to change tack and take up a government post in wartime.

It is also possible, however, that Collingwood was remembering his own government service at the Admiralty over twenty years before, and he would surely have recollected that what eluded him then was a link between theory and practice that he could find plausible. As Collingwood later described his state of mind at that time, the disengaged intellectual was at odds with the philosophy he believed in. We can be reasonably certain that the idea that the complete life must also be the united life is an aspiration Collingwood never lost. It is present in his admiration for Lord Milner's Kindergarten and we find it, too, in his praise for D. G. Hogarth, Collingwood's "bold revolutionary",[2] mentor of T. E. Lawrence and "a man of letters with an immense knowledge of a wide range of subjects, and yet, when the moment required it, a man of action".[3] The hero as polymath is a tempting portrait of Hogarth, and of Collingwood, too, but with one notable difference. For Hogarth it was the force of personality and will that led to the successful welding together of literature and life. By contrast, Collingwood, as a philosopher, aimed to apprehend his time in thought. No synthesis of theory and practice would be complete if philosophy and history were absent. But towards the end of his life the specialisation that Collingwood had always sought to overcome had penetrated philosophy itself. Philosophers saw themselves as under-labourers modestly finding clarity and precision in the ways we speak rather than as public intellectuals volubly warning the city at the first sign that it is under threat. We can think of the Peace Conference as the attempt to grasp its political moment in thought. In playing a part in its preparations Collingwood contributed to the vast amount of information that government agencies, American, French and Italian, as well as British, provided for the decision-makers. At the time, the ideals and hopes of Paris 1919 were Collingwood's, too. Later, and especially as the 1930's took their bleak and seemingly pre-determined course, he came to share in the prevalent post-war disillusionment. Collingwood did not believe that history was either plotted in advance or an arbitrary jumble of events. His philosophy of history together with his account of historical method and also his Anglicanism saved him from these errors. But in 1919 his sense that history could be brought into a fruitful relation with politics was not ready to be tested either by events or the logic of his own arguments. Collingwood came to think of his life at that time as a life divided. He lived as if the separation of thought and life was true, whereas his philosophy told him it was false. At that time, however, his attempt to forge a link between philosophy and history was largely undeveloped. In 1940 by contrast Collingwood possessed the authority that comes from speaking in a voice that was exclusively his own. A life that is lived in compartments can be explained away, but in 1940 with his thought mature, if not complete, Collingwood felt able to rely on his own resources. The study that Collingwood feared in 1919 now became a campaign headquarters. Government service of the kind Collingwood dutifully performed in the First War had to be set aside. Collingwood determined to do what he was good at. For the professorial goose the moment to cackle had come.

Endnotes

1   R. G. Collingwood to T. M. Knox, 6 January 1940, see Peter Johnson, *The Correspondence of R. G. Collingwood*, 1998, K2xxx.

2   R. G. Collingwood, *An Autobiography*, pp17, 82.

3   Phillip Knightley and Colin Simpson, *The Secret Lives of Lawrence of Arabia*, Thomas Nelson and Sons Limited, London, 1969, p20.

APPENDIX

The following is a sketch of Collingwood's work done during his time at the Admiralty:

27 February 1916: "John Ruskin" paper read to the Eranos Society, Rugby School.

March/April 1916: six lectures on "The Philosophy of Religious Evolution", delivered at the Foyer d'Etudiants, Kingsway.

May 1916: "The Devil" published in *Concerning Prayer* (first edition dated May, 1916). In a letter to Macmillan, dated 13 July 1916, Collingwood wrote:

> I have in preparation a book of about 78,000 words on the philosophy of religion, and I should be glad to know whether you would like to see it with a view to publication. You have recently published an essay of mine on the same subject in a volume entitled "Concerning Prayer" edited by Canon Streeter, and you may be able to judge from that whether you could wish to publish anything else of mine. If so, I will send a specimen chapter immediately, or the whole manuscript in a few weeks, for your consideration. I regret that owing to Govt. work I am unable at present to call on you in person.

See Peter Johnson, *The Correspondence of R. G. Collingwood, An Illustrated Guide*, The Collingwood Society, 1998, M1i, and also letters M1ii to M1v.)

12 August 1916: *Religion and Philosophy* sent to the printers.

Autumn 1916: *Religion and Philosophy* published.

December 1916: Lecture on Nationality and Ethics, Foyer d'Etudiants. "The Exploration of the Roman Fort at Ambleside, Report on the Third Year's Work (1915)", *Transactions of the Cumberland and Westmorland*, (2) xvi, 1916, pp1–62.

6 May 1917: Address to the Student Christian Movement, St Mary's, Oxford.

3 June 1917: Address to St Hughes Christian Union.

23 August to 6 September 1917: *Truth and Contradiction* written, revised 6 and 7 January 1918. (Later destroyed, but Chapter 2 survives. Letter to Macmillan offering them *Truth and Contradiction*, dated 8 January 1918, See Johnson, M1vi.)

6 February 1918: Collingwood sends manuscript to Macmillan, "I should be sorry to delay its publication until after the war".

15 February 1918: Review of May Sinclair, *The New Idealism* in *The Oxford Magazine*.

31 May 1918: Review of J. N. Figgis, *The Will to Freedom: or, The Gospel of Nietzsche and the Gospel of Christ*, in *The Oxford Magazine*.

13 September 1918: completes "Words and the Tune".

4 October 1918: "Christianity in Partibus" published in *Challenge*.

October and December 1918: lectures at the School of Economics. Talk on the Philosophy of St Paul, Somerville College, Oxford, 1918.

14 February 1919: Review of Bertrand Russell, *Mysticism and Logic*, in *The Oxford Magazine*.

7 May 1919: lecture on the "Spiritual Basis of Reconstruction".

24 May 1919: lecture on "Money and Morals".

8 August 1919: *Ruskin's Philosophy*. Lecture "Christian Attitude to Pain", address at Lady Margaret Hall Chapel; also talk on "Religious Intolerance".

31 October 1919: essay entitled "A Footnote to Future History".

December 1919: lectures on the Ontological Proof (written December 1919, for delivery in the Hilary Term 1920). Started translating de Ruggiero *Modern Philosophy*.

1919: Obituary of Francis Haverfield, Proceedings of the Society of Antiquaries of Newcastle, IX, 117-18.

BIBLIOGRAPHY

Primary sources

Archives

Abbot Hall Art Gallery and Museum of Lakeland Life, Kendal
  W. G. Collingwood Archive.

The Bodleian Library Oxford
  The Papers of R. G. Collingwood (as listed in Ruth A. Burchnall, *Catalogue of the Papers of R. G. Collingwood 1889–1943*, Dep. Collingwood 1–26, 1994).

British Library
  Letters from R. G. Collingwood to Macmillan and Co. Ltd, 13 July 1916 to 10 October 1931, Add. Mss 55270f.

Cumbria Record Office, Kendal
  Collingwood Family Archive.

Leeds University Library
  Arthur Ransome Papers, Brotherton Collection, C20 manuscripts, Ransome.

National Archives, Washington, D. C.
  Records of the Inquiry
  Inquiry Document 984, Confidential Report on the Arrangements made by the British Government for Collating Data for the Peace Conference, June 1918.

Printed material

A Manual of Belgium and the Adjoining Territories, I. D. 1168, prepared by the Geographical Section of the Naval Intelligence Division, Admiralty, HMSO, London, 1918, pp1–595.

Manual of Belgium Atlas, I. D. 1168A, Naval Staff Intelligence Division, Admiralty, February 1918, HMSO, London 1918, nineteen maps.

A Manual of Alsace-Lorraine, I. D. 1211, Naval Staff Intelligence Department, Admiralty, June 1919, HMSO, London, 1919, pp1–422.

A Manual of Alsace-Lorraine Atlas, I. D. 1211A, prepared by the Geographical Section of the Naval Intelligence Division, Admiralty, HMSO, London, 1919, twenty maps including a relief panorama.

Belgium, Handbooks Prepared Under The Direction Of The Historical Section Of The Foreign Office, No. 23, April 1919, pp1–220 plus folding map.

Alsace-Lorraine, Handbooks Prepared under The Direction Of The Historical Section Of The Foreign Office, No. 28, February 1919, pp1–121 plus folding map.

Question of the Scheldt, Handbooks Prepared under the Direction of the Historical Section of the Foreign Office, No. 25, December 1918, pp1–22 plus folding map.

Slesvig-Holstein, Handbooks Prepared under The Direction Of The Historical Section Of The Foreign Office, No. 27, April 1919, pp1–26 plus folding map.

The Geographical Work of the Naval Intelligence Division, Naval Staff, 1915–1919, Technical History Section, Admiralty, December, 1919, ADM 223/90 303399.

Works by R. G. Collingwood

Books

Religion and Philosophy, Macmillan, London, 1916.

Speculum Mentis, Clarendon Press, Oxford, 1924.

An Essay on Philosophical Method, Clarendon Press, Oxford, 1933.

Roman Britain and the English Settlements (with J. N. L. Myres), Clarendon Press, Oxford, 1936.

The Principles of Art, Clarendon Press, Oxford, 1938.

An Autobiography, Oxford University Press, Oxford, 1939.

The New Leviathan, Clarendon Press, Oxford, 1942.

The Idea of History, edited with an introduction by T. M. Knox, Clarendon Press, Oxford, 1946.

The Roman Inscriptions of Britain (with R. P. Wright), Clarendon Press, Oxford, 1965.

The New Leviathan, revised edition with a new introduction and additional material edited by David Boucher, Clarendon Press, Oxford, 1992.

The Idea of History, revised edition, edited with an introduction by Jan Van Der Dussen, Clarendon Press, Oxford, 1993.

"The Function of Metaphysics in Civilization", as reprinted in R. G. Collingwood, *An Essay on Metaphysics*, revised edition, edited with an introduction by Rex Martin, Clarendon Press, Oxford, 1998.

The Principles of History, edited by W. H. Dray and W. J. van Der Dussen, Oxford University Press, Oxford, 1999.

"Man Goes Mad", as reprinted in R. G. Collingwood, *The Philosophy of Enchantment*, edited by David Boucher, Wendy James and Phillip Smallwood, Clarendon Press, Oxford, 2005.

(As translator) Benedetto Croce, *The Philosophy of Giambattista Vico*, Howard Latimer, London, 1913.

Articles, essays, pamphlets and reviews

"Report on the Excavations at Papcastle 1912", *Transactions of the Cumberland and Westmorland Antiquarian and Archaeological Society*, vol. 13, 1913, pp131–41.

"Report on the Excavations of the Roman Fort at Ambleside 1913 (with Professor F. Haverfield) with a Preliminary Report of the Excavation in March and April 1914 (with L. B. Freeston)", *Transactions of the Cumberland and Westmorland Antiquarian and Archaeological Society*, vol. 14, 1914, pp433–65.

"The Exploration of the Roman Fort at Ambleside, Report of the Second Year's Work (1914)", *Transactions of the Cumberland and Westmorland Antiquarian and Archaeological Society*, vol. 15, 1915, pp1–62.

"The Exploration of the Roman Fort at Ambleside: Report on the Third Year's Work (1915)", *Transactions of the Cumberland and Westmorland Antiquarian and Archaeological Society*, vol. 15, 1915, pp56-90.

"The Devil", in B. H. Streeter and Lily Dougall (eds), *Concerning Prayer*, Macmillan, London, 1916, pp449-75.

"Lectures on the Philosophy of St Paul, Somerville College, Oxford 1918", Collingwood Manuscripts, DEP 1/3.

Review of J. N. Figgis, "The Will to Freedom: or the Gospel of Nietzsche and the Gospel of Christ", in *The Oxford Magazine*, 31 May, 1918, p299.

"Christianity in Partibus", *The Challenge*, vol. 9, no. 232, 4 October 1918, p323.

Review of Bertrand Russell, *Mysticism and Logic*, in *The Oxford Magazine*, 14 February 1919, p129.

"Footnote to Future History" 1919, Collingwood Manuscripts, DEP 12/1.

"The Spiritual Basis of Reconstruction" Address to the Belgian Students Conference at Fladbury, 10 May 1919, as reprinted in R. G. Collingwood, *Essays in Political Philosophy*, edited with an introduction by David Boucher, Clarendon Press, Oxford, 1989.

Obituary of Francis Haverfield, *Proceedings of the Society of Antiquaries of Newcastle* (third series), vol. 9, 1919, pp117-18.

"Luxemburg" *Encyclopaedia Britannica*, 12th edition, 1920, pp811-12.

Ruskin's Philosophy [1922] as reprinted in Alan Donagan (ed.), *Essays in the Philosophy of Art by R. G. Collingwood*, Indiana University Press, Bloomington, 1964, pp5-41.

"Note to the Second Edition" in the Catalogue of the Roman Inscribed and Sculptured Stones in the Carlisle Museum Tullie House by the Late F. Haverfield, second edition, Public Library and Museum Committee, Titus Wilson and Son, Kendal, 1922 (not in I. A. Richmond, "R. G. Collingwood: Bibliography of Writings on Ancient History and Archaeology", *Proceedings of the British Academy*, vol. 29, 1943, pp19-23; Taylor, *R. G. Collingwood A Bibliography*, 1988; or Christopher Dreisbach, *R. G. Collingwood, A*

Bibliographic Checklist, Philosophy Documentation Centre, Bowling Green State University, Bowling Green, Ohio, 1993).

"Skipness Castle" (with Angus Graham), *Proceedings of the Society of Antiquaries of Scotland*, 57, 1922-3, pp266-87.

Review of *Map of Roman Britain*, second edition, Southampton Ordinance Survey of the United Kingdom, 1928, *The Geographical Journal*, vol. 77, July to December 1928, pp565-6.

The Book of the Pilgrimage of Hadrian's Wall July 1st to 4th, *Society of Antiquaries of Newcastle upon Tyne, Cumberland and Westmorland Antiquarian and Archaeological Society*, 1930.

"List of Work Done" (Booklet), 1930/1, Collingwood Manuscripts, DEP 22.

"War in its relation to Christian Ethics", Paper read to The Group, 17 November 1932, Collingwood Manuscripts, DEP 1/8.

"In Memoriam", *Proceedings of the Cumberland and Westmorland Antiquarian and Archaeological Society*, vol. 33, 1933, pp308-12.

"Obituary of W. G. Collingwood", *The Times*, Monday 3 October, 1933, p9.

Secondary sources

Works on Collingwood

Books

Boucher, David, *The Social and Political Thought of R. G. Collingwood*, Cambridge University Press, Cambridge, 1989.

Browning, Gary K. *Rethinking R. G. Collingwood, Philosophy, Politics and the Unity of Theory and Practice*, Palgrave Macmillan, London, 2004.

Connelly, James, *Metaphysics, Method and Politics, The Political Philosophy of R. G. Collingwood*, Imprint Academic, Exeter, 2003.

Donagan, Alan, *The Later Philosophy of R. G. Collingwood*, Clarendon Press, Oxford, 1962.

D'Oro, Giuseppina, *Collingwood and the Metaphysics of Experience*, Routledge, London, 2002.

Dray, William H., *History as Re-enactment, R. G. Collingwood's Idea of History*, Clarendon Press, Oxford, 1995.

Freeman, P. M. W., *The Best Training Ground for Archaeologists: Francis Haverfield and the Invention of Romano-British Archaeology*, Oxbow Books, Oxford, 2007.

Helgeby, Stein, *Action as History, The Historical Thought of R. G. Collingwood*, Imprint Academic, Exeter, 2004.

Inglis, Fred, *The History Man, The Life of R. G. Collingwood*, Princeton University Press, Princeton, 2009.

Johnson, Peter, *R. G. Collingwood: An Introduction*, Thoemmes Press, Bristol, 1998.

Johnson, Peter, *The Correspondence of R. G. Collingwood, An Illustrated Guide*, The Collingwood Society, 1998.

Johnston, W. M., *The Formative Years of R. G. Collingwood*, Martinus Nijhoff, The Hague, 1967.

Olivetti, Alessandra Greppi, *Due Saggi Su R. G. Collingwood*, Liviana Editrice, Padova, 1977.

Patrick, James, *The Magdalen Metaphysicals, Idealism and Orthodoxy at Oxford 1901–1945*, Mercer University Press, Macon, 1985.

Rubinoff, Lionel, *Collingwood and the Reform of Metaphysics: A Study in the Philosophy of Mind*, University of Toronto Press, Toronto, 1970.

Taylor, Donald S. *R. G., Collingwood, A Bibliography*, Garland Publishing, New York and London, 1988.

Van Der Dussen, W. J., *History as a Science, The Philosophy of R. G. Collingwood*, Martinus Nijhoff Publishers, The Hague, 1981.

Articles

Bates, David, "Rediscovering Collingwood's Spiritual History (in and out of context)", *History and Theory*, vol. 35, February 1996, pp29–55.

Collini, Stefan and Williams, Bernard, "Collingwood, Robin George 1889-1943", *The New Oxford Dictionary of National Biography*, online edition, Oxford University Press, October 2008.

Connelly, James, "Art Thou The Man: Croce, Gentile or de Ruggiero", in David Boucher, James Connelly and Tariq Modood (eds), *Philosophy, History and Civilization, Inter-disciplinary Perspectives on R. G. Collingwood*, University of Wales Press, Cardiff, 1995, pp92–114.

Connelly, James, "Natural Science, History and Christianity", *Collingwood Studies*, vol. 4, 1997, pp101–32.

Connelly, James, "Collingwood and his Contemporaries: Responses to Critics 1918–1928", *Collingwood Studies*, vol. 7, 2000, pp72–93.

Connelly, James (and Peter Johnson), "R. G. Collingwood's 'Christianity in Partibus'", *Collingwood Studies*, vol. 6, 1999, pp166–71.

Donagan, Alan, "Collingwood and Philosophical Method", in Michael Krausz (ed.), *Critical Essays on the Philosophy of R. G. Collingwood*, Clarendon Press, Oxford, 1972, pp1–19.

Johnson, Douglas H., "W. G. Collingwood and the Beginnings of the Idea of History", *Collingwood Studies*, vol. 1, 1994, 1–26.

Knox, T. M., "Collingwood, Robin George 1889-1943" *The Dictionary of National Biography 1941–1950*, pp168–70.

Martin, Rex, "Collingwood's Logic of Question and Answer, its relation to Absolute Presuppositions: A Brief History", *Collingwood Studies*, vol. 5, 1998, pp122–35.

McCallum, R. B., "Robin George Collingwood 1889-1943", *Proceedings of the British Academy*, vol. 29, 1943, pp463–68.

McCallum, R. B., "R. G. Collingwood 1889-1943", *The Oxford Magazine*, 4 February 1943, p160–01.

Patrick, James, "Eliot and the New Idealism: Poetry and History at Oxford 1914-1915", *Collingwood Studies*, vol. 7, 2000, pp1–31.

Peters, Rik, "Collingwood's Logic of Question and Answer, its relation to Absolute Presuppositions: another brief history", *Collingwood Studies*, vol. 6, 1999, pp1–28.

Rubinoff, Lionel, "The Relation between Philosophy and History in the Thought of R. G. Collingwood", *Collingwood Studies*, vol. 3, 1996, pp137–73.

Rubinoff, Lionel, "Review Article: R. G. Collingwood, Religion and Philosophy", *Collingwood Studies*, vol. 4, 1997, pp157–82.

Vigorelli, Amadeo, "Lettere di R. G. Collingwood a Benedetto Croce (1912–1939)", *Rivista di storia della filosofia*, vol. 3, 1991, pp545–63.

Works on naval intelligence, peace planning and the Paris Peace Conference

Books

Andrew, Christopher, *Secret Service, The Making of the British Intelligence Community*, William Heinemann Ltd, London, 1985.

Beesley, Patrick, *Very Special Intelligence, The Story of the Admiralty's Operational Intelligence Centre 1939-1945*, Hamish Hamilton, London, 1977.

Beesley, Patrick, *Room 40, British Naval Intelligence 1914–18*, Hamish Hamilton, London, 1982.

Deacon, Richard, *A History of the British Secret Service*, Frederick Muller, London, 1969.

Dockrill, Michael and Goold, Douglas J., *Peace without Promise, Britain and the Peace Conferences 1919–1923*, Batsford Academic and Educational Ltd. London, 1981.

Freeman, T. W., *A History of Modern British Geography*, Longman, London, 1980.

Gelfand, Lawrence E., *The Inquiry, American Preparations for Peace 1917–1919*, Yale University Press, New Haven and London, 1963.

Goldstein, Erik, *Winning the Peace, British Diplomatic Strategy and the Paris Peace Conference*, Clarendon Press, Oxford, 1991.

Hinsley, F. H., *British Intelligence in the Second World War*, vol. 1, HMSO, London, 1979.

Jaffe, Lorna S., *The Decision to Disarm Germany, British Policy Towards Post war German Disarmament 1914–1919*, Allen and Unwin, London, 1985.

Jellicoe of Scapa, Viscount, *The Crisis of the Naval War*, Cassell and Company Ltd, London, 1920.

Judd, Alan, *The Quest for Mansfield Cumming and the Founding of the Secret Service*, Harper Collins, London, 1999.

Lord, R. H., *Some Problems of the Peace Conference*, Harvard University Press, Cambridge, Mass.,1920.

Macartney, C. A., *Survey of International Affairs 1925*, Oxford University Press, London, 1928.

Macmillan, Margaret, *Peacemakers, Six Months That Changed The World*, John Murray, London, 2002.

McLachlan, Donald, *Room 39, Naval Intelligence in Action 1939–1945*, Weidenfeld and Nicolson, London, 1968.

Marder, Arthur J., *From the Dreadnought to Scapa Flow, The Royal Navy in the Fisher Era 1904-1919*, vol. 2, *The War Years to the Eve of Jutland*, Oxford University Press, London, 1965.

Marder, Arthur J. *From the Dreadnought to Scapa Flow, The Royal Navy in the Fisher Era 1904-1919*, vol. 3, *Jutland and After May 1916–December 1916*, second edition, revised and enlarged, Oxford University Press, London, 1978.

Morley, Sir James Headlam, *A Memoir of the Paris Peace Conference 1919*, edited by Agnes Headlam Morley, Russell Bryant and Anna Cienciala, Methuen, London, 1972.

The Navy List, HMSO, London, 1918.

Nicolson, Harold, *Peacemaking 1919*, revised edition 1943, Methuen, London, 1964.

Stafford, David, *Churchill and Secret Service*, John Murray (Publishers), London, 1997.

Temperley, H. W. V., *A History of the Peace Conference of Paris*, vol. 2, *The Settlement with Germany*, Oxford University Press, London, 1920.

Toynbee, Arnold J., *Survey of International Affairs 1920–1923*, Oxford University Press, London, 1925.

Wells, A. R., *Studies in British Naval Intelligence*, (Ph.D. thesis) University of London, 1972.

Articles

Abbenhuis, Maartie, "Caught between the Devil and the Deep Blue Sea: Some Problems with Dutch Neutrality in the Great War 1914–1918", Paper presented to the Inaugural European Studies Conference, National Centre for Research on Europe, Christchurch, New Zealand, May–June, 2002.

Andrew, C. M., "The Mobilization of British Intelligence for the Two World Wars" in N. F. Dreisziger (ed.), *Mobilization for Total War, the Canadian, American and British Experience 1914–1918, 1939–1945*, Wilfred Laurier University Press, Waterloo, Ontario, Canada, 1981.

Anon, "Geography at the Congress of Paris 1919", *The Geographical Journal*, vol. 55, no. 4, April 1920, pp309–12.

Beesley, Patrick, "British Naval Intelligence in Two World Wars — Some Similarities and Differences", in Christopher Andrew and Jeremy Nokes (eds), *Intelligence and International Relations 1900–1945*, Exeter Studies in History no. 15, Exeter, 1987.

Clout, Hugh and Gosme, Cyril, "The Naval Intelligence Handbooks: a monument in geographical writing", *Progress in Human Geography*, vol. 27, no. 2, 2003, pp153–73.

Cubitt, B. B., "War Work of the Society", *The Geographical Journal*, vol. 53, no. 5, May 1919, pp336–39.

T. D., "Handbooks of the Geographical Section, Naval Intelligence Division, Admiralty", *The Geographical Journal*, vol. 57, no. 1, January 1921, pp51–2.

Darby, H. C., "Academic Geography in Britain 1918–1946", *Transactions of the Institute of British Geographers*, new series, vol. 8, no. 1, 1983, pp14–26.

French, David, '"Had We Known How Bad Things Were In Germany, We Might Have Got Stiffer Terms" Great Britain and the German Armistice', in Manfred F. Boemeke, Gerald D. Feldman and

Elizabeth Glaser (eds), *The Treaty of Versailles, A Reassessment after 75 Years*, German Historical Institute, Washington D. C. and Cambridge University Press, Cambridge, 1998.

Freshfield, Douglas W., "Address at the Anniversary General Meeting", *The Geographical Journal*, vol. 48, no. 1, 1917, pp2–5.

Goldstein, Erik, "Hertford House: the Naval Intelligence Geographical Section and Peace Conference Planning 1917–1919", *The Mariner's Mirror*, vol. 72, 1986, pp85–8.

Goldstein, Erik, "Historians Outside the Academy: G. W. Prothero and the Experience of the Foreign Office Historical Section 1917–1920", *Historical Research*, vol. 63, no. 151, June, 1990, pp195-211.

Gosme, Cyril, "The Naval Intelligence Handbooks Series (Great Britain 1941–1946): a description and a call for comments", *Cybergio, European Journal of Geography*, article 137, 2007, pp1–21.

Heffernan, Michael, "Geography, Cartography and Military Intelligence: the Royal Geographical Society and the First World War", *Transactions of the Institute of British Geography* (new series), vol. 21, 1996, pp504–33.

Heffernan, Michael, "The Politics of the Map in the Early Twentieth Century", *Cartography and Geographical Information Science*, vol. 29, no. 3, 2002, pp207–26.

Mair, L. P., "The Scheldt Controversy", *Economica*, vol. 24, 1928, pp351–69.

Marks, Sally, "Behind the Scenes at the Paris Peace Conference of 1919", *Journal of British Studies*, vol. 9, no. 2, 1970, pp154–89.

Wark, W. K., "British Military and Economic Intelligence: assessments of Nazi Germany before the Second World War", in C. Andrew and D. Dilkes (eds), *The Missing Dimension, Governments and Intelligence Communities in the Twentieth Century*, University of Illinois Press, Urbana and Chicago, 1984.

Memoirs and biographies

Books

Altounyan, Taqui, *In Aleppo Once*, John Murray, London, 1969.

Altounyan, Taqui, *Chimes from a Wooden Bell*, A Memoir, I. B. Tauris, London, 1990.

Amery, L. S. The Rt Hon. C H, *My Political Life*, Volume 2, *War and Peace 1914–1929*, Hutchinson, London, 1953.

Amery, L. S. The Rt Hon. C H, *The Leo Amery Diaries*, vol. 1, *1896–1929*, edited by John Barnes and David Nicholson, Hutchinson, London, 1980.

Bridge, Ann, *Portrait of My Mother*, Chatto and Windus, London, 1955.

Bridge, Ann, *Moments of Knowing, Some Personal Experiences Beyond Normal Knowledge*, Hodder and Stoughton, London, 1970.

Brogan, Hugh, *The Life of Arthur Ransome*, Jonathan Cape, London, 1984.

Carritt, E. F., *Fifty Years A Don*, privately printed, 1960.

Chambers, Roland, *The Last Englishman, The Double Life of Arthur Ransome*, Faber, London, 2009.

Cropper, Margaret, *Evelyn Underhill 1875-1941, An Introduction to her Life and Writings*, Mowbrays, London, 1975.

Fitzgerald, Penelope, *The Knox Brothers*, Coward, McCann and Geoghegan, New York, 1977.

Furbank, P. N., *E. M. Forster A Life*, vol. 2, Oxford University Press, Oxford, 1979.

Graham, Angus, *Skipness, Memoirs of a Highland Estate*, Canongate Academic, Edinburgh, 1993.

Grundy, G. B., *Fifty-Five Years at Oxford, An Unconventional Autobiography*, Methuen Ltd, London, 1945.

Hardyment, Christina, *Arthur Ransome and Captain Flint's Trunk*, Jonathan Cape, London, 1984.

Haslam, Jonathan, *The Vices of Integrity, E. H. Carr 1892–1982*, Verso, London, 1999.

Hibberd, Dominic, *Wilfred Owen, A New Biography*, Phoenix, London, 2003.

BIBLIOGRAPHY

Hilton, Tim, *John Ruskin, The Later Years*, Yale University Press, New Haven and London, 2000.

James, Admiral Sir William, *The Eyes of the Navy, A Biographical Study of Admiral Sir Reginald Hall*, Methuen and Co. Ltd, London, 1953.

Keynes, Geoffrey, *The Gates of Memory*, Clarendon Press, Oxford, 1981.

Keynes, Margaret Elizabeth, *A Home by the River, Newnham Grange to Darwin College*, Darwin College, Cambridge, 1976.

Lawrence, A. W., *T. E. Lawrence by his Friends*, Jonathan Cape, London, 1937.

Lawrence, Michael Asher, *The Uncrowned King of Arabia*, Penguin Books, London, 1999.

Lawrence, T. E., *The Letters of T. E. Lawrence*, edited by David Garnett, Jonathan Cape, London, 1938.

Lear, Linda, *Beatrix Potter, A Life in Nature*, Allen Lane, London, 2007.

Leigh, Margaret, *The Fruit in the Seed Chapters of Autobiography*, Phoenix House Ltd, London, 1952.

Matheson, P. E., *The Life of Hastings Rashdall, DD*, Oxford University Press, London, 1928.

McGuiness, Brian, *Young Ludwig, Wittgenstein's Life 1889–1921*, with a new preface, Clarendon Press, Oxford, 2005.

Michael Millgate, *Thomas Hardy A Biography*, Oxford University Press, Oxford, 1985.

Monk, Ray, *Ludwig Wittgenstein, The Duty of Genius*, Jonathan Cape, London, 1990.

Monk, Ray, *Bertrand Russell, The Spirit of Solitude*, Jonathan Cape, London, 1996.

Owen, Wilfred, *Collected Letters*, edited by Harold Owen and John Bell, Oxford University Press, London, 1967.

Pollock, John, *Kitchener*, Robinson, London, 2002.

Ramsay, David, *"Blinker" Hall Spymaster The Man Who Brought America Into World War One*, revised edition, Spellmount, The History Press, Stroud, 2009.

Ransome, Arthur, *The Autobiography of Arthur Ransome*, Prologue and Epilogue by Rupert Hart-Davis, Jonathan Cape, London, 1976.

Ransome, Arthur, *Signalling from Mars, The Letters of Arthur Ransome*, selected and introduced by Hugh Brogan, Jonathan Cape, London, 1997.

Rhees, Rush (ed.), *Ludwig Wittgenstein, Personal Recollections*, Basil Blackwell, Oxford, 1981.

Russell, Bertrand, *The Autobiography of Bertrand Russell*, vol. 2, 1914–1944, George Allen and Unwin, London, 1968.

Sayers, Dorothy L., *The Letters of Dorothy L. Sayers 1889–1936*, edited by Barbara Reynolds, Hodder and Stoughton, London, 1995.

Smith, A. L. (Mrs), Arthur Lionel Smith Master of Balliol (1916–1924), *A Biography and Some Reminiscences by His Wife*, John Murray, London, 1928.

Thwaite, Ann, *A. A. Milne, His Life*, Faber, London, 1990.

Toynbee, Arnold J., *Experiences*, Oxford University Press, London, 1969.

Wakefield, Dick, *The Collingwoods at Lanehead*, unpublished manuscript.

Wardale, Roger, *Nancy Blackett, Under Sail with Arthur Ransome*, Jonathan Cape, London, 1991.

Wilson, Jeremy, *Lawrence of Arabia, The Authorised Biography of T. E. Lawrence*, Heinemann, London, 1989.

Winstone, H. V. F., *The Illicit Adventure*, Jonathan Cape, London, 1982.

Woodward, E. L., *Short Journey*, Faber, London, 1942.

Woolf, Virginia, *The Letters of Virginia Woolf*, edited by Nigel Nicolson, vol. 2, *1912–1922*, The Hogarth Press, London, 1976.

Woolf, Virginia, *The Diary of Virginia Woolf*, edited by Anne Olivier Bell, vol. 1, *1915–1919*, The Hogarth Press, London, 1977.

Articles

Anon. "Obituary of W. G. Collingwood", *Nature*, vol. 130, 15 October 1932, pp571-2.

Anon. "Obituary of Lily Dougall 1858-1923", *Christian World*, vol. 18 October 1923.

Anon. "Obituary of Lily Dougall", *The Times*, 13 October 1923.

R. N. R. B., "Obituary Dr Henry Newton Dickson CBE", *The Geographical Journal*, vol. 59, no. 6, June 1922, p479.

Dearden, James S., "Collingwood, William Gershom 1854-1932", *The New Oxford Dictionary of National Biography*, online edition, Oxford University Press, 2004.

Dunbar, J. G., "Angus Graham", *Proceedings of the Society of Antiquaries of Scotland*, vol. 111, 1981, pp1-6.

Garnett, Jane, "Rashdall, Hastings 1858-1924", *The New Oxford Dictionary of National Biography*, online edition, Oxford University Press, 2004.

Gordon, Joanna, "The Objects Themselves: A Short Note on the Life and Ideas of Angus Graham", *The Review of Scottish Culture*, vol. 6, 1990, pp1-6.

Graham, R. B., "W. G. Collingwood: A Memoir", *Journal of the Rock and Fell Climbing Club of the English Lake District*, vol. 9, 1932, pp194-6.

Green, Dana, "Underhill, Evelyn Maud Bosworth 1875-1941", *New Oxford Dictionary of National Biography*, online edition, Oxford University Press, 2004.

Maddrell, Avril M. C., "Ormsby, Hilda 1877-1973", *New Oxford Dictionary of National Biography*, online edition, Oxford University Press, 2004.

MacCall, H. B., "Obituary of W. G. Collingwood", *Yorkshire Archaeological Journal*, vol. 31, 1934, pp192-3.

A. S., "Obituary of Henry Newton Dickson", *The Scottish Geographical Magazine*, vol. 38, 1922, pp183-4.

Smith, Teresa, "R. G. Collingwood: 'This Ring of Thought': Notes on Early Influences", *Collingwood Studies*, vol. 1, 1994, pp27–43.

Walsh, W. H., "H. J. Paton 1887–1969", *Proceedings of the British Academy*, vol. 56, 1970, pp293–308.

Other works

Philosophy

Books

Baldwin, Thomas (ed.), *The Cambridge History of Philosophy 1870–1945*, Cambridge University Press, Cambridge, 2003.

Collingwood, William, *The Value and Influence of Art as a Branch of General Education*, W. Kent and Co., London, 1862.

Collingwood, W. G., *The Art Teaching of John Ruskin*, Percival and Co. London, 1891.

Hacker, P. M. S., *Wittgenstein's Place in Twentieth Century Analytical Philosophy*, Blackwell, Oxford, 1996.

Hinchcliff, Peter, *God and History, Aspects of British Theology 1875–1914*, Clarendon Press, Oxford, 1992.

Ruskin, John, *Works*, library edition, edited by E. T. Cook and Alexander Wedderburn, George Allen, London, 1903.

Russell, Bertrand, *Mysticism and Logic*, Longmans Green and Co., London, 1918.

Articles

Boys-Smith, Rev. J. S., "The Interpretation of Christianity in Idealistic Philosophy in Great Britain in the Nineteenth Century", *The Modern Churchman*, vol. 21, 1941, pp251–73.

Conant, James, "Philosophy and Biography", in James C. Klagge (ed.), *Wittgenstein, Biography and Philosophy*, Cambridge University Press, Cambridge, 2001, pp16–56.

Hewison, Robert, "Ruskin Tomorrow", Lecture to the Royal Society of Arts (19 April 2000).

MacKinnon, D. M., "Some Aspects of the Treatment of Christianity by the British Idealists", *Religious Studies*, vol. 20, 1984, pp133–44.

Monk, Ray, "Philosophical Biography: The Very Idea", in James C. Klagge, *Wittgenstein, Biography and Philosophy*, Cambridge University Press, Cambridge, 2001, pp3–15.

Paton, H. J., "Fifty Years of Philosophy", in H. D. Lewis (ed.), *Contemporary British Philosophy, Personal Statements*, third series, George Allen and Unwin Ltd, London, 1956.

Sell, Alan P. F., *The Philosophy of Religion 1875–1980*, Thoemmes Press, Bristol, 1988.

Sell, Alan P. F., *Philosophical Idealism and Christian Belief*, University of Wales Press, Cardiff. 1995.

Streeter, B. H. (ed.), *Foundations*, Macmillan, London, 1913.

Williams, Bernard, *The Sense of the Past, Essays in the History of Philosophy*, with an introduction by Miles Burnyeat, Princeton University Press, Princeton, 2006.

Wittgenstein, Ludwig, *Culture and Value*, revised edition, edited by G. H. von Wright, translated by Peter Winch, Blackwell Publishers, Oxford, 1998.

History

Books

Barker, Ernest, *Linguistic Oppression in the German Empire*, Longmans Green and Co., London, 1918.

Best, Geoffrey, *Humanity in Warfare*, Weidenfeld and Nicolson, London, 1980.

Collini, Stefan, *Absent Minds, Intellectuals in Britain*, Oxford University Press, Oxford, 2006.

Cowling, Maurice, *Religion and Public Doctrine in Modern England*, Cambridge University Press, Cambridge, 1980.

Fair, John D., *Harold Temperley, A Scholar and Romantic in the Public Realm*, University of Delaware Press, Newark, 1992.

Frere, Sheppard, *Roman Britain since Haverfield and Richmond*, A Lecture given in All Souls College, 23 October 1987.

Haverfield, F., *The Roman Occupation of Britain*, Clarendon Press, Oxford, 1924.

House, Colonel, *The Intimate Papers of Colonel House*, arranged as a narrative by Charles Seymour, vol. 3, *Into the World War April 1917–June 1918*, Ernest Benn Ltd., London, 1928.

Keegan, John, *The First World War*, Hutchinson, London, 1999.

Kramer, Alan, *German Atrocities 1914 A History of Denial*, Yale University Press, New Haven and London, 2001.

Kramer, Alan, *Dynamic of Destruction, Culture and Mass Killing in the First World War*, Oxford University Press, Oxford, 2007.

Liddell Hart, B. H., *The Real War 1914–1918*, Faber, London, 1930.

Pickering, Henry, *Chief among the Brethren*, Pickering and Inglis, London, 1918.

Rae, John, *Conscience and Politics, The British Government and the Conscientious Objector to Military Service 1916–1919*, Oxford University Press, London, 1970.

Rothwell, V. H., *British War Aims and Peace Diplomacy 1914–1918*, Oxford University Press, London, 1971.

Seligmann, Matthew S., *Spies in Uniform, British Military and Naval Intelligence on the Eve of the First World War*, Oxford University Press, Oxford, 2006.

Spears, Major-General Sir Edward, *Liaison 1914*, second edition, Eyre and Spottiswoode, London, 1968.

Stevenson, David, *1914 1918 The History of the First World War*, Penguin Books, London, 2004.

Strachan, Hew, *The First World War*, vol. 1, *To Arms*, Oxford University Press, Oxford, 2001.

Terraine, John, *White Heat The New Warfare 1914–1918*, Guild Publishing, London, 1982.

Townend, Matthew, *The Vikings and Victorian Lakeland: The Norse Medievalism of W. G. Collingwood and His Contemporaries*, Cumberland and Westmorland Antiquarian and Archaeological Society, extra series, vol. 34, Titus Wilson and Son, Kendal, 2009.

Toynbee, Arnold J., *A Study of History*, Oxford University Press, London, 1954.

Wallace, Stuart, *War and the Image of Germany, British Academics in Wartime Whitehall 1914–1918*, John Donald Publishers Ltd., Edinburgh, 1988.

Whitehouse, J. Howard, *Ruskin, Contemporary Addresses*, Oxford University Press, London, 1919.

Wilkinson, Alan, *The Church of England and the First World War*, SPCK, London, 1978.

Willis, James F., *Prologue to Nuremburg The Politics and Diplomacy of Punishing War Criminals of the First World War*, Greenwood Press, Westport, Connecticut, 1982.

Articles

Crawley, C. W., "Sir George Prothero and His Circle", *Transactions of the Royal Historical Society*, fifth series, vol. 20, 1970, pp101–27.

Gusewelle, Jack. K., "Science and the Admiralty during World War 1", in Gerald Jordan (ed.), *Naval Warfare in the Twentieth Century, Essays in Honour of Arthur Marder*, Croom Helm, London, 1977, pp105–17.

Marks, Sally, "The Luxemburg Question at the Paris Peace Conference and After", available at www.f1wi.ugent. 1970.

Stevenson, D., "Belgium, Luxemburg and the Defence of Western Europe 1914–1920", *International History Review*, vol. 4, 1982, pp504–23.

Winter, J. M., "Oxford and the First World War", in Brian Harrison (ed.), *The History of the University of Oxford*, vol. 8, *The Twentieth Century*, Oxford University Press, Oxford, 1994, pp3–27.

INDEX

Albert Memorial, 2, 96
Alexander, S. 1, 48
Alsace-Lorraine, 49, 62, 65, 66, 67, 78, 80, 83–5, 91, 107, 129, 134
Altounyan, A. A. 93–4
Altounyan, E. H. R. 55, 92–5, 98–9
Altounyan, T. 30, 93, 98
Ambleside, 35, 36, 40, 41, 42
Angell, N. 101
Aristotle, 35
Arnold, M. 127
Atrocities, 66, 73, 93, 105

Barker, E. 87
Belgium, 41, 49, 62, 64–6, 68–9, 70, 74–7, 83, 88, 107, 134
Boer War, 38, 43
Bradley, F. H. 127
Bridge, A. 100
Buchan, J. 34

Calder, W. 48
Carr, E. H. 71, 77
Cheeseman, G. L. 137, 142
Christianity, vi, 4, 12, 22, 24, 25, 36, 85, 88, 114, 116, 120, 123, 126-3
Churchill, W. 54, 56, 68
Collingwood, B. 40, 57–8, 59, 60, 74, 95
Collingwood, D. 74, 93, 98
Collingwood, R. G.
    An Autobiography, vi, 6–10, 13, 16, 19, 20, 23, 25, 27, 31–3, 38, 41, 43–5, 55, 57, 60, 72, 75, 77, 103, 104, 108, 114, 117, 123, 144–6
    An Essay on Metaphysics, 108, 132
    Guide to the Roman Wall, 3
    Manual of Alsace-Lorraine, 75, 80, 86–9, 105, 109, 129, 136
    Manual of Belgium, 62–3, 65, 76, 84, 86, 88, 110, 137, 141
    The New Leviathan, 43–4, 69, 89, 109–10, 145

INDEX

   Religion and Philosophy, 15, 31, 35, 57, 94–5, 103, 105, 113, 118, 132, 147
   Roman Britain and the English Settlements, 41
   Roman Inscriptions of Britain, 135, 141
   Ruskin's Philosophy, 13, 29, 32, 33, 125–128, 132
   Speculum Mentis, 32, 37, 88, 90, 96, 108–09, 111, 116–18, 120–121, 123, 126–7, 136–8, 141–3
Collingwood, W. G. 30, 59, 73, 90–99
Collingwood, W. 22, 30
Conscription, 36, 37, 42, 87
Cozens-Hardy, W. H. 50, 61
Croce, B. 6, 13, 35, 40, 41, 94, 140, 143
Cumnor Circle, 112, 122

Dickson, H. N. 46, 47, 48, 50, 52, 55, 59, 61, 67, 73, 79, 85, 86, 96, 134
Donagan, A. 126–8, 132
Dougall, L. 112, 122

First World War, v, 1, 10, 34, 37, 45, 46, 49, 103, 105, 108
Forster, E. M. 97–8
Freeston, L. B. 36, 40
French, Sir J. 68

Goldstein, E. 44, 46, 51, 53, 54, 55, 59, 62, 67, 71–9, 86, 96, 142
Graham, A. 99, 100
Graham, E. W. 100
Green, T. H. 23, 117, 121
Grundy, G. B. 48–9, 55

Hall, Admiral R. 45, 48–9, 71, 79, 134, 144
Haverfield, F. 35, 41, 42, 95, 135, 138, 141, 142
Heffernan, M. 44, 50, 61, 62, 75, 77, 80, 83, 85, 87
Hegel, G.W. F. 6, 31, 117, 140, 143
Hertford House, 44, 48, 49, 53, 54, 57, 59, 73, 75, 77, 86, 90
Hitler, A. 105
Hobbes, T. 2
Hogarth, D. G. 50, 55, 145

I. D. 25, 3
I. D. 32, iii, 1, 2, 44–9, 52–55, 58–9, 60–63, 65– 9, 70–75, 79, 81–4, 86, 90, 92, 95, 97, 115, 134, 144
Inquiry, 47, 49, 58, 65, 67

Jesus, 25, 31, 123
Johnson, Major D. 47, 65, 67

Kant, I. 6
Kemp Smith, N. 48
Knox, T. M. 44, 145, 146

Lawrence, T. E. 50, 55, 95, 97, 99, 145, 146
League of Nations, 39, 44, 84, 85, 88, 103–09
Leigh, M. 42, 49, 55
Liberalism, 4, 38, 85, 129–31
Lloyd George, D. 88, 91, 142
Logic of question and answer, 2, 33, 96
Luxemburg, 63–4, 73, 74, 83, 88, 91

McCallum, R. B. 44, 60, 67, 68, 69, 73, 75, 76, 141
Milner, Lord 145
Monk, R. 113–14

Naval Intelligence Division, iii, 1, 34, 40, 45–52, 55, 57, 60, 63, 64, 65, 72, 78, 81, 82, 142, 144
Nicolson, H. 51, 56, 81, 87
Nietzsche, F. vi, 119, 122

Official Secrets Act, 63, 108
Ormsby, H. 72
Owen, W. 5, 90, 91, 96

Papcastle, 35, 40
Parker, A. 79, 86
Paton, H. J. 1, 48, 54, 82, 83, 87, 102
Peace Conference, v, 1, 3, 5, 12, 24, 37, 40, 45, 46–56, 60– 63, 68–9, 71, 74, 77– 97, 100, 134–9, 140, 144
Plato 117, 140
Protheroe, G. 79
Prussianism, 4, 38, 39, 64, 68

Ransome, A. 41, 72, 93, 95, 98, 99, 102
Ransome, G. 41
Rashdall, H. 1, 48, 54
Realism, 6, 18, 20, 23, 26, 27, 28, 29, 39, 40, 95, 102–03, 139,
Royal Geographical Society, 2, 46, 49, 50, 59, 60, 71, 78, 81
Rubinoff, L. 24–5, 31, 124, 132
Ruggiero, G. de 6, 43, 87, 140, 143, 148
Ruskin, J. 9, 13, 29–30, 32, 33, 73, 125–32, 140, 143
Russell, B. 7, 11, 12, 15, 17, 19, 22, 23, 37, 42, 89, 113–16, 120–21

Salter, E. G. 58
Scheldt, River 63, 69, 70, 71, 74, 76–88, 107, 134
Second World War, v, 2, 37, 52, 54, 55, 72, 103, 144
Simpson, A. 90
Simpson, F. G. 31
Smith, J. A. 121, 122
Socrates, 126
Survey of International Affairs, 10, 77

Temperley, H. W. V. 139, 142
Toynbee, A. 11, 13, 52, 77, 88, 142
Treaty of Versailles, 12, 43, 74, 134

Underhill, E. 58, 72

Vico, G. 35, 41, 94

War crimes, 84
Wilson, Woodrow 91, 105
Wittgenstein, L. 2, 5, 7, 12, 14, 15, 16, 17, 19, 20, 22, 23, 114–20, 124
Woolf, L. 98
Woolf, V. 97–8

Zimmern, A. 13, 52